Regionalism and Globalism in Southeast Asia

Also by Eero Palmujoki

VIETNAM AND THE WORLD: Marxist–Leninist Doctrine and the Changes in International Relations

Regionalism and Globalism in Southeast Asia

Eero Palmujoki
Senior Fellow
Tampere Peace Research Institute
University of Tampere
Finland

palgrave

First published 2001 by
PALGRAVE
Houndmills, Basingstoke, Hampshire RG21 6XS and
175 Fifth Avenue, New York, N. Y. 10010
Companies and representatives throughout the world

PALGRAVE is the new global academic imprint of St. Martin's Press LLC Scholarly and Reference Division and Palgrave Publishers Ltd (formerly Macmillan Press Ltd).

ISBN 0–333–73477–7

This book is printed on paper suitable for recycling and made from fully managed and sustained forest sources.

A catalogue record for this book is available from the British Library.

Library of Congress Cataloging-in-Publication Data
Palmujoki, Eero, 1958–
Regionalism and globalism in Southeast Asia / Palmujoki, Eero.
p. cm.
Includes bibliographical references and index.
ISBN 0–333–73477–7 (cloth)
1. Asia, Southeastern—Politics and government—1945–
2. Asia, Southeastern—Economic conditions. 3. Regionalism–
–Asia, Southeastern. I. Title.

JQ750.A58 P35 2001
327'.0959—dc21

2001034817

10 9 8 7 6 5 4 3 2 1
10 09 08 07 06 05 04 03 02 01

Printed and bound in Great Britain by
Antony Rowe Ltd, Chippenham, Wiltshire

Contents

Acknowledgements

This study is an outcome of several research projects carried out at the Department of Political Science and International Relations and at the Tampere Peace Research Center (TAPRI) within the University of Tampere. The main sources of funding have been three research projects sponsored by the Academy of Finland, namely: "Regionalism and globalism in Southeast Asia", "Regionalism, globalism and the development of the inter-state system in Southeast Asia" and "The Regional and local policy impacts of the global environmental and climate regimes". The initiative for the research originated in 1996 from the Finnish Ministry for Foreign Affairs, which made it possible to start the project and supported it during the entire research period. A senior fellowship at TAPRI enabled me to finalise this book.

Owing to these three projects, several persons have inspired the ideas for my study. Inevitably, the book includes thoughts and views of my colleagues in our Southeast Asia project: Annamari Antikainen-Kokko, Janne Jokinen, Anisa Doty and Teemu Tuominen. Although the project was sometimes difficult to administer, the effort as such was stimulating, operating among three universities (Universities of Tampere, Turku and Abo Akademi University) and three departments. In addition, with the particular support of the Foreign Ministry, it differed from more conventional academic research projects. Indeed, the interests and support of the Foreign Ministry staff for our network were very important. Hannu Mäntyvaara and Mikko Jokela flexibly connected the need for policy information to academic interests and Paula Parviainen and Markku Heiskanen, among many other officials at the Foreign Ministry, gave an important practical policy perspective on Southeast Asian affairs.

The research project included three research trips to Southeast Asia. I am indebted to several colleagues and friends in Malaysia, the Philippines, Singapore and Thailand for their hospitality and help. Here I would also like to thank: Miriam Coronel Ferrer, Derek da Cunha, Jalil Miswardi and Hong Chee, Suthiphand Chirathivat, Yupin Chancharoensin and Yeo Lay Hwee. I would particularly like to mention the help of librarians at the Institute of Southeast Asian Studies in Singapore, at the library of Chulalongkorn University in Bangkok and at the Institute of Strategic and International Studies in Kuala Lumpur.

I have also received important practical help in my research. Riitta Lehtimäki at the Department of Political Science and International Relations has patiently administrated my projects and Erja Yläjärvi collected material on the Asian economic crisis. Joan Lofgren, Virginia Mattila and Tina Parke-Sutherland did a lot of work in editing my English. Finally, Marita Alanko professionally prepared the manuscript for the publisher.

To carry out an academic research project is often a stressful job of combining intellectual intentions and financial realities. I am thankful to my wife, Sirkku, for understanding this insecurity. I am also very much obliged to my colleagues at the Department of Political Science for their support: Pertti Lappalainen, Juha Holma, Tarja Seppä, Tapani Turkka and Pekka Virtanen, from whom, I am afraid, I have got more than I have given.

A part of the material presented in this book has appeared in other publications. The earlier version of the first chapter, "Integration and Fragmentation in Southeast Asian Regionalist Discourse", was published previously in a Special Issue of the *Journal of the Finnish Anthropological Society*, Volume 25 No. 2 (June 2000), pp. 76–88 and a shorter version of Chapter Five has appeared as "EU-ASEAN Relations: Reconciling Two Different Agendas" in *Contemporary Southeast Asia*, Volume 19, No. 3, December 1997, pp. 269–285. Reproduced here with the kind permission of the publisher, Institute of Southeast Asian Studies, Singapore.

Abbreviations

ACU	ASEAN Currency Unit
ADB	Asian Development Bank
ADS	*ASEAN Document Series*
AEM	ASEAN Economic Ministers (meeting)
AFMM	ASEAN Finance Minister's Meeting
AFTA	ASEAN Free Trade Area
AIA	ASEAN Investment Area
AIPO	ASEAN Inter-parliamentary Organization
AMM	ASEAN Ministerial Meeting
APEC	Asia-Pacific Economic Cooperation
ARF	ASEAN Regional Forum
ASCU	ASEAN Surveillance Coordinating Unit
ASEAN	Association of Southeast Asian Nations
ASEAN-ISIS	ASEAN Institutes of Strategic and International Studies
ASEM	Asia-Europe Meeting
ASEP	ASEAN Subregional Environment Program
ASFOM	ASEAN Senior Finance Official's Meeting
ASTSU	ASEAN Surveillance Technical Support Unit
CBM	Confidence-building measure
CDC	Committee on Development and Cooperation (the EU Parliament)
CEER	Committee on External Economic Relations (the EU Parliament)
CEPHCP	Committee on the Environment, Public Health and Consumer Protection (the EU Parliament)
CEPT	Common Effective Preferential Tariff
CER	Closer Economic Relations (between Australia and New Zealand)
CFSP	(European Union's) common foreign and security policy
CLOB	Central Limited Order Book
CSCA	Conference on Security Cooperation in Asia
CSCAP	Council for Security Cooperation in the Asia Pacific
CSCE	Conference on Security and Cooperation in Europe
EAEC	East Asian Economic Caucus
EAEG	East Asian Economic Grouping
EC	European Community
EEC	European Economic Community

EPC	European Political Cooperation
EU	European Union
FAB	*Foreign Affairs Bulletin* (the Thai Ministry of Foreign Affairs)
FAC	Foreign Affairs Committee (the EU Parliament)
FAM	*Foreign Affairs Malaysia* (the Malaysian Ministry of Foreign Affairs)
FAN	*Foreign Affairs Newsletter* (the Thai Ministry of Foreign Affairs)
FDI	Foreign Direct Investments
FEER	*Far Eastern Economic Review*
FSC	Forest Stewardship Council
FTA	Free trade area
GATT	General Agreement on Tariffs and Trade
GDP	Gross domestic production
HPEA	High performing Asian economies
HS	Harmonized Commodity Description and Coding System
IAI	Initiative for ASEAN Integration
IMF	International Monetary Fund
IPE	International political economy
ISO	International Standard Organization
IT	Information technology
ITO	International Trade Organization
ITTO	International Timber Trade Organization
KLSE	Kuala Lumpur Stock Exchange
MAI	Multilateral Agreement on Investments
MERCOSUR	Mercado Común del Sur
MNC	Multinational company
NAFTA	North American Free Trade Agreement
NAM	Non-Aligned Movement
NEP	New Economic Policy
NGO	Non-governmental organization
NIC	Newly industrialized country (in Asia)
NTB	Non-tariff barrier
OECD	Organization for Economic Cooperation and Development
PAP	People's Action Party
PBEC	Pacific Basin Economic Council
PECC	Pacific Economic Co-operational Council
PIWP	ASEAN Customs Policy Implementation and Work Programme

PMC	(ASEAN) Post-Ministerial Conference
PRC	People's Republic of China
PTA	Preferential trade arrangement
RHAP	Regional Haze Action Plan
SAL	Structural Adjusted Loans
SEOM	(ASEAN) Senior Officials Meeting
SLORC	State Law and Order Restoration Council
STABEX	Stabilization of export earning scheme
TAC	Treaty of Amity and Cooperation in Southeast Asia
UMNO	United Malays National Organization
UNEP	United Nations Environment Program
UNTAET	United Nations Transitional Administration in East Timor
WTO	World Trade Organization
ZOPFAN	Zone of Peace, Freedom and Neutrality

1 Introduction: Analyzing Southeast Asian Regionalist Efforts

NEW REGIONALISM AND THE REGIONALIST DEBATE

This book examines the regionalist debate in Southeast Asia from the end of the Cold War up to the beginning of the new millennium. In this era the Association of Southeast Asian Nations (ASEAN) developed from a Cold War alliance into a regional organization emphasizing its originating idea of gathering all Southeast Asian countries together under the same co-operational organization. Rapid economic growth and increasing political self-confidence among the ASEAN members also characterize this period. While in the 1970s and 1980s the growing economic might of ASEAN countries highlighted the distinctive character of Southeast Asian regionalism, the Asian economic crisis in 1997 and the resulting restructuring of Asia-Pacific economic and political systems, forced the rethinking of many assumptions behind Southeast Asian regional development.

The destruction of the Cold War bipolar structure and the emergence of regional systems turned analysts' interests away from the geo-strategic approaches of the superpowers toward regional developments. Trying to distinguish between European integration and the post-Cold War regional processes they examined, the new studies introduced the concepts of *old* and *new regionalism*, emphasizing the qualitative differences between regionalism in new and emerging regions and on the old continent. The studies published on Southeast Asian regional systems particularly highlighted differences and emphasized two important factors determining the shape of regional development. The first determinant is the structure of the international system. This thesis has been advocated particularly by Björn Hettne and his colleagues in their grandiose research program, the new regionalism, the results of which have been published in five volumes covering regional developments in all the continents.[1] The program theorized a larger systemic context for regionalization rather than concentrating on regions as such.[2] Hettne asserts that old regionalism was created in the bipolar world of the Cold War, whereas new regionalism originates in the much more pluralistic situation of the post-Cold War period and makes possible much more spontaneous developments.[3] The second determinant applies specifically to European integration and Asia-Pacific regionalism. This thesis, introduced by Norman Palmer, points to qualitative differences between European and Southeast Asian regionalism. According to Palmer, old regionalism is characterized by the tendency toward integration, federalism, and diminishing national sovereignty. On the other hand, two other tendencies drive new regionalism – nationalism and interdependence.[4] Palmer's arguments about the distinct character of ASEAN regionalism vis-à-vis European regionalism have been shared by many Southeast Asian and Western analysts.[5]

This study considers Southeast Asian regionalism from a different point of view. Contrary to the thesis of new regionalism, the central argument of this book is that the Southeast Asian regionalist debate includes mostly the same theoretical elements as the European regionalist debate. "Regionalist debate" is defined here as a kind of academic and political discussion which is concerning regional – political and economic – cooperation in a given geographical area. European and Southeast Asian regionalism do differ qualitatively.[6] Regionalism is developing along different paths in Southeast Asia than in Europe. Nevertheless, this study argues that common fragmenting and integrating forces shape both European and Southeast Asian regionalist endeavors. It is the intensities of the common integrating and fragmenting pressures as well as the specifics of their content that varies between Europe and Southeast Asia. An analysis of the nature of these differences in intensity and content sheds light on the contents of the concepts, on regionalist approaches, and on integration theories.

If the developmental stage of regional organizations and institutions in Europe and in the Third World are compared, the thesis of Norman Palmer and his followers is relatively easy to justify. However, when the regionalist debates in Europe and in Southeast Asia are examined, the similarities are much more obvious than the differences. Concepts may differ, but similar ideas and approaches can be found in both regions. The emphases are, of course, different, and some concepts, such as the idea of federalism, disappear in the Southeast Asian regionalist debate.

In the discussion of European regionalism several approaches are used: functionalist and neo-functionalist approaches are seen as normative theories which have been realized in the development of the European Community and the European Union. Federalism can be understood as a political incarnation of neo-functionalist theories. Hence, the supranational institutions have replaced some functions of nation-states. Realist and institutionalist approaches in regionalist debates emphasize inter-governmental relations as a political arrangement between regional states. In the 1970s the concepts of interdependence and the international political economic (IPE) approach, which emphasize the development of the global economy, also established footholds in European regionalist discussion.

It comes, therefore, as no surprise that this book has its particular interest in the regionalist ideas and political arguments for cooperation in the ASEAN context and not in the concrete records of Southeast Asian regionalism. As the book aims to analyze how Southeast Asian regionalism is constructed, the political contexts in which the arguments are made and the debates conducted, of course, become important. Therefore the arguments of Southeast Asian scholars and other experts are examined as well as those of political elites and members of governments.

In practical politics the starting points of regionalist ideas differ slightly from those in academic and expert discourse. However, the three elements figure into both the ASEAN regionalist discussion and the national discourse in the ASEAN countries. These political contexts have reference to academic discussion: Realism and neorealism were fertilized in the Cold War's two-bloc system, and IPE emerged both from Third Worldism and economic development in Southeast Asia. Similarly, the unique economic development in Southeast Asia inspired institutionalist and constructivist views on regional development. The fourth element of regionalism – integration – is a newcomer to Southeast Asian regionalist discourse, despite the fact that functionalist ideas have been present since the early days of ASEAN.

THEORETICAL PATTERNS OF SOUTHEAST ASIAN REGIONALIST DISCOURSE

In general, researchers use two main approaches when studying regionalism. The functionalist and neo-functionalist approaches were especially created to explain European integration while the International Political Economy (IPE) approach focuses both on European integration and on regionalism in the developing countries. The functionalist and neo-functionalist approaches presume that cooperation across national borders (particularly in the economic field) spreads out to other sectors. This *spill-over* effect leads finally to the formation of supranational institutions and to the diminishing role of the nation-state.

While functionalism examines regionalism as a natural product of economic integration, IPE considers regionalism a by-product of globalization and the nation-states' attempts to counter it. Broadly speaking, the concepts of *new* and *old regionalism* fall within these IPE approaches. Different political and academic currents can base their arguments on IPE. Owing to its diversity as an academic research program, IPE has provided useful theoretical frameworks for various political and academic projects; most approaches to the study of Southeast Asian regionalism make use of the idea of IPE. From this standpoint, globalism is seen as a social process catalyzed by the world's technological development. This development accelerates the integration of the world's economy and trade as the barriers to trade and capital flows disappear. Accordingly, this paradigm constructs regionalism as a state-led project, in which the regional states try to organize their reciprocal relationships in order either to take advantage of globalization tendencies or to resist these tendencies.[7]

In the theoretical debate on regionalism the (neo)realist school has also gained a foothold, particularly in the inter-governmentalist approach in the political debate, which understands regionalism merely as an instrument in alliance-building. As the main interest of political realism has been in the role of nation-states in international politics, the theoretical regionalist debate is not its main area of concern. As realism emphasizes the sovereignty of nation-states in international systems, its thrust can be considered as working to fragment regionalist ideas. In the Southeast Asian regionalist discourse, however, realism has taken on a rather important role, since the development of supranational institutions remains slow.

Without a doubt, in European academic discourse the functionalist and realist approaches are very much joined to the political trends – federalism and inter-governmentalism – of European integration. Thus the intellectual development of regionalist thinking in Europe can hardly be kept separate from political development. In this sense, the direction of the influence between European politics and theoretical thinking is difficult to discern.

In the context of ASEAN, federalism and inter-governmentalism appear in neither political nor academic discourse. ASEAN has developed on the basis of rather loose declarations (Bangkok 1967, Kuala Lumpur 1971 and Bali Declarations of 1976). The first very modest steps toward institution-building were taken in Bali in 1976 when the ASEAN Secretariat was established. Integration in any serious sense cannot be spoken of before 1992, when the ASEAN Free Trade Area (AFTA) was established. As a parallel to European discourse, Amitav Acharya suggests two approaches to Southeast Asian regionalism: Realism and institutionalism. Realism corresponds to the concept detailed above. Institutionalism in Acharya's terms approaches functionalism in certain ways, although it is closer to inter-governmentalism than to federalism. The theoretical background is constructivist, not particularly characteristic of a functionalist approach. For Acharya, institutionalism has a strong constructivist leaning as it refers to the importance of socialization, norms, and identity over legalistic and bureaucratic practices.[8] Acharya's division is important, in spite of the fact that it has already been used in regional theories and in European security cooperation, the least developed area in the European Union's cooperation.

Even though the term "federalism" is not relevant to the Southeast Asian situation and the term "functionalism" does not appear in the Southeast Asian discussion, clear undercurrents of functionalist ideas run through the theoretical constructions, particularly in the most recent economic discussion of the post-economic crisis situation in Southeast Asia.

Thus at least three or four theoretical approaches appear in Southeast Asian regionalist discussions. The fact that Southeast Asian regionalism has been a state-led project explains the strength of the (neo)realist school, although the form of realism used in the Southeast Asian debate differs essentially from the realism appearing in the Western academic debate. The differences between the ideas of realism used in these two debates hinges on the history of nation-building in the Southeast Asian countries and its theoretical premises, which refer particularly to domination theories. Similarly, the boundaries between IPE and domination theories tend to blur. Thus, anti-colonial rhetoric softens the theoretical outlines of realism and IPE. This parlance, including realism and anti-colonial rhetoric, seems to suggest fragmentation from the global point of view. In regard to ASEAN cooperation, theorists often refer to the institutionalist basis of cooperation. Southeast Asian regionalist debate reveals, thus, a strong constructivist undercurrent.

Although most of the political arguments in Southeast Asian regionalist discussion derive from these approaches, the functionalist point of view does surface, particularly in Southeast Asian academic discussions. As functionalism emphasizes economic as well as political integration, it can be seen as tracing a tendency opposite to realism. In recent Southeast Asian discussions, functionalist, constructivist and IPE approaches often overlap.

Functionalism and Institutionalism in Southeast Asian Regionalism

In European integration, the theoretical basis for federalism relies on functionalist and neo-functionalist theories. Functionalist theories emphasize how cooperation and integration in a certain sphere spread out to other sectors. The starting point is economic cooperation and integration, which demands legislative cooperation and harmonization within the participating countries. In order to control and execute harmonization, a common institution is needed, and a common institution presupposes even closer cooperation at the political level. As this *spill-over* continues, national sovereignty diminishes and common regional institutions take over the role of the state in various sectors.

The history of the European Union (EU) illustrates this process exactly. The EU started from the European Coal and Steel Community (1951) which was designed to establish a common market for coal and steel and to allow common control and exploitation of these materials. This establishment of a supranational institution and later the spread of cooperation among the member countries to other sectors – first to the European Defense Community (1952) and then to the treaties of Rome (1957) and the creation of the European Economic Community (EEC) – meant the enforcing of a supranational approach. Due to stagnation of the integration process, the intergovernmental approach gained strength during the 1960s and 1970s. However, the Single European Act of 1987 and the creation of the European Union meant that European integration reached into many and diverse areas, fulfilling the federalist plans of the 1950s and the 1960s and cutting nation-states' roles in many important sectors.

The development of nation-states in Southeast Asia has not so far supported such theories. Regionalism has been a state-led political project in which economic integration played no role before the 1990s. Surprisingly, however, the first noteworthy study on Southeast Asian regionalism, Estrella Solidum's *Towards A Southeast Asian Community* (1974), depended on functionalist starting points. Solidum's study is based on her Ph.D. dissertation (Solidum 1970) which was completed only a few years after the first steps toward ASEAN were taken. In *Towards A Southeast Asian Community* she examined whether the functional cooperation had *spill-over* impacts leading to integration. Although her answer was negative,[9] her approach was greatly influenced by the integration studies dealing with the European Community.

Solidum found three principal elements behind the political cooperation in Southeast Asia – namely external threat, internal stability and economic development.[10] The first refers to the Cold War's political context. The second and third provide points of departure for the "Asian" politico-economic model, which was central to the ASEAN organization's identity-building during the notable period of economic development in Southeast Asia in the 1980s and 1990s.

The findings of Solidum's work on Southeast Asian regionalism have been repeated in numerous studies. The model of ASEAN's decision-making through consensus, possibly the most repeated finding, provides a stronghold for the constructivist approach in Southeast Asian regionalist studies. In this model, ASEAN member states try to make decisions through the concepts of *mushawarah* (consultations) and *mufakat* (consensus) on matters where unanimity is possible. While this kind of decision-making system is not efficient, every decision made this way enforces the unity of the organization. According to Solidum's second finding, the organization does not aim at institutional development, but at functional cooperation.[11] Later studies of Southeast Asian regionalism have often emphasized and even idealized both of these characteristics.[12]

However, post-Cold War ASEAN studies have ignored the third characteristic highlighted by Solidum, the condition of nation-building and the colonial past. In fact, as Solidum points out, the first two characteristics follow as consequences of the third.[13] From the point of view of integration, the colonial past and nation-building conditions in Southeast Asia work as fragmentative factors and have necessitated an intensive identity-building effort in ASEAN in order to accommodate this element in regional cooperation. Solidum herself turned more to ASEAN's decision-making, in which functionalist ideas are obscured.

Whether Solidum's study has had an impact on ASEAN's development is an open question. Certainly she influenced Southeast Asian regionalist discussion. However, when, after the Cold War, the discussion on economic cooperation and possible economic integration in the ASEAN area really started, she did not take part in it, as she continued to focus on constructivist starting points.

The establishment of the Free Trade Area (AFTA) in 1992 provided a springboard for new discussion on integration. In general, AFTA can be examined from the point of view of functional cooperation, as it focused on economic cooperation. This economic cooperation has created a new kind of discussion emphasizing the *spill-over* effects of functional economic cooperation for other sectors.[14]

The functionalist starting points leading toward deeper economic and political integration have particularly interested Southeast Asian economists. Pressure for ASEAN's integration has been felt first of all in the area of economic legislation, beginning with issues of customs and foreign trade and moving into more profound domestic legislation. In this process, the European Community and then the European Union have served as examples.[15] Economic interdependence is leading to the harmonization of domestic institutions as well as toward greater adherence to democratic principles in Southeast Asian countries.[16]

While this Southeast Asian model differs markedly from neo-functionalism, in which harmonization is conducted by common institutions, the claim that integration is not part of Southeast Asian regionalism becomes harder and harder to support. In discussions of Southeast Asian regionalism, AFTA is seen as "as a step toward economic integration", in which "market forces are already driving economic integration in ASEAN without reference to the political readiness of the member states to yield part of state sovereignty to a larger unit".[17] Thus, "[i]f successfully implemented, AFTA will be another facet of growing ASEAN economic interdependence and integration".[18]

After the Asian economic crisis and partly owing to ASEAN's inability to handle it, calls for more coherent integrative efforts were made by Southeast Asian experts and academics. The new suggestions have included both shifting from the old ASEAN idea of consensus toward more effective decision-making processes and moving toward supra-regional institutions. [19]

Regional cooperation leading to institution-building has not played a similar role in the constructivist approach as it has in functionalism. Nevertheless, constructivism does also emphasize institution-building, although not the kind that entails common institutions and diminishing national sovereignty. The constructivist approach emphasizes the importance of rules, norms, institutions and identities in driving human behavior. In a more political framework, this approach is thus called institutionalism. In ASEAN cooperation, behavioral norms, rather than formal rules and regulations, occupy a central position. These characteristics of ASEAN regionalism – emphasizing common norms and basing decision-making on *mushawarah* and *mufakat* rather than building organizational structures – strongly support the constructivist research enterprise. Often called the "ASEAN way", these special elements come together to suggest that a regional identity has already emerged. These identity-forming "soft features" make up the essence of ASEAN, while the "hard features", such as geography (ten Southeast Asian countries)[20] and the ASEAN treaties, form the contextual framework of the organization.[21]

Solidum, who turned from a functionalist enterprise to a more constructivist approach, emphasized the necessity of enforcing certain cultural elements as "a regional culture will necessarily be the cement that binds the peoples of the five states".[22] However, as Solidum pointed out, even though member nations believe that "the ASEAN way" has developed from cultural values shared among the ASEAN states, the fact is that these elements also derive from principles appearing in ASEAN declarations made by the organization's leaders. Therefore an extra-cultural component coming from the region's top political elite has had a role in constructing a common ASEAN culture. Solidum contemplated such methods of introducing the ideas of the elite to the ordinary ASEAN citizens and concluded that a select strata in member countries – including political elites, interest groups, and businesses as well as universities – should indoctrinate ASEAN norms of behavior into the general population. In this process, the "ASEAN way" should be presented as the "prototype of an ASEAN culture".[23]

As Solidum's example shows, the scholars and expertise groups have taken part in ASEAN's identity-building. In fact, the concept of epistemic communities includes the constructivist idea. At ASEAN's track two meetings, particularly among the network of the ASEAN Institutes of Strategic and International Studies, ASEAN-ISIS, institutionalist ideas have been constantly repeated. The norms and rules in ASEAN's decision-making institutions have been focused on in numerous studies of ASEAN scholars and think-tanks. During the 1990s, the discussion of ASEAN's enlargement, rather than an attempt to strengthen regional integration, directed this focus.[24] This was due to the clearly lower economic levels of the new member candidates, which would have the difficult task of integrating into the regional economic system. For institutionalists, the interest lies not in economic and political integration, but in cooperation between the national states. Institutionalists believe that "the security of all of Southeast Asia is inter-linked, that the comprehensive security and prosperity of each of the states of the region is very closely tied to the comprehensive security and prosperity of the entire region".[25] In this belief, institutionalists follow quite closely the official line of the organization.

Nevertheless, the dividing line between institutionalism and functionalism is sometimes difficult to find. For example, the institutionalists often urge a strengthening of ASEAN's decision-making processes, while suggesting partly to abandon consensus decision-making in order to make ASEAN's organization more effective, thus approaching the idea of neo-functional integration. An effective decision-making system relying on majority decisions necessitates nation-states giving up part of their sovereignty. Such a move clearly means integration in a neo-functionalist mode.[26]

International Political Economy and Southeast Asian Realism

International Political Economy: the Prospects for Regionalism

All the theories of IPE originate from the assumption that economic matters play the central role at global, regional, and local levels, having thus a crucial impact on political development. From this kernel, the IPE studies advance in different directions, from liberal theories through domination theories. The other variable in these studies is the role of the nation-state and the government; whether it is an initiating force in the development or whether it only executes the will of the economic forces. Therefore, the questions of fragmentation and integration particularly divide the debate in the IPE context.

The relevance of IPE in Southeast Asian regionalism lies in the fact that the arguments supporting the need for a regional organization, ASEAN, closely parallel IPE's central premises and concepts. These arguments have been outlined in the ASEAN documents and treaties, particularly in the Bali treaties and declarations. From the very beginning ASEAN adopted such concepts as interdependence, self-reliance, and self-resilience, common concepts within the Third World Movement. The concept of interdependence, which was a negative force in the domination theories, has a positive connotation in ASEAN's vocabulary.

Interestingly enough, at the beginning of mutual co-operation, the ASEAN countries did not focus on economic aspects at all; they did not even mention trade liberalization and integration in their agenda. The Southeast Asian countries and the ASEAN organization adopted the general goals of the Third World Movement, which emphasized establishing self-reliant national economies and sovereign governments.

However, the examination of the ASEAN countries only as a part of general Third World currents obscures the particular characteristics of their strategies. The means taken by the ASEAN countries to achieve strong economies and politically sovereign governments differ from the general trend among Third World countries. The ASEAN countries did not take an active part in the Third World front and claim better terms of trade under the rubric of the New International Economic Order for the countries producing raw materials. Instead, the ASEAN countries in their national policies chose the way which some new East-Asian economies, first Japan and then South Korea, Taiwan and Singapore, chose earlier. The basic principle of their strategy was to adjust their economies and societies to the needs of global trade by encouraging investments in export-intensive industries. Although various ASEAN countries applied the new Asian approach differently, the general point of departure was to take advantage of the globalizing trends of the world economy and politics, not to resist them. When economic cooperation was later taken into ASEAN's agenda, it became the organization's main mantra. As a result, Southeast Asian regionalism has not reinforced the fragmentation of the world economy, but rather staged a managed effort at adapting into the world economy. In fact, Southeast Asian regionalism has been followed, particularly during the 1980s, by other regional agreements in the Third World which aim at integration into the global economy by first liberating regional trade.[27]

Although economic cooperation did not become the practical policy of ASEAN until the 1990s, economic factors became undercurrents in political legitimization in Southeast Asian countries. It is, therefore, difficult to analyze to what extent the ASEAN experts are repeating the mantras of the ASEAN governments and what can be considered as a part of their own ideas and knowledge. Starting from economic forces, however, very different political lines originate with the ASEAN experts and academics. Andrew MacIntyre, when exploring the communities of Indonesian economic experts, found three groups with different views on national- and regional-level economic policy.[28] He studied only the expertise quite close to the government and did not mention the radical trends occurring in academic circles and particularly in the NGOs. An examination extended to cover all of Southeast Asia includes a much larger number of different intellectual communities. In order to collect these many approaches, I outline three categories which illustrate the various uses of economic bases to defend or reject regional cooperation.

In the first ASEAN interpretation of regionalism, the role of sovereign states is reinforced by regional cooperation. This interpretation follows the premises of the NIC countries in which the necessity for international trade is recognized, but the sovereignty of the state is also emphasized. Regionalism and regional cooperation accommodate the national economies to the global economy and protect the nation-states' autonomy against global pressures.

These nationalist-regionalists sometimes sing the same tunes as leftist academics or NGO groups. On the political level, its purest representative is the Malaysian Prime Minister, Mahathir Mohamad. In fact, Mahathir's loudly voiced ideas have found their way into the work of many Southeast Asian academics.[29] The main emphasis of this understanding of Southeast Asian regionalism does not rest on regional economic cooperation, let alone on economic integration, but on the region's attempt to resist the negative impact of globalization, particularly the threat posed to national sovereignty, local culture, and national economies.

According to the nationalist-regionalist paradigm, the particular need for regional cooperation originates from geographical factors, since the Southeast Asia cultural currents and trade routes from the West, South, and East Asia meet. Since the area has attracted modern Western imperialist and militarist powers, who have tried to spread their military, economic and cultural domination throughout the region, a regionalist approach should not be limited to the Southeast Asian region, but may also include East-Asia. The main concern of the nationalist-regionalist expertise group is the possibility of the US seeking to control East- and Southeast Asia by both military and economic means.[30] Thus nationalist arguments on regionalism made by Southeast Asian academics combine both neo-colonial critique, pan-Asianism, nationalism and regionalist ideas. [31]

Whether this position means fragmentation is a matter of question. From the point of view of globalization, it is evidently a fragmentative tendency. However, from the point of view of regionalism, the question is much more complicated. On the one hand, it can be argued that this approach enforces regional cooperation but does not mean integration and not necessarily ASEAN cooperation. From the nationalist point of view, the approach emphasizes nation-state-based cooperation in ASEAN.

In spite of the fact that this approach deals with both organization and regionalism, the single state remains the basic unit.[32] Hence, this group is rather close to neorealist theories in which the state is an actor in a complex interdependence of international systems. However, two developments in the 1990s forced even these nationalist-regionalists into taking ASEAN into consideration as an organization, namely the enlargement of ASEAN and changes in the global economy. Asia-Pacific economic development, particularly Asia-Pacific Economic Co-operation

(APEC), the formation of the European Union, and the Asian economic crisis more recently also brought organizational questions to the fore.

Their positions on these questions of globalism separate nationalist-regionalists from two other communities, leftist anti-globalists and liberal globalists. Despite their anti-Western and sometimes anti-colonial rhetoric, the Southeast Asian nationalist-regionalists have never been anti-globalist like the leftist anti-globalists, nor have they accepted unlimited economic freedom as a driving force for their national development. In leftist discourse, regionalism is not the most popular topic, but it is not totally rejected. It connects anti-colonial rhetoric and neo-colonialist critique with an emphasis on national sovereignty. In this way, it approaches nationalist rhetoric.

Interestingly enough, the two extreme points on the continuum of this discussion, radical neo-colonialist critique and economic and political liberalism, can be found in the Filipino discourse. Undoubtedly, both were spawned in the particular political and academic conditions in the Philippines. The political pluralism of the Philippines, on the one hand, and the special relationship with the USA, on the other, is reflected in academic discourse. Hence American-style political liberalism is challenged by nationalist and leftist thinking based on the neo-colonialist critique.

The extreme ends of Filipino discourse stand out in relief in the discussion of the general issues of globalization. The major proponents of neo-colonialist critique can be found in academic circles. There the discussion blends with nationalistic tendencies, particularly when the discourse focuses on political aspects. According to nationalist thinking, globalization tries to demolish all the borders which separate Philippine society from the global capitalist system. Throughout its history, Philippine society has opposed this tendency: "the major impetus for most if not all nationalist mass movements in the country is the struggle against colonial and capitalist domination.... Globalization and imperialism, therefore, can be viewed as major stumbling blocs in the realization of Philippine nationalist aspirations."[33] Globalization, while derailing national economic and social policies, brings capitalist and neo-colonialist fluctuations and cultural and political dependency on the Asia-Pacific economic superpower, the United States. Thus, in this context globalization is often understood as "Americanization".[34]

The advocates of free trade and globalization have a rather different point of departure. Some of them refer to an ideal version of the Asian model, according to which trade and investments become the crucial keys for economic growth in the Asia-Pacific region. However, these liberalist thinkers do not depend solely on economic arguments to promote free trade, but also on a more political point of view. In his analysis, a Filipino academic, Julius Caesar Parreñas, approaches European functionalists: He argues that economic interdependence reduces the possibility of military conflicts between nations which are in economic cooperation. Thus, he concludes, "[o]pen borders and markets temper the need for absolute control over territory and convert border areas from barriers into bridges for trade between countries. This is especially significant for the Asia-Pacific, where potential conflicts over various unresolved territorial disputes abound."[35]

In fact, similar borderlines can be seen when dealing with regionalism. From the liberalist point of view, as regionalism is only a springboard for globalism, regional organizations should definitely not attempt to create trading blocs. Therefore Parreñas maintains that the Philippines also has interests in 'open' regionalism on a global basis "instead of an exclusive Asia-Pacific trading bloc". Thus, he prefers trade liberalization on a global scope and "facilitation of trade and investment flows, rather than one that is limited only to the region".[36] Accordingly, his arguments for the advantages of globalization include both peace and welfare, as opposed to neo-colonialist critique.

(Neo)realist Discourse: the Nation-state and Regional Cooperation

Although realist theory ignores regionalism as an alternative to the nation-state system and deals with regional cooperation as a form of alliance-building, a remarkable part of Southeast Asian regionalism can be understood only in light of realist discourse. ASEAN is characteristically an intergovernmental organization. Its starting point is to support Southeast Asian nation-building. The premises of neorealism, which acknowledge the concept of interdependence, but also the interests of sovereign states, seems to support Southeast Asian regionalist endeavors.

However, as one Southeast Asian analyst put it: "regionalism is more than *realpolitik*; it is also commitments to certain ideals and principles of cooperation".[37] In reverse, it is also obvious that realist discourse is held in a regionalist context. Nevertheless this approach refers to cooperation on the governmental level and strictly from the point of view of national interests.

ASEAN's common policies toward external actors such as the EU, and its negotiations in the World Trade Organization (WTO) have enforced realist premises. The enlargement of ASEAN with new members

– first with Vietnam in 1995, then with Laos and Myanmar (Burma) in 1997, and at last with Cambodia in 1999 – has further reinforced the realist point of view over institutionalist and functionalist considerations. The Western critique of Myanmar's membership, due to its bad human rights records, stimulated ASEAN's need to unite itself against foreign pressure. Similarly, the differences between these new members and the old ASEAN members in terms of socio-economic underdevelopment do not support ASEAN's institution-building efforts, but rather fit more into ASEAN's geostrategic considerations.

The inclusion of the new members into ASEAN raises two issues: the norms of cooperation and the political power of the organization. In the epistemic community, more interest is devoted to the first; among the political circles, the emphasis has been on the second. Southeast Asian experts have referred particularly to the different politico-cultural experience of the new members and thus their possible problems in adopting ASEAN norms. From the point of view of political power, the arguments have been made that the process of ASEAN enlargement has united the organization. The fact that all Southeast Asian countries are now members enhances the bargaining position of regional countries in international organizations, such as the WTO.[38] Similarly, the enlarged organization helps to resist the foreign influence particularly posed by the US and the EU. However, the Southeast Asian experts' position against the membership of Myanmar refers to the same argument of *realpolitik*: ASEAN stands to lose its international influence because of Myanmar's membership.[39]

Security issues have become a part of the discussion of ASEAN enlargement and economic cooperation, opening up ASEAN cooperation on a broader regional and global basis. Economic and security issues combine with questions of military power and economic influence to produce a complex formula among Southeast Asian politicians and academics.

There seem to be two main trends in that discussion. The first pays attention to the growth of the military in the Asia-Pacific area, particularly to the growing might of the PRC's army, while the second focuses on the economic influence of the US, especially after the Asian economic crises. The latter discussion includes elements of IPE discourse, and in it the lines between IPE and neorealism blur.

Characteristically, neorealist discourse emphasizes a broader regional sphere than solely ASEAN cooperation. The point of departure is that ASEAN countries are far too weak in economic, political, and military terms to develop a regional organization which can protect the members against external economic and security threats. Thus, for example, the participants in the security forum organized by ASEAN, the ASEAN Regional Forum (ARF), are not only the ASEAN countries, but also the major Asia-Pacific and global actors. Again, the ARF does not aim at supra-national institution-building, but at flexible rules which stabilize the political and strategic system in the area. This orientation seems to be evident both in the work of the decision-makers and the scholars who prefer Southeast Asian political cooperation.[40] Similarly, as there is no common base for concrete military cooperation between the ASEAN countries, the organization is seen as a mechanism of dispute settlement and an institution for confidence-building.[41]

However, there is, from the realist standpoint, a hard critique against the Southeast Asian security mechanism which pushes aside traditional military alliances, particularly the U.S. role in the area. In fact, this critique parallels the argument that views ASEAN economic integration as insignificant due to the size and the weakness of regional economies. Interestingly enough, whereas the economic argument prefers ASEAN's integration into a greater East-Asian economic system in order to resist US economic power, the security argument insists that the US military presence is necessary in order to balance the PRC's or Japan's military supremacy in the area.[42] In fact, the ARF is criticized as a neo-Wilsonian idea, totally incompatible with Southeast Asian security needs. The multilateral forums, where other than regional countries are involved, give external powers with direct political interests, such as China, a chance to enact a policy of divide and rule.[43]

REGIONALIST DISCOURSE IN POLITICAL CONTEXT: A HISTORICAL PERSPECTIVE

Despite certain links between academic regionalist discourse and the political development of the ASEAN organization, academic views of regionalist endeavors in ASEAN differ in many respects from the views of national governments and leaderships. Many factors account for these differences. First of all, before the 1990s important national decisions were made outside the context of the organization. Excluding ASEAN's common position on the Kampuchean conflict, the organization never made a decision against the interests of any of the member countries. Particularly in the early days, the organization seemed not to have any specific aim, and it was criticized as a mere discussion club.

Nevertheless, more positive estimations see ASEAN's loose organizational structure as a strength. In the context of a changing international system, its only slightly institutionalized decision-making system has been viewed positively. The concept of new regionalism, advocated particularly by Norman Palmer, emphasizes this flexibility. In fact, ASEAN has developed from many different elements inside a changing international context. In 1967, when the Bangkok Declaration was launched, two factors were obvious: The role of Southeast Asian countries in the Cold War's two-bloc system and their role in the post-colonial economic system. The first factor located the ASEAN countries in the Western camp, while the second forced these countries to search for positions in the Third World movement. A third element emerged during the 1970s and the 1980s, namely, economic development in the East and Southeast Asia. The rapid economic development gave a new context to the Southeast Asian regional organization. This latter part of the chapter examines how regionalism was justified in ASEAN vis-à-vis political developments before the Asian economic crisis in 1997.

Realism as a Cold War Heritage in Southeast Asian Political Discourse

When ASEAN was established during the intensive phase of the Vietnam war, the organization was generally considered both in the Western and Eastern camps as a minor actor and a minor Western ally in the Cold War struggle in Asia. The view of ASEAN as an anti-communist bloc in Southeast Asia further solidified when the ASEAN countries rejected Vietnam's invasion of Democratic Kampuchea and formed an international front against Vietnam's Indochina policy during the 1980s.[44]

In fact, despite ASEAN's common stance against Vietnam's policy, the individual ASEAN countries held different views on Vietnam. Nevertheless, rationalist arguments emphasizing power relations in Southeast Asia gained strength and dominated the parlance of the leaders of the ASEAN countries. Realism, understanding power relationships as a basic element in interstate relations, shapes the ideas of many Southeast Asian politicians. The premises of realism contribute most obviously to the thinking of Singaporean first generation leadership. Together with their Premier Lee Kuan Yew, Singaporean cabinet members often argued their views on regional issues by referring clearly to power relations, sometimes in a very naturalistic manner. According to realist analysis, the international system is constituted by sovereign states which are, at least potentially, in conflict with each other.[45] This possible conflict is obvious not only between the regional states, but also between superpower(s) and regional state(s). The superpowers can destabilize the regional systems particularly by intervening into affairs of the regional states. Although dominant in Singaporean political parlance, realist arguments are not ignored by other Southeast Asian politicians either.[46]

The interesting thing is how realist ideas have worked in regionalist thinking. Of course, in certain historical situations realist arguments have stood out in high relief – a fact which should be noticed when generalizations are made. Similarly, it is important to notice whether these arguments refer to regional interstate relations or the region's external relations. For regional interstate relations, the nation-building process and the conflicts between regional states have strengthened realist ideas. For the region's external relations, the superpower relations and the Cold War conflict have equally supported realist arguments.

In Southeast Asia, the economy serves as a bridge between regionalism and realism. Characteristically, economic strength has always been considered an important part of political power in Southeast Asian realist thinking. In this way, such thinking approaches neorealism. Accordingly, economic situations affect political relations in the region in various ways. First, economic underdevelopment and instability undermine existing political systems and fertilize revolutionary movements. Political instability in one country can threaten interstate relations in the region. Furthermore, both domestic and interstate conflicts give opportunities to foreign powers to intervene in Southeast Asian affairs.[47]

A political solution to these potential problems involves the development of national and regional economies and blends Southeast Asian realist thinking with functionalist ideas. In this approach the most important task is to develop national economies to the phase where the basic needs of the population are satisfied and the revolutionary energy of internal movements can be absorbed. Also important is positive economic interdependence between the regional states, which provides common incentives to maintain stable and peaceful development in the area.[48] The task of regional organization is to catalyze this kind of development in the region. If the organization did make modest attempts at harmonizing ASEAN's internal trade, no serious common efforts for liberalizing intra-ASEAN trade had been made before the 1990s. ASEAN was seen as a mechanism for reconciling the interests of regional states.

In realist parlance, regionalism has been seen as an alliance of like-minded states and governments in a region. However, regional organization alone cannot sufficiently guarantee regional stability; such stability calls for national measures, first of all economic, but also those involving national defense and relationships with foreign powers. In these very important political and strategic arenas, the ASEAN countries have had serious difficulties adjusting national views to fit the policies of ASEAN. In spite of the fact that the main documents of ASEAN include the idea of absorbing the influence of the external powers in the area, the national governments have very different views about how such a goal can be realized.

All the national governments of the ASEAN countries embraced the same priority – to prevent any foreign power from intervening into Southeast Asian affairs. However, each member country differed from every other in terms of its particular government, its position inside the Southeast Asian regional system, and its relations to the superpowers. As a result, the Southeast Asian countries made their own unilateral defense and security commitments which, if not threatening the security interests of others, were difficult to harmonize into a general ASEAN line.

The most obvious difference among ASEAN countries has been their position toward external powers. When the Bangkok Declaration was signed in 1967 and even when the Kuala Lumpur Declaration was accepted by the ASEAN governments in 1971, two member countries, Thailand and the Philippines, had military treaties with the US; Malaysia and Singapore were linked to Great Britain through the Five Powers Treaty. The second factor influencing the attitude toward external powers was the position of the ASEAN members in the Third World movement, primarily among the Non-Aligned Movement (NAM). Even though these politico-military factors determined member countries' relationships with external powers, the theoretical arguments used to justify these relationships shed interesting light on the nature of Southeast Asian realism.

The common attempt of the ASEAN countries to avoid superpower interference focused on the concept of neutrality or, better, "neutralization". A paragraph in the Bangkok Declaration asserted that foreign military bases in Southeast Asia should be temporary, and the Kuala Lumpur ZOPFAN (Zone of Peace, Freedom and Neutrality) Declaration made an even more straightforward claim for neutrality. However, through a political compromise, the various ASEAN countries retained the right to interpret individually exactly what "neutralization" might mean.[49]

In brief, there were three kinds of answers to the question of the external powers' role in Southeast Asian regionalism. First, Indonesia answered this question by maintaining that external powers should not have any kind of role in Southeast Asia. Second, Malaysia proposed that the external powers should guarantee Southeast Asian neutrality. Last, other countries supported the view that the balanced presence of the external powers in the area should secure regional peace in Southeast Asia.[50]

Particularly in the rhetoric of Singaporean leaders, the need for external powers to play a balancing role in Southeast Asia appears in very clear form. When, for example, the Malaysian view emphasized the need to maintain a neutral stance toward outside powers,[51] the Singaporean approach emphasized the need for external powers to intervene when there is a danger that some power – external or regional – threatens Southeast Asian regional order. This Singaporean analysis is based purely on the balance of power in Southeast Asia.[52] Since the pursuit of power is universal, the intentions of regional as well as foreign powers could prove equal threats to the existing regional order.

The Singaporean analysis was not easy to accept – particularly in Indonesia and Malaysia.[53] However, Malaysian thinking did not totally reject the role of external powers, as "[r]ealistically, however, such disengagement [of external powers] cannot be expected until and unless South East Asia develops national and regional resilience. Without such resilience, many South East Asian countries would not forego the security insurance that external power presence appears to provide."[54] The Kampuchean conflict, which united ASEAN's external policy and supported Singapore's argument to accept the US presence in Southeast Asia, also pushed the question of the content of neutralism largely aside. Nonetheless, this sometimes latent contradiction between ASEAN's declared project of neutralization and the realities of the role of foreign powers in Southeast Asia has came to the fore from time to time – most recently in the 1990s.[55]

The Vietnamese invasion of Democratic Kampuchea in December, 1978, and the military incidents at Thailand's border which followed, reinforced realist parlance among the ASEAN countries. ASEAN based its common stance toward the Kampuchean question strictly on the respect for national sovereignty and non-interference in internal affairs. This position put aside the humanitarian arguments which supported the defeat of Pol Pot's administration and the Vietnamese invasion. Similarly détente between the ASEAN countries and Vietnam was frozen. ASEAN policy considered Vietnam's move as power politics to be balanced only by correspondingly strong countermeasures. These countermeasures called for, first of all, the united ASEAN stand in which both Malaysia's and Indonesia's sympathetic attitude toward Vietnam gave way to Singapore's and Thailand's hard-line policy. In taking such a stand,

ASEAN gave at least partial approval to the Singaporean analysis of the balance of power in Southeast Asia.[56]

The realist parlance focused on governmental cooperation and political harmonization on the diplomatic front. As in realist theory, Southeast Asian politicians' rationalist arguments are based on the concept of sovereign states which are eager to pursue political power and hegemony. Characteristically, however, Southeast Asian political power is not based solely on military power, but also on economic development and growth. Here again, the role of governmental cooperation in Southeast Asia is to support the economic development of the nation-states and the economic growth of the whole region.

The question is, what kinds of elements are left in Southeast Asian realism after the end of the Cold War? As realism relied firmly on the Cold War's international structure, is there any relevance for it in the present situation? At least two main elements have disappeared from the Southeast Asian political theatre: The Vietnamese domination of Indochina and the Soviet Union's presence in Southeast Asian politics. In this altered post-Cold War situation, Southeast Asian countries enjoyed an economic boom and then suffered the 1997 crisis. What is the realist view on regionalism in this new context of the 1990s and the 2000s?

From Post-Colonial Economic Status to Southeast Asian Economic Miracle: Functionalism and IPE

Although the ASEAN organization has been based on intergovernmental cooperation among sovereign states, the political vocabulary which developed in ASEAN's cooperation and treaties strayed rather far from traditional realism. Despite its obvious rationalism, closer reference can be found to economic theories and functionalism. Similarly, the neorealist approach, which developed later, adopted ideas such as interdependence, which were already familiar both in dependence theories and in ASEAN cooperation.

Certain sources contributed richly to ASEAN's political vocabulary. Most of the Southeast Asian countries were old colonies, and three of the ASEAN countries were members of the Non-Aligned Movement. The anti-colonialist tradition ran particularly strong in Indonesia, where former president Sukarno was a prominent figure in the Third World movement. During his presidency, Indonesia was one of the leading countries in the Non-Aligned Movement, in which a neutralist approach blended with some anti-Western tendencies. Despite their Western orientation, an anti-colonialist tendency can be found also in the Malaysian and the Philippine leadership and among the first generation Singaporean leaders.[57]

Whether or not Sukarno's nationalism and populism showed Marxist influences is not the question of main importance. Surely he was anti-colonial and anti-Western. Sukarno followed the non-aligned mainstream thinking in which non-alignment did not mean absolute neutrality in the global system. Hence, this rhetoric drew a dividing line between independence and colonialism: "In every single case, the cause, the root of international tension, is imperialism and colonialism and the forcible division of nations. ... History in the past and the realities of today prove that different social systems can co-exist, but there can be no co-existence between independence and justice on one side and imperialism-colonialism on the other side."[58]

In spite of the fact that other Southeast Asian governments did not accept Sukarno's *konfrontasi*[59] in Southeast Asia and its anti-Western orientation and were not sorry for Sukarno's fall, anti-colonialism still prevailed among the politicians of Western-oriented governments. Even the Singaporean People's Action Party, which turned anti-Communist, was influenced by anti-colonialism.[60] Long-standing Malaysian premier Mahathir Mohamad adopted Sukarno's rhetoric, at least partly, from the former Indonesian leader.[61] During the 1970s, when developing Southeast Asian countries became industrial competitors with European countries in some sectors, industrializing Southeast Asian countries reintroduced an anti-colonial vocabulary. In this discourse, ASEAN's role as a tool for cutting ties with old colonial masters was emphasized.[62]

Neutralism, which was an important part of Southeast Asian regionalism, refers also to the Third World movement. Indonesia, particularly, tried to attract two non-aligned Southeast Asian countries, Laos and Burma, to the new organization, in order to avoid pro-Western leaning in ASEAN.[63] Similarly, the concept of neutrality and ZOPFAN, discussed earlier, can be understood in the context of the Non-Aligned Movement. The concept was even adopted into the Political Declaration of NAM's Algiers Conference of 1973, but rejected at the following Conference owing to pressure from Laos and Vietnam.[64] As the content of neutrality of ZOPFAN varied according to which Southeast Asian country defined it, its meaning could not be directly derived from the NAM, but from the broader two-bloc structure in Southeast Asia.

However, the line between anti-colonial rhetoric and new economic parlance in ASEAN is very obscure. The ASEAN declarations adopted several terms already familiar in Sukarno's *Pancasila*. Together with *gotong royong* (collective activity, collective effort for a common goal), *mushawarah* and *mufakat,* several other ideas of Indonesian nation-building ideology were used to describe ASEAN cooperation. Owing to these ideas, which emphasize economic growth as a central part of nationalism, ASEAN cooperation partakes of many functionalist elements. In fact, in Southeast Asian regionalist thinking dependence theories were turned upside down: global capitalism should be taken advantage of and old colonial dependencies should be replaced or balanced by regional cooperation. On the other hand, nationalism and the strong emphasis on sovereignty made enacting regional cooperative ideas seriously difficult in ASEAN.

The idea is that national strategies should be realized also at the regional level. Thus economic interdependence which integrates national units also has positive economic effects on the whole Southeast Asian region. In terms of nation-building, regional interdependence was seen as a desirable alternative to dependence on Western economic powers. When connected to the export-oriented economic model, the economic idea was emphasized in Southeast Asian regionalist thinking, separating it further from traditional anti-colonialism.

However, as mentioned above, national policies remained obstacles. The Southeast Asian countries made better competitors than collaborators in the global and regional markets, and the governments (especially Indonesia and Malaysia) had big national plans for industrialization. The various governments resolved the issues of national and foreign political and economic ties in different ways: the Philippines and Thailand maintained their traditional connection to the US; Malaysian Premier Mahathir separated from the old British connections by turning toward Japan;[65] and Indonesia continued its old national projects. Only Singapore seemed ready for comprehensive regional trade arrangements.

Despite the difficulties of integrating Southeast Asian economies under a regional organization, the intention of creating Southeast Asia as a self-reliant and cooperative area remained in the vocabulary of the ASEAN declarations and documents. Similarly functionalist ideas emphasizing regional interdependence can be found in the rhetoric of the ASEAN leaders and political elites. Characteristically, functionalist elements were mixed with anti-colonial rhetoric. Neocolonialism was seen as a serious danger for the Third World countries. However, Southeast Asian regionalism would provide a convenient tool to avoid neocolonialist dominance. Accordingly, Southeast Asia has "gone further in this direction [regionalism] than . . . most Third World countries", which have failed to forge a compromise between nationalism and regionalism and with that failure continue to "provide opportunities for intervention by and dependence on outside powers".[66]

In the early days of ASEAN these functionalist ideas were put into practice by establishing committees to aid cooperative efforts. These committees included: food production; civil air transport; communication; air traffic services; and meteorology. Committees for shipping and commerce and industry were also established. After 1975 the number of these functionalist committees grew significantly.

Although these committees imply the intention for cooperation more than they imply intense and effective cooperation itself, several elements seem to be clear among the Southeast Asian political elite. First, state sovereignty cannot be maintained in isolation, since global interdependence calls for regional cooperation. The circumstances promoting national sovereignty can best be realized through peaceful and stable development in the area. Second, functional cooperation means common organizations. Even though public debate has yet to include a discussion of what kind of common authorities should be established and what their competence should be, the willingness to cross national boundaries exists. After the Bali Summit of 1976, a Singaporean cabinet member commented on the industrial projects launched in Bali by referring to "the market in ASEAN" which "covers 200 million people whose potential purchasing power is enormous". He added that "those in Bali realized that the regional market by itself was not enough and that the order of priorities was to be first the national market, then the regional market, and finally the world market".[67]

In fact, the Bali Declaration of ASEAN Concord meant that economic functional cooperation grew remarkably. After the Declaration, ASEAN played a different kind of economic role than it had earlier. The ASEAN countries used the ASEAN organization as a pressure group in their dealing with the European Community. When the United Kingdom joined the EC in the beginning of the 1970s and had to cut down preferential trade agreements with her old colonies, the ASEAN countries tried to get equal treatment with the Lomé countries, albeit without great success.[68]

Similarly, the ASEAN countries started to act as one group toward other external powers, particularly toward Japan. The growing economic and political relations between Japan and the ASEAN countries came in the wake of the American disengagement from Southeast Asia. The growing interest of Japan toward the ASEAN countries was thus welcomed in the area. The new relations between Japan and the ASEAN countries produced the stabilization of export earning scheme (STABEX) between

Japan and the ASEAN countries in 1977. This is particularly important, as the STABEX was an institutionalization of the Lomé convention which ASEAN failed to accomplish with the EC.[69] An equally important experience was that, in its relations toward the EC and Japan, ASEAN turned from consultation to common action.

Besides these external developments, the ASEAN countries signed a Preferential Trade Arrangements (PTA) agreement in Manila on 24 February 1977, which provided for the reduction of tariffs in intra-ASEAN trade on an item-by-item basis. The principle of the agreement was important, although it never catalyzed intra-regional trade in ASEAN because it covered only a limited range of products. In fact, after PTA, intra-ASEAN trade dropped below pre-PTA levels, as the Exclusion List left out enough important products to water down the idea of PTA.[70] Thus, particularly during the 1970s and the 1980s, ASEAN developed into a pressure group in the international arena rather than becoming a regional organization aiming to arrange inter-state economic and political relations among its member countries.

A modest step for the institutionalization of ASEAN was taken in Bali, when a permanent ASEAN secretariat was established. The role of the secretariat was, however, limited to working as an administrative organ in ASEAN's activities and projects. Its authority did not challenge national governmental bodies which decide on regional cooperation.[71] Therefore neither economic integration nor institutionalization of the ASEAN organization supported functionalist parlance in ASEAN cooperation.

From this point of view, interestingly enough, together with the general economic emphasis, functionalist elements survived in the parlance of Southeast Asian political elites. Nevertheless, ASEAN's external relations determined regionalist discourse during the 1970s and 1980s. Hence, anti-colonial rhetoric was a useable tool in bargaining over international economic issues with the Western countries, and realist arguments were strongly supported by Cold War conflicts and particularly by the Cambodian question.

Constructing regionalism in Post-Cold War Southeast Asia

The Vietnamese withdrawal from Cambodia in October 1991 and the Paris Peace Accords on Cambodia meant the end of the Cold War in Southeast Asia. The disappearance of the Soviet Union was only the symbolic end of the era. This change in ASEAN's external circumstances put Southeast Asian regionalism in a new situation. The old realist arguments of regionalist thinking lost their relevance. Southeast Asian politicians acknowledged the need to create a new basis for regionalist thinking. In an interview published just before the Vietnamese withdrawal from Cambodia and which was read widely in Southeast Asia, Singaporean Prime Minister Lee Kuan Yew warned that ASEAN might disintegrate with the disappearance of the uniting factor – fear of communist expansionism – and the end of the Cambodian conflict. An experienced statesman, Premier Lee introduced the theme which would replace the Cambodian question as a uniting factor for ASEAN. He suggested that the ASEAN member countries should "increase their bargaining strength against developed countries and fight against protectionism and other economic harassments".[72] Together with more political issues, this global economic point of view became the central element in ASEAN's unity in the post-Cold War situation.

Although ASEAN's role as an economic pressure group stood out in this new era, ASEAN regionalism took on other seemingly new characteristics in the 1990s. In fact, most of these characteristics echoed earlier themes, albeit carrying altered weights. The starting point in constructing ASEAN's regionalist thinking focused on the organization's uniqueness and emphasized two particular points: First, the Third World experience distinguished Southeast Asian regionalism from European regionalism. Second, the peculiar social, political, and economic order in the ASEAN countries fostered a regionalism which diverged even further from European models.

Owing to the first characteristic, Southeast Asian regionalism, which emphasizes both national sovereignty and regional order, has been difficult for Westerners and particularly European observers to understand.[73] The Third World experience refers both to the common approach toward developed countries as well to the principles of regional cooperation. By using a regional organization, the Southeast Asian countries have tried to defend their economic independence and resist cultural and political pressures from the developed West. Under the guidance of founding Southeast Asian leaders, ASEAN took on this role early, and the role was again emphasized after the end of the Cold War. As the basis for realist arguments bound to the two-bloc structure disappeared, realism turned, as Lee Kuan Yew suggested, from security questions toward economic matters. Therefore the global role of ASEAN as a politico-economic pressure group was defended by realist arguments of universal power interests, mixed with some strains of anti-colonial rhetoric.

As a consequence, functionalist thinking was, if not rejected, pushed into the background. Even in intra-ASEAN cooperation, the main interest turned toward ASEAN's enlargement. Functionalist ideas could be seen at work in the realization of AFTA, but this was not emphasized by the ASEAN governments. Only after the Asian economic crisis did functionalist ideas emerge as part of the re-formulation of Southeast Asian regionalism. Therefore, the discussion of bringing in new members reinforced the old ASEAN principles of regional cooperation. The principles of national sovereignty, non-interference in internal affairs, and regional resilience again dominated debates as ASEAN prepared to bring the Indochinese countries and Myanmar, with their different political and economic systems, into ASEAN's cooperation. The organization adopted a new concept, constructive engagement, as a tool to help new members adjust to ASEAN cooperation. The concept of constructive engagement asserted that the positive encouragement of countries with human rights problems would lead them to abandon negative practices better than would pressure and isolation.

The second element figuring large in the post-Cold War reconstruction of Southeast Asian regionalism is associated with the first. As part of defending their economic, cultural, and political independence, some Southeast Asian leaders started to introduce ideas which they claimed originated in indigenous politico-cultural backgrounds. Accordingly, the peculiarity of Southeast Asian regionalism comes from the distinct social order in the regional countries which has guaranteed long and steady economic growth and survival through the Cold War.

The distinct social orders of some ASEAN member states put the authoritarian or semi-authoritarian political system in a positive light. While the Philippines and also Thailand to some extent pursued more democratic systems, Singaporean, Malaysian, and Indonesian leadership relied on authoritarian order, justifying it with economic growth. In the beginning of the 1990s, this authoritarian tendency prevailed in Southeast Asian regionalism. In the beginning of the decade, Philippine democracy was weak and its economy in turmoil. Similarly, Thai society seemed unable to offer an attractive alternative to the other authoritarian but stable Southeast Asian countries.

The authoritarian tendency in New Asian thinking was fed by growing global economic competition and by the rejection of the Western emphasis on democracy and human rights in the post-Cold War situation. In fact, even early in the two-bloc system some arguments justified authoritarian rule as more suitable for Southeast Asian countries than participatory democracy. The defenders of authoritarian governments argued that the strict control of the governments over politics was the reason that the Southeast Asian dominoes did not fall, as predicted, in the face of Communist expansion in Asia. The situation would have been different if the Southeast Asian countries had adopted democratic systems. As Singaporean Rajaratnam put it, democratic doctrine is "something of a [sic] handicap in the deadly game of power politics".[74] Using the same rationalism, some Southeast Asian leaders argued that long and steady economic growth is not possible in a situation in which the governments would be democratically elected. To support this claim, they refer particularly to the Filipino situation after the fall of Marcos.

Authoritarian political doctrine, before it made its way into regional discussion in the beginning of the 1990s, was developed particularly in Singapore. National ideology in Singapore began in anti-communism and developed through pragmatism and rationality toward a communitarian ideology of shared values. In Singapore, where 75 per cent of the population is Chinese, Confucianism was adopted as a value base of the city-state.[75] This focus on Confucianism as a shared ideological base led to the discussion on common Asian values, first in Singapore and then in other Asian countries. Although official ASEAN documents never introduced this Confucian model, the model underlay many comments by ASEAN leaders and ASEAN joint statements.

At the core this ideology Asian politico-cultural values and the Asian politico-economic model were represented. In economic terms, international financial institutions have considered the model in positive ways. According to the Asian Development Bank (ADB) it includes six characteristics: 1) Export promotion, 2) development led by the private sector, 3) agricultural transformation, which means that in East Asia the growth in agricultural productivity has been higher than in other parts of the developing world, 4) high saving rates, 5) skill accumulation and 6) economic flexibility.[76] In economics, in general, globalization and economic interdependence are seen merely as positive phenomena in the Asian economic model, growing out of export-oriented production and the ability to adopt new production technologies and new branches.

However, from the political point of view of global financial institutions, first of all the IMF, the Asian model may include elements which are inconsistent with the concept of transparency. According to the ADB, only Hong Kong, Japan and Singapore have developed legal standards comparable to those in western industrialized countries.[77] This fact, coupled with most nation-states' attempts to protect new production sectors and to develop national financial institutions, works against the openness of the global economy.

The political aspect of the Asian model refers to the particular characteristics of East Asian political culture. These politico-cultural characteristics include "post-Confucian blossoming", emphasizing Confucian political, moral, and family values; a stable core of leaders with vision; a single dominant party; a meritocratic development state; docile virgin labor; and low state welfare. These characteristics add up to an authoritarian political system which centers on continuity, stability and the determination for economic growth.[78]

Before the Asian economic crisis, the ASEAN political leaders did not publicly disagree on the Asian model, although in academic and NGO discourse several opinions were presented. In these quarters the discourse focused on the following issues: 1) democracy/stability, 2) equality/ efficiency 3) freedom/responsibility and 4) globalization/sovereignty. The first three dichotomies clearly originated in the post-Cold War discussion on human rights and democracy and between "Western" and "Eastern" political and social values. The fourth is much more general and originated both in anti-colonialism and in the Japanese example of expressing both globalization and national self-determination in the world's economic relations.

As the first three issues originated in the same discourse, their separation into different categories may be somewhat artificial. However, these questions have dominated discussion both in academic and in political circles. The debate began in the ASEAN countries in the middle of the 1980s and gathered force a couple of years later when the Kampuchean question started to disappear from the ASEAN agenda. The political initiative was followed by the ASEAN NGOs bringing to the discussion a wide range of opinions. Some of them follow government views rather closely, but more critical approaches have also been presented.

The main argument in ASEAN's official line has been that the regional governments have to concentrate all their efforts on economic growth and increased general social welfare. By doing this, the ASEAN governments add stability to their societies, and stability is a basic condition for democracy and human rights. In this argument, the development of political freedoms and democracy should follow general social and economic development. These arguments are clearly presented in the Bangkok Declaration on Human Rights adopted by the representatives of Asian states in 1993.[79]

However, several ASEAN NGOs responded angrily to the ASEAN governments' attempts to prioritize economic growth over democracy and human rights, although attitudes have varied in different ASEAN countries. [80] For example, the influential Malaysian NGO, Just World

Trust,[81] follows closely the Malay government's delineations, while Indonesian and particularly the Filippino NGOs have taken on rather critical views. The academic and the think tank discourse also confirms the lack of unanimity on the Asian model, and the debate is loudly echoed by some Asian governments and several Western scholars.

Defending the Asian model against liberal democratic arguments, Southeast Asian scholars have compared the Asian experience of Japan, where one-party democracy represents stability and economic growth, to the Filipino system, which copied American political institutions and liberal democracy, and which represents chaos and anarchy as well as inefficiency so rampant that not even an authoritarian government (Marcos) could correct it. These scholars also offer the similar example of Indonesian parliamentary democracy in the early fifties, which is described as "a period of political chaos," followed by Suharto's authoritarian regime where "[t]he strong state and use of state enterprises as well as joint private-public enterprises have been sparkplugs of Indonesian development".[82] Instead of speaking of the Asian model, the leader of the prominent Singaporean research institute, Chan Heng Chee, speaks of Asian democracy, which includes respect for authority and hierarchy as well as a communitarian ethic according to which the individual is important as part of a group rather than as a centerpiece of democracy. A dominant party which can remain in power several decades creating a centralized bureaucracy and a strong state is typical of Asian democracy. Chan Heng Chee points out that the Asian states, including Southeast Asia, are developing their own model of democracy which has so many common characteristics that one can speak of Asian democracy.[83]

ACADEMIC AND POLITICAL DISCOURSE ON SOUTHEAST ASIAN REGIONALISM: SOME CONCLUSIONS

Regionalism involves two elements: The relations among nation-states within a particular region and the relationship between a particular region and the global system. Both of them characterize the nature of regionalism. These two elements stand out in both academic and political discourse in Southeast Asian regionalism. The interplay between a region's internal and external relations figures prominently in the various analytical approaches to regionalism.

The modern history of Southeast Asia supposes both integrative and fragmentative aspects for the region. The colonial past and the area's geographical position between Chinese and Indian cultures call for a common identity, but different economic development and political systems together with different security interests, serve to fragment Southeast Asian regionalism. Political discourse clearly reflects this tension, as do academic discussions.

Clear differences exist between the experts' discussions on regionalism and the politicians' arguments for the need for regionalism. The experts' views are based on different theoretical orientations and include the political connotations implicit in them. Not surprisingly, political arguments are theoretically, even philosophically, much more mixed. It is clear that even the theoretically colored arguments of regional leaders are closely bound to actual political contexts.

The most evident common denominator in regionalist discourse, whether among theoretical experts or in first track political discussion, is the economy. Therefore the main theoretical pattern of Southeast Asian regionalist discourse seems to be IPE, with most arguments for regionalism being drawn from regional and global economic developments. However, IPE, as a general research paradigm, offers a too heterogeneous orientation to analyze Southeast Asian discourse effectively, since that discourse includes elements of realist and functionalist reasoning. Moreover, depending on the issue areas, (neo)realist trends seem to be rather strong among Southeast Asian experts. Here, Southeast Asian specialists differ from European federalists. Although some functionalist trends can be found in Southeast Asian academic and expert communities, such communities are not particularly the advocates of supra-national institutions in ASEAN. Although the issues of supra-nationalism and sovereignty are not always clearly expressed, they are the basis for both political and theoretical divisions in the Southeast Asian regionalist debate. Hence, it overlaps with the general discussion of integration. Therefore, this study asks how issues of supra-nationalism and sovereignty are dealt with in ASEAN cooperation.

The mainstream of Southeast Asian experts prefers Southeast Asia's integration into a global economy over the formation of a regional bloc. Despite the critical views on the possibilities of free international trade to solve regional problems, only minor nationalists and leftists among the NGO groups oppose globalization itself. However, rather strong regionalist trends among expertise communities can be considered fragmentative from the viewpoint of globalists. These communities assert that in order to better respond to global challenges, the Southeast Asian countries should engage in a stronger regional integration process. It is rather unclear whether these arguments should be considered as functionalist or as general trends of IPE, but such views can be found among academics and in second track discussions.

Even though some Southeast Asian voices have encouraged the development of the common regional institutions which challenge national sovereignty, most Southeast Asian expertise groups support a regionalism composed of strong nation-states. In this support they follow the general political trend in the area. Only the Southeast Asian economic crisis has disrupted this general trend and opened the debate on possible supra-national development.

Three elements stand out in constructing Southeast Asian regionalism in the post-Cold War situation: 1) ASEAN as a politico-economic pressure group; 2) ASEAN as a unique political alliance between Southeast Asian countries with different kinds of political and economic systems; and 3) the challenge of the integration of the ASEAN states. The first theme refers to ASEAN as a global actor and to its external relations, the second refers to the inter-state system in Southeast Asia, and to the institutionalist theme, which also includes the idea of ASEAN as a politico-cultural entity. The third theme challenges the system of sovereign states. The first two themes ignore regional integration understood as a development of supra-national institutions, an oversight that seems particularly biased when AFTA is considered.

This study asks how the above three elements are represented in ASEAN regionalism. It suggests that, despite the fact that economic integrative policies were implemented in ASEAN, the three first themes have dominated the discussion of Southeast Asian regionalism. Moreover, the study suggests that the Asian economic crisis, which broke out in June 1997, acted as a turning point in Southeast Asian regionalism. Consequently, the final part of the study asserts that the new post-crisis situation calls for different kinds of approaches and an attempt to reconstruct regionalism in Southeast Asia.

The following chapters analyze regionalist discourse in concrete settings. The first two chapters deal with ASEAN internal discussion on the nature of ASEAN cooperation in political and economic fields. The third chapter deals with ASEAN interstate relations, but expands the ASEAN debate to include a broader a geographical area with a discussion of security issues. The next two chapters discuss ASEAN's external relations in an Asia-Pacific context and relations with the EU. The last part of the book examines ASEAN cooperation and cooperative initiatives during and after the Asian economic crisis.

Part I
The Principles of ASEAN's Interstate Relations in Practice

2 Widening or Deepening Regional Cooperation?

This chapter deals with the Southeast Asian post-Cold War era debate on political and economic cooperation in ASEAN. The debate focuses mainly on two questions – one on the enlargement of ASEAN with new members, and the other on measures for deepening regional cooperation. ASEAN's attempts to create an ASEAN free trade area, AFTA, were important, although expansion also involved economic issues. The attempts at expanding ASEAN, on the one hand, and deepening economic cooperation, on the other, can be seen as competing strategies for developing the organization, even though both aims were accepted by all six ASEAN members. The concrete steps for deepening economic integration came first when the ASEAN free trade agreement, AFTA, was signed at the Singapore Summit in 1992. However, from the broader perspective, it is fair to say that the question of expanding ASEAN dominated the regionalist debate in Southeast Asia during the 1990s.

An emphasis on sovereignty is part of Third World nationalism, which during the 1950s, 1960s and up to the 1970s took on a particularly strong anti-colonial and anti-Western tone. This anti-colonialism originated in radical political movements in these countries as well as in their internal national structures. Typically, many Third World countries, although relying on the concept of the nation-state, are not nation-states at all. Even in some leading Southeast Asian countries, colonial borders, not the national background of the population, determine the state's territory. Reacting against this history of imperialism, the leaders of the new states try to find ideologies, alternative to liberal capitalism and liberal democracy, which allow and even encourage competition and the negotiation of conflicting interests.[1] In Southeast Asia, the artificial nature of the nation-state is evident in Indonesia, but also in Malaysia. Therefore, national sovereignty remains a central ideological issue of the governments and thus is emphasized in Southeast Asian regional cooperation – as it is in Third World regionalism in general – and shapes a kind of regional cooperation different from the market-driven regionalism of, for example, the European Community.

The founders of ASEAN relied on the Charter of the United Nations and on the Bandung Declaration when formulating the principles of Southeast Asian regional cooperation. The Bandung Declaration established the basic rules of the Third World Movement. These principles, summarized in ASEAN's Treaty of Amity and Cooperation in Southeast Asia (TAC), altogether emphasize national sovereignty and non-interference.[2] The principles appearing in the TAC fix the limits beyond which cooperation may not extend. New candidates for membership must accede to these principles before they can join ASEAN. Still, ASEAN declarations and treaties remain too general to set practical rules of cooperation. The notion of *bhinneka tunggal ika,* "unity in diversity", shapes general principles and informal decision-making patterns and justifies the independence of the members inside the organization. The Bangkok Declaration, the Kuala Lumpur Declaration and the Bali Treaties of 1976, the three basic documents of ASEAN, articulate the central vocabulary of Southeast Asian regionalism and emphasize the founding principle of *bhinneka tunggal ika,* but they do not offer any direct and practical procedures for decision-making. Instead, these founding documents outline the central aim of strengthening national and ASEAN resilience by developing awareness of regional identity, thus forging a strong ASEAN community. This identity-building connects to the more concrete aim of strengthening political solidarity "by promoting the harmonization of views, coordinating positions and, where possible and desirable, taking common action".[3] The founding documents define ASEAN activities as state-led efforts – not the products of any formal and permanent decision-making ASEAN institutions.

Decisions concerning the organization and member countries are made either in annual or special ministerial meetings, complemented by informal ministerial meetings which exert a roughly equal influence on ASEAN's decision-making procedures. The informal rules of decision-making, formulated along constructivist lines, refer to common, culturally-based behavior and contain the principles of interstate relations – *Gotong royong*, *mushawarah* and *mufakat.* These principles assure the absolute sovereignty of the member countries and reiterate the idea that decisions of the organization should not harm the interests of any of its members. The inviolability of member interests has been manifested in different ways. In some situations it has forced the ASEAN countries to sort out vital from non-vital interests among the members. In the Cambodian conflict, for example, Thailand's vital security interests dictated ASEAN's stance. The inviolability of member interests can also prevent ASEAN from taking action if member interests come into sharp conflict, or it can lead to the creation of new procedures aimed at circumventing such serious conflict.

In ASEAN meetings the need to develop the organization was widely recognized. In the early 1990s context of developing global economic regimes and newly emerging regional systems, the end of Cold War divisions and the unification process in the European Community toward the Union challenged ASEAN most directly. However, the organization formulated no definite plan to direct its own development. In July 1990, the ASEAN foreign ministers referred to post-Cold War world developments and asserted that it was "imperative for ASEAN . . . to adopt a more flexible and forward-looking approach to prepare itself for the challenges of the 90s, and in particular to strengthen itself and intensify intra-ASEAN cooperation".[4]

The ministers' statement left unclear exactly what strengthening itself and intensifying intra-ASEAN cooperation should mean. Since in 1990 the Cambodian question remained unsettled and Vietnam's relations with ASEAN had yet to take shape, deepening cooperation rather than broadening it seemed to be what the foreign ministers intended. Indeed, the foreign ministers welcomed the measures aimed at enforcing the ASEAN secretariat. Similarly they proposed "to take more concrete steps towards more effective intra-ASEAN cooperation".[5]

In fact, ASEAN was in danger of dropping out of the race toward general regional cooperation. The supporters of regional cooperation referred to the developments among the European Community and the North American Free Trade Agreement (NAFTA). In 1989 a new Asia-Pacific organization for economic cooperation was established. Originally created as a loose consultation forum for Asia-Pacific countries, Asia-Pacific Economic Cooperation (APEC) began in the early 1990s to develop into a more institutionalized economic organization. At the same time, Malaysian Prime Minister Mahathir Mohamad raised his proposal for an East Asian regional arrangement, the East Asian Economic Grouping (EAEG). Mahathir's new initiative took the position that regional arrangements in Southeast Asia could not deal effectively with economic and political situations arising from the newly emerging world order. The vision of broader East Asian economic and political integration behind Mahathir's proposal reflected clearly the strategic problems inherent in Southeast Asian regionalist development. Mahathir's initiative coupled a strong wish to achieve regional economic and political independence from the world's main economic powers with a recognition of Southeast Asia's deep dependence on Japan. However, a caveat was expressed that integration with powerful East Asian economies might eventuate in the neglect of Southeast Asia's own regional development. Mahathir's suggestions for untying this strategic knot followed the ASEAN way of handling difficult issues – moving in directions in which unanimity would be reached and avoiding issues which threatened to expose differences. Thus ASEAN took both economic and political tacks by enforcing economic cooperation on the one hand and by swelling the ranks of ASEAN membership on the other.

TAKING THE POLITICAL APPROACH: ASEAN AND THE NEW MEMBERS

The political approach which sought to bring all Southeast Asian countries into the ASEAN organization seemed to follow institutionalist lines, at the same time as it satisfied member states' needs to maintain national sovereignty vis-à-vis regional organization.

This debate includes elements interesting from the point of view of international relations theories, particularly theories dealing with regional cooperation. The arguments for broadening regionalist cooperation grow out of ASEAN's traditional institutionalist approach. Institutionalism emphasizes the role of common values, norms and rules in international interaction. This theoretical framework has traditionally structured ASEAN political cooperation. However, in security questions and particularly in dealings with Western economic and political powers, the emphasis on sovereignty and national interests reflects realist arguments, colored by anti-colonialist rhetoric. Realist arguments also inform questions of ASEAN enlargement. Several studies have argued that, in joining ASEAN, new members acted out of political motives; they had no intentions of giving away their sovereign power to a regional organization.

Functionalism, which focuses on functional cooperation, especially on economic cooperation which would spread to other sectors, has not been easy to identify in the Southeast Asian regionalist debate. Nevertheless, when the new members joined ASEAN, the discussions did take into consideration the dynamic between new economic relations and continued political sovereignty.

Functionalist Ideas in the Early Phase of ASEAN Enlargement

Nevertheless, some functionalist aims motivate the ASEAN countries' turn towards Indochina in the late 1980s and early 1990s. In fact, functionalist lines of reasoning became discernible even while the Cambodian question remained unresolved and the ASEAN countries were at a diplomatic stalemate with the Indochinese. As Thai Prime Minister Chatichai Choonhavan declared his intention of transforming Indochina from a battlefield into a market place, he emphasized the functionalist ideas of economic interdependence and peace. Although Chatichai's ideas were perhaps not thoroughly thought out, the functionalist bias was obvious in his vision of the ASEAN and Indochinese countries closely linked together with Burma "through ties of trade, investment, communications and telecommunications".[6] Similar concepts of interdependence were crucial in many other arguments for closer ASEAN Indochina ties in the early 1990s.

Chatichai's proposal came at a bad time, however. It surprised the other ASEAN countries, and they did not respond positively to it before the Paris Peace Accords on Cambodia in October 1991. The Cambodian conflict had so segmented the ASEAN governments that debate about including Indochinese countries in the organization or about integrating their economies with other Southeast Asian economies could not go forward during this period.

The Paris Peace Accords opened up a new era in Southeast Asian regionalism. As the Cold War constellation broke down, the possibility of extending ASEAN cooperation toward Indochina became a realizable vision. On the political level, after the ASEAN Singapore Summit in January 1992, discussion of enlarging ASEAN membership from six to ten countries began in earnest. A larger ASEAN would bring both political and economic benefits.[7] The question of Vietnam's membership in ASEAN had emerged earlier, but now all the ASEAN countries accepted the idea.

Interestingly enough, functionalist ideas surfaced often in the Vietnamese political discourse on its Southeast Asian policy even before the Paris Peace Accords. These ideas were reinforced by the economic trend in the Vietnamese political leadership, manifested in Vietnamese Premier Vo Van Kiet's visit to all six ASEAN countries during 1991 and 1992 – a trip interpreted as "an economic-led diplomatic tour".[8] In fact, these ideas took root in the *doi moi* (renovation) campaign which started in Vietnam after the 6th Party Congress in 1986 and followed Gorbachev's *perestroika* in the Soviet Union.

In the Vietnamese renovation, *doi moi tu duy,* international relations, played an important role. New Gorbachevian thinking on international relations involved the concept of interdependence as a crucial part of a new international order. On a theoretical level these concepts fit better with the theories of IPE than with functionalist integration theories. Nevertheless, they included the functionalist idea of the important relationship between economic interdependence and peace. The Vietnamese Foreign Ministry, a stronghold of new ideas, adapted these concepts and connected them to Vietnam's policy toward Southeast Asia.

The reformist wing in the Foreign Ministry and the Vietnamese Communist Party worried particularly about Vietnam's poor economic performance, her heavy dependence on Soviet economic aid and her isolated international position. Pragmatic reformists looked toward capitalist Southeast Asian countries in order to overcome their international isolation and vitalize their weak economy. But, because of the Cambodian question, their hopes did not materialize before the Paris Peace Accords. However, during the years 1986–1993 Vietnamese political thinking took on board new elements which supported Vietnam's policy of joining ASEAN.

On the other hand, Vietnamese Marxist-Leninist theoreticians had rather big problems translating the old political doctrine of the two roads of development into a new vocabulary. While in the old doctrine the crucial concept had been struggle, *dau tranh*, the new thinking adopted such concepts as interdependence, *su le thuoc lan nhau*, internationalization, *xu the quoc te hoa,* and an international order, *mot trat tu quoc te,* as well as later the concept of globalization, *toan cau hoa.* Conservative elements wanted to hold firm to the old Vietnamese Marxist-Leninist doctrine, while new influences and reformist political doctrine threatened its disintegration.[9]

In any case, a discussion on regionalism emerged which aimed at Vietnam's closer relations with the ASEAN countries. The concept of regionalism, *chu nghia khu vuc*, was introduced by Vietnam's Foreign Minister Nguyen Co Thach in the late 1980s. Thach used a definition of regionalism very similar to the one used in International Political Economy. He emphasized that regionalism is a product of economic forces offering neighboring countries new possibilities for cooperation which go beyond the existing political and military alliances – "a new specific trait of an international division of labor".[10]

Thus a strong economic undercurrent runs through the first phase of Vietnam's integration into ASEAN. This economic factor turned Vietnam's foreign relations toward the Asia-Pacific Region and supported Vietnam in taking advantage of economic growth in the area. Although the figurehead of this orientation, Nguyen Co Thach, lost the power game in the Vietnamese Communist Party and had to leave the Politburo and the

Foreign Ministry, the influences of this trend remained in the Party and in the Foreign Ministry.

The security dimension played a role which was even more important than the economic dimension in Vietnam's rationale for ASEAN membership. After the sacking of Nguyen Co Thach, the Vietnamese leadership engaged in a modest rapprochement with China, but soon began to doubt the efficacy of such a move, owing to China's hardline policy toward the disputed Spratly Islands in the South China Sea. The turn toward China can be seen as a reaction against Thach's "Western-oriented" policy as well as an attempt, on the part of conservative circles, to find an ideological ally in China after the collapse of the Soviet Union. However, when ideological fraternity did not extend to *realpolitik,* the Vietnamese abandoned the Chinese orientation and sought a security background from Southeast Asia.[11]

After the Paris Peace Accords, the ASEAN countries were eager to realize Chatichai's vision of turning war-torn Indochina into a marketplace. In point of fact, the ASEAN leaders articulated Chatichai's vision on several occasions prior to Paris.[12] In August 1991, a symposium between Vietnamese and ASEAN experts and politicians gathered in Hanoi, their main consideration being how to integrate Vietnam's economy into the economies of the ASEAN countries. Negotiations for a free trade area in ASEAN, to be established half a year later, worked as a springboard for these discussions. Both the Vietnamese and ASEAN arguments referred to changes in the world economy. For example, they pointed, on the one hand, to the tendency toward protectionism between the regions and, on the other hand, to the liberation of trade in the region. Both the Vietnamese and ASEAN sides reached the conclusion that economic integration of the Vietnamese economy into the region, as well as the development of regional integration as a whole, were both desirable and necessary.[13]

The symposium thus emphasized Vietnam's integration into ASEAN through economic channels. The need for supranational institutions was not raised, but the functionalist idea of intensified political cooperation through economic integration was clear. This emphasis can be explained largely by the optimism which prevailed when possibilities for new kinds of interaction opened up between Vietnam and the ASEAN countries. Similarly, the expectations for the emerging free trade area were rather high among the Vietnamese and the ASEAN experts. This optimism declined a few years later, and the Vietnamese Deputy Foreign Minister reiterated the functionalist argument just before Vietnam joined ASEAN. According to his argument, a failure, to integrate into the regional community would lead to the isolation of the country. Such isolation must be avoided since "[r]egional integration and participation in the game of global liberalized trade are unavoidable challenges for a state if it wants to exist and develop in the new world conjuncture".[14]

Vietnam and the ASEAN Rules of the Game

Nonetheless, it can be argued that the tendency toward deeper integration was stronger at the beginning of the 1990s than a few years later. The functionalist arguments for Vietnam's membership vanished both from the Vietnamese and from the ASEAN side after the Singapore ASEAN Summit in 1992. In the report of the ASEAN-Vietnam study group in February 1993, functionalist ideas likewise disappeared. The study group, led by Malaysian Finance Minister Anwar Ibrahim, emphasized that "Southeast Asia must strive to be, not a supranational community as envisaged by proponents of the European Community's Maastrich Treaty, but a community of different peoples with their own identities, their own domestic arrangements and economic development, and their own patterns of external affiliations and connections".[15] Therefore, the report asserted, Southeast Asia should be "a pluralistic community" in which national policies remain sacrosanct. The ASEAN members should ensure "constructive engagement" to establish common positions and coordinate policy.[16]

Two factors account for this conceptual shift. First, even though hopes for integrating member economies came mainly from the Vietnamese side, which expected ASEAN's help with her miserable economy, the changes in Vietnamese political leadership and her unsuccessful flattery of Beijing turned Hanoi's interest away from economy and toward security. Secondly, finding "common shared values" in ASEAN remained easier than engaging in important economic arrangements in the region. The limits of the ASEAN free trade area (AFTA) became rapidly visible after the Singapore Summit.

In spite of the fact that economic trends in Vietnam's foreign policy had to give way to a more conventional approach, Hanoi's expectations for economic gains as a result of its membership in ASEAN remained high. Despite the modest volume of intra-ASEAN trade, the Vietnamese had a particularly keen interest in AFTA. The liberal thinkers in Vietnam also anticipated the stimulating effect of Southeast Asian foreign direct investments (FDI) on Vietnam's economy.[17]

Counterbalancing the liberalizing tendencies of economic cooperation, the Vietnamese leadership worried about how internationalization and opening to the outside world would affect Vietnam's political stability. To name this threat, the Communist Party adopted the concept of "peaceful evolution", *dien bien hoa binh,* from the Chinese political vocabulary, by which they referred to the disintegration of Communist rule owing to the influence of Western ideas of democracy, human rights and political freedom. The linkages to Beijing's rhetoric notwithstanding, the concept does parallel the ideas of some Southeast Asian leaders on the differences between Western and Asian political and social values.

The main thesis presented by Anwar Ibrahim's prestigious study group matches Vietnamese conservative ideas with ASEAN cooperative practices. The Vietnamese Communist Party leadership and particularly its conservative wing obviously tried to maximize the security elements of ASEAN and minimize political influences allowing for the opening up of Vietnam to other Southeast Asian countries. Despite the Foreign Ministry's enthusiasm regarding emerging ASEAN relations, in the power center of the Communist Party, the role imagined for ASEAN in Vietnam's development was quite modest. ASEAN is only one component in Hanoi's foreign relations – for example, the Political Report of the Eighth Party Congress in 1996 mentioned this regional organization only three times.[18] The Report was a revision of an earlier draft version which did not to mention ASEAN at all in its foreign policy section. The original report was amended after criticisms from the ASEAN ambassadors pointed out that the document failed to mention Vietnam's membership in ASEAN.[19]

For all of these reasons, institutionalist cooperation, emphasizing the principles and values of interaction, was the easiest way to start the concrete process of Vietnam's entrance into ASEAN. The ASEAN principle of avoiding domestic issues of member countries particularly delighted the Vietnamese leadership. Although the study group recognized the need for the concrete integration of Vietnam into Southeast Asia through economic relations, its report focused on the principles of cooperation. The four principles presented by the group can be derived from the master principle of "unity in diversity". According to this vision, as stated above, ASEAN should be a "pluralistic community" allowing different kinds of political and economic systems for its members. However, the three following principles link the members together for purposes of "common security", "common prosperity" and "shared opportunities".[20] Common security underscores the fact that a security problem, economic or political, in one of the members reflects on all Southeast Asian countries. Therefore ASEAN should constantly aim at regional regime-building "[b]ut more formal structures of cooperative relationship need not be confined to regional regime building. Expressed consensus and official agreements among regional states in key questions can also serve a similar function."[21] Thus ASEAN did not need to make profound integrative efforts with the new member; the goal of "common prosperity" sufficed – and reinforced the institutionalist starting points of the organization.

Owing to the limits placed on integration, the "structures of shared values and interests" are particularly important when dealing with extra-regional partners. "Shared values and interests" are enforced by "shared opportunities", which, on the one hand, guarantee the Southeast Asian community's participation in global economic development and, on the other hand, help maintain national autonomy in decisions regarding national development according to the chosen paths of the members.[22]

Institutionalist starting points were reinforced in the diplomatic rapprochement between ASEAN and Vietnam. Vietnam acceded to the Treaty of Amity and Cooperation (TAC) together with Laos in 1992, and both countries achieved observer status in ASEAN. In the Bali Treaties and in TAC particularly, the basic ASEAN rules of the game were written. They included strict non-interference in the internal affairs of the member countries, respect for the independence of the fellow members, respect for each other's territorial interdependence and the peaceful settlement of disputes. The basis for cooperation, shared interests and shared values, would be further underscored by *constructive engagement*, a strategy for cooperative influence whereby ASEAN members, by virtue of their economic and political practices, provide positive models for other members.

Unresolved security questions also prompted ASEAN governments to prefer the modest political approach. Vietnam had fishing disputes in the Gulf of Thailand with Thailand, and more importantly, the contest over the Spratly Islands between Vietnam, Malaysia, the Philippines and China continued to threaten regional peace. ASEAN's calm approach to the dispute helped maintain the status quo in the South China Sea and defended Hanoi's policy to resist Chinese claims on the Spratlys.

Vietnam's admission to ASEAN took place at the 28th ASEAN Ministerial Meeting in Bandar Seri Begawan, Brunei on 28 July 1995. Despite some critical expectations, Vietnam's first years in ASEAN were remarkably smooth.[23] During the negotiating process, Vietnam had made clear its intention to take part in AFTA as soon as possible and also its readiness to learn the ASEAN decision-making style of consensus-seeking.

Even though institutionalist theory does not adequately explain the motives either of Vietnam or the ASEAN countries for promoting Vietnamese membership in the organization, it does explain the form in which Vietnam and the ASEAN countries were willing to cooperate. The interests of both parties lie in realizing the economic and security benefits of economic cooperation typical of a functionalist approach – even urging the establishment of supranational arrangements. But security factors and ASEAN's external factors led ASEAN into an institutionalist way of constructing the organization.

ASEAN Enlargement and the Independence of Southeast Asia

At the fifth ASEAN Summit in Bangkok in December 1995, the ASEAN leaders adopted a Bangkok Summit Declaration which paved the way for further expansion of the ASEAN grouping. The main theme of the Summit Declaration was "the speedy realization of an ASEAN comprising all Southeast Asian countries as it enters the 21st century". That goal thus overtook other important tasks of ASEAN such as identity-building, functional cooperation and economic integration.[24] However, despite the publicly expressed unanimity of the ASEAN governments on expanding ASEAN from seven members to ten, much more criticism surrounded the entrance into the association of Cambodia, Laos, and Myanmar than had accompanied Vietnam's membership a couple of years before.

Two factors account for the strength of this critique. First, although AFTA had not fulfilled all the expectations governments had for it, a strong tendency to deepen cooperation prevailed within ASEAN. Critics claimed that the entrance of the three countries into the association would slow down that desired economic integration. Second, although bringing the Indochinese countries into ASEAN did not pose such a threat, Southeast Asian expert groups saw Myanmar's membership as problematic.[25] Myanmar's candidacy for membership caused open conflict between ASEAN and its Western partners – first of all the US, but also the European Union. This last factor carried important political weight. In fact, as is argued here, the opposition of the West resolved the question of membership for the new candidates.

Even though Malaysia was most active among the old ASEAN members in urging enlargement, the Malaysian government did not see the enlargement of ASEAN as the best way to develop Southeast Asian regional cooperation in the early 1990s. On the contrary, Malaysian Prime Minister Mahathir Mohamad openly doubted the benefits of expanding membership of ASEAN both in economic terms and political influence. Mahathir's primary intention was to establish an East Asian economic grouping (EAEG) in order to defend East Asian interests in the global economy – in this way his arguments originated in political economy. He claimed that European Union and US policy in particular aimed at preventing the developing countries in Asia from achieving a developed status by imposing upon them both political as well as economic restrictions. [26]

When it became clear that other ASEAN countries and particularly Japan were not ready to adopt the EAEG proposal to the extent the Malaysians wanted, Mahathir turned to his second option – the enlargement of ASEAN. Together with moderating his own organizational concept (the acronym changed to East Asian Economic Caucus, EAEC) Mahathir abandoned his earlier preference for a weak ASEAN. Mahathir's foreign minister argued that "together as ASEAN Ten we can make a powerful difference. At present we have a combined GDP in purchasing power parity terms valued at US$1.617 billion. That could still make us smaller than the NAFTA economies, China, the European Union or Japan, but we will not be bit players anymore either. Flourishing in a free trade area of over a half billion people and fortified by other bonds of economic and functional cooperation as well, we would count as hefty middleweights."[27] Similarly, the Malaysian economist, Mohamed Ariff, argued that instead of deepening ASEAN cooperation, widening it would be more profitable. He warned that deepening ASEAN relations would be "a costly affair" since the outside world would ignore ASEAN if it turned inward. By comparison, expanding ASEAN was "a better option, as it would only entail some additional budgetary allocations, a small price worth paying for the increased political clout and leverage it could bring."[28]

Political issues were involved in the criticism of the expansion of ASEAN, especially with reference to the situation in Myanmar. The political criticism from the West allowed Mahathir to continue his anti-colonialist rhetoric and emphasize the rights of the East Asian and Southeast Asian countries to defend their sovereignty against Western powers.[29] Finally, at the fifth ASEAN Summit in Bangkok in December 1995, Mahathir pronounced that the rationality of an enlarged ASEAN with Laos, Cambodia and Myanmar lay in ASEAN's enhanced ability to resist Western countries in global political and economic issues. Therefore he urged that "the ASEAN Ten should become a reality quickly, not slowly".[30]

Nevertheless, the Bangkok Summit left open both the timing and the procedure for joining. The vision of ASEAN joining together all ten Southeast Asian countries became a reality in the first informal ASEAN heads of government meeting in Jakarta, 30 November 1996, when the ASEAN leaders decided to embrace all the member candidates simultaneously.[31] This decision ran counter to the earlier schedule, according to which Cambodia and Laos would be accepted first and Burma's membership would take place at a more appropriate time.[32]

The defense of ASEAN's sovereignty as a starting point in ASEAN's expansion came onto the agenda in a natural way. In ASEAN's dialogue with the European Union and the US, the Western partners of ASEAN argued against Myanmar's membership. The negative attitude of the West against Myanmar's membership was due to Rangoon's bad human rights record and the repression of political opposition. The contrasting approaches to human rights questions of ASEAN and the Western countries had already surfaced in the ASEAN Post-Ministerial Conference in Kuching in 1990, where ASEAN and its Western dialogue partners disagreed over ways to deal with the Chinese human rights situation after the Tiananmen Square incident.

The determination to defend the sovereignty of the ASEAN member countries became a uniting factor during the discussions on human rights issues, as Western opposition to the inclusion of Myanmar strengthened ASEAN's resolve to complete its expansion plans. In this way the ASEAN response to Western arguments against Myanmar's membership stimulated rather than delayed the process. As Sukhumbhand Paribatra noted, "[p]ride is parent to prejudice, because the message 'do not do' the proud ASEAN governments seem to feel they must do what they have been told not to do".[33] Thus, the necessity of defending ASEAN sovereignty and its insistence on taking care of its own business occluded members' arguments against enlargement.[34]

Nevertheless, countries with stronger traditions of civic debate such as Thailand and also the Philippines voiced particularly strong opposition to Myanmar's membership. In Malaysia, the government spoke loudly for the membership, and Singapore together with Indonesia followed the policy of expansion. The expertise and NGO groups in Thailand criticized the official argument that enlargement would strengthen ASEAN, asserting that the membership of Myanmar would weaken ASEAN diplomatic power and cohesion. Myanmar's membership would diminish ASEAN's credibility as an international actor, since ASEAN's main Western partners opposed it. Furthermore, critics warned, including Myanmar would weaken ASEAN's internal cohesion owing to suspicion between Myanmar and Thailand. Several security and policy issues between Thailand and Myanmar needed to be resolved before Myanmar joined the association. This view paralleled the EU's enlargement procedure, which urged establishing some preliminary requirements before membership negotiations could start.[35] Opposite to views that ASEAN Ten would enforce regional security, it was also argued that the security environment in ASEAN would become even more complex since the relationship of the Rangoon Junta, the SLORC (State Law and Order Restoration Council), with China would make the PRC even more involved in ASEAN's internal situation.[36]

On the other hand, others defended Myanmar's membership by referring to ASEAN's role as a confidence-builder and a conflict management mechanism. Following this line of reasoning, Burma's presence in the organization would increase regional stability rather than decrease it.[37] The critics of Myanmar's membership countered that the new member could impact negatively on the organization. Acceptance of a *pariah* state like Myanmar might lead ASEAN into the position of a *pariah* organization. It would be wiser, then, to wait until Myanmar reformed itself before bringing it into ASEAN.[38]

Supporters of Myanmar's membership defended the ASEAN concept of *constructive engagement* as a more suitable tool to incorporate Myanmar into the Southeast Asian state system than political or economic pressure. As the concept supposes, regional cooperation would lead to stronger interdependence, economic growth and political stability for Myanmar. The country's new strength would pave the way for it to adopt common and more acceptable practices towards its own population. On the contrary, isolation and economic blockade, as practiced by the Western powers, would hinder economic growth and lead to poverty and political instability and to even more repressive measures by the ruling junta.[39] The argument continued that, as long as other countries refrained from interfering in Myanmar's domestic affairs, growing external contacts could encourage smooth change in the government. However, counter arguments asserted that the ASEAN principle of non-interference could not be applied to Myanmar, because Myanmar's junta was legitimate neither in the Western liberal democratic sense nor in the ASEAN sense. *Constructive engagement* could, therefore, not work as ASEAN's policy towards Myanmar.[40]

Myanmar's qualifications for ASEAN membership were not publicly discussed in ASEAN's organs and summits. On the contrary, the ASEAN Standing Committee's Annual Report 1996–1997 emphasized only the technical compatibility between the existing ASEAN countries and Myanmar, a compatibility based on its wide knowledge of English and Myanmar's familiarity with modern international trade and economic rules owing to its membership in the WTO.[41] However, in an informal meeting in Jakarta in the end of November 1996, ASEAN's leaders heard various views from member countries. The Philippines and Thailand wanted to delay Burmese entrance into ASEAN, while the host, Indonesia, strongly favored Burmese membership. Philippine President Fidel Ramos was reported as saying that there was only one voice at the Summit and this "was articulated by Indonesia". Indonesian dominance came partly from the prominence of the East Timor question, in the forefront because of Portugal's active role in the EU.[42] Therefore the argument of rejecting external interference in ASEAN's internal affairs was particularly strong at the Jakarta Summit. In the end, the consensus was formulated: ASEAN leaders "reaffirmed their strong commitment to the speedy realization of an ASEAN comprising all ten Southeast Asian countries. They agreed that Cambodia, Laos and Myanmar be admitted as ASEAN members simultaneously."[43] In this way the diplomatic pressure of the US and the EU, which culminated in the Spring of 1997 in direct diplomatic efforts by the US toward Thailand, failed to realize – and even worked against – its own goal. ASEAN persisted in its stand of accepting Myanmar together with Laos and Cambodia.[44]

But ASEAN Ten was not realized according to schedule at the ASEAN Annual Ministerial Meeting in Kuala Lumpur in July 1997, where only Myanmar and Laos were accepted. The military coup of Hun Sen in Cambodia postponed Cambodia's membership until April 1999. Reversing their former practice of non-interference in each other's domestic affairs, the ASEAN leaders argued that Cambodia had to put its house in order before it could be accepted as a member of the organization. The ASEAN leaders tried to explain that their decision did not constitute involvement in Cambodia's internal affairs, but amounted to a technical matter only. ASEAN's reaction reflected its frustration with the demolishing of the Cambodian coalition agreement which the ASEAN governments had strongly backed.[45]

Cambodia participated in the Sixth ASEAN Summit in Hanoi in December 1998 at a particular 9+1 meeting arranged by the host country, Vietnam. The Summit officially permitted Cambodia's entrance into the organization. Vietnam was particularly active in supporting Cambodia for membership. It took advantage of the position of the host country and managed to do away with doubts concerning Cambodia's membership. Although the coalition agreement was not rehabilitated as such, the general elections and formation of the new Hun Sen government assured the ASEAN members that stability and normalcy would return to Cambodia.[46] Cambodia was accepted without great publicity into ASEAN in the Admission Ceremony in Hanoi, 30 April 1999.

Fear for ASEAN's credibility greatly enhanced support for Cambodia's membership. As the inclusion of all the Southeast Asian countries before the end of the old millennium was one of the main aims of ASEAN, the question also concerned the organization's prestige. After fulfilling its goal and assuring its prestige with Cambodian membership, ASEAN could now turn to the demanding tasks of deepening cooperation "in all areas and at all levels".[47]

THE RATIONALITY OF INTRA-ASEAN ECONOMIC COOPERATION

Functionalist and neo-functionalist theories suppose that economic cooperation spreads to other social sectors and that this *spill-over* effect leads to overall regional integration. However, the official ASEAN cooperative schemes have hardly acknowledged the pursuit of economic integration, let alone political integration. ASEAN ideology has emphasized *national resilience*, accompanied by *regional resilience*. The concept of *resilience* includes strong national sovereignty. Thus even economic cooperation, requiring national economies to adapt, to some degree, to regional adjustments, has been difficult for the ASEAN countries. The ASEAN PTA and the failures of some common investment projects provide good examples of the way national interests have watered down any serious attempts to create supranational economic cooperation in ASEAN.

Taking these failures into account, it is interesting to note that some experts and retired ASEAN statesmen strongly urged economic integration with strengthened political cooperation as early as the late 1980s and early 1990s.[48] The proponents of the regional free trade area (FTA) were disappointed in the Third ASEAN Summit in Manila when the ASEAN leaders could not agree on the FTA. Although the ASEAN governments had committed to increased intra-ASEAN trade in the ASEAN Concord in Bali in 1976 and put it into practice by signing ASEAN Preferential

Trading Agreements in 1977, ASEAN records in liberalizing regional trade were far from promising.

The ASEAN PTA failed. In relative terms, intra-ASEAN trade dropped from 19.7 percent to 17.7 percent between 1985 and 1990.[49] In absolute terms, intra-ASEAN trade grew 14.8 percent during the same period, but when the huge transition trade through Singapore is taken into account, overall growth in ASEAN exports to the rest of the world accounts for the increases.[50] This growth in exports without any regional free trade agreement did not, of course, support serious efforts for economic integration in the region. The failure of the PTA can be seen as a symptom of conflicting national interests among the ASEAN members, but it also reflects the limits of the institutional approach in regional cooperation.

In fact, the proponents of the concept of *new regionalism* argue that the pursuit of regional economic integration which aims to expand intra-regional trade is not part of the Third World's regional strategy. According to this reasoning, Third World countries no longer fear their growing dependence on rich developed countries; instead they fear being excluded from the global economy. That's why the *new regionalism* is also called an *open regionalism*.[51] Therefore, intra-regional trade arrangements do not promote the main interests of Third World countries, while integration into the global economy does. Although this analysis provides a rather simplistic view of Southeast Asian regionalism and ignores anti-colonial undercurrents still existing in ASEAN regionalism, *open regionalism* is an important concept in present-day ASEAN economic cooperation.

Institutionalism and pre-AFTA Discussion of Economic Regionalism

According to neo-functionalism, economic integration does not progress, after a certain stage, in the system of nation-states without the help of supranational organizations and the active role of governments. Without supranational organizations backed by governmental support, integration is blocked by particular national interests. In the original ideas of ASEAN cooperation, national interests received primary acknowledgment, and, because of this fact, liberalization of regional trade did not become their main form of cooperation. However, the idea of the ASEAN PTA, signed in February 1977, was to provide the ASEAN member countries a mechanism for regional trade liberalization. Nevertheless, the PTA grew out of a general ASEAN decision-making system in which national interests provide the general basis for a common consensus.

It can be argued that the PTA was an institutionalist attempt to boost intra-ASEAN trade, based on a voluntary approach. Formally the member countries agreed on the products which should have preferential trade treatment. However, the item-by-item negotiations produced such huge exclusion lists, that in the late 1980s the PTA covered only five percent of total ASEAN trade. Very permissive criteria were used to formulate the exclusion list. Products on which substantial import revenues were collected got placed on the list as well as products which were important for employment. In fact, nearly any product could be listed for exclusion. Moreover, the voluntary selection of the items assured their very low trade content. In keeping with national interests, the PTA did not intend to establish a system of substantial tariff reductions. National trade policies prevailed and the average margins of preference varied from Singapore's two percent to Thailand's 30 percent. And in the end, the modest progress in the growth of the PTA items was watered down by the increase of non-tariff trade barriers.[52]

Although free trade through the PTA was never acknowledged as the major ASEAN aim of economic cooperation, the rhetoric of the ASEAN leaders cast the PTA as a significant step toward closer economic cooperation.[53] In opposition to the official approval, the ASEAN experts sharply criticized the PTA system and contemplated alternatives, the most popular being a free trade area and a customs union. But establishing either a common market or an economic union calls for extensive political and economic integration unrealistic for the ASEAN countries. A common market requires free capital, labor and enterprise mobility among participating countries, while an economic union requires unified fiscal, monetary and social policies.

Preferential trading arrangements are designed to reduce trading barriers rather than eliminate them. However, the benefits of the PTA for ASEAN internal trade were very small. The purpose of both a customs union and a free trade area is to eliminate tariffs between members. According to economic theory, elimination of tariffs would lead to more effective allocation of economic forces in the region and stimulate economic growth. However, while a customs union eliminates tariffs between the members, it sets common tariffs against the outside world. In a free trade area arrangement members eliminate tariffs among themselves but can freely and individually determine tariffs against the outside world.[54] The proponents of the concept of *open regionalism* argue that this openness is the characteristics of the *new regionalism* in Southeast Asia and distinguishes it from the *old regionalism*: The members of the FTA try to take advantage of global economic development and are not turning inwards to create blocs.

Although the FTA fits nicely into the concept of open regionalism, ASEAN experts, interest in a free trade area did not grow out of an appreciation of this theoretical congruence but rather out of an awareness of the difficulty ASEAN countries would have agreeing to the common external tariffs necessary for a trade union. For example, Singapore, as a center where products are received for regional import and export, is dependent on entrepôt trade and is also completely dependent on world and local markets. Even fairly reasonable common tariffs would have ruined its duty free markets. Similarly, very low common external tariffs, which would be in harmony with the concept of open regionalism, would have been unacceptable for the other ASEAN members.

The essential difference between a customs union and a free trade area lies in the question of the sovereignty of each member. A customs union would have provided ASEAN members with greater economic advantages. The member countries would not need to create a complex system of rules of origin, as common external tariffs prevent the exploitation of tariff differentials. Similarly, a customs union with fairly moderate common external tariffs would attract foreign investments to the area more readily than a free trade area would, although proponents of the ASEAN FTA also claimed this benefit. A customs union, however, would have removed the members' sovereignty over their external tariffs against non-members. This kind of limit on national decision-making was incompatible with the traditional ASEAN institutionalist approach.

Nevertheless, the temptation to move toward a customs union remained strong, even though devising a system of rules of origin would not be an easy task in the FTA arrangements, and union would lead to bureaucracy, resulting in smaller benefits to the members – as happened with the PTA. Several proposals among Southeast Asian experts suggested various combinations of a customs union and the FTA. In 1987 the Institute for Southeast Asian Studies Colloquium proposed a system in which the four countries of Indonesia, Malaysia, the Philippines and Thailand would form a customs union and Singapore and Brunei would be linked to it with a free trade area.[55] In a FTA, the rules of origin should accompany the determination of the domestic content requirement in order to avoid trade deflection (the exploitation of tariff differentials) in real or in factitious production. This system would add national control to intra-ASEAN trade. On the other hand, the level of domestic content requirement would be difficult to determine. A high domestic content requirement would effectively water down the benefits of the free trade area. The FTA aims to better allocate resources and to encourage production and trade. But the ASEAN markets are limited and they need new production technologies and new production sectors which do not exist in the region. Therefore, demanding domestic content requirements would effectively hinder technological development in the FTA countries.

There were only few purely economic estimations of the effects of a possible free trade area. The experts concluded that a free trade area was the easiest way to develop intra-regional trade and was necessary in order to deepen ASEAN cooperation. Earlier proposals had tried to develop the PTA through various supporting measures,[56] but in the beginning of the 1990s it became obvious that these measures were not enough. The ASEAN economists did not expect that the FTA would have revolutionary effects on intra-ASEAN trade. The study by Pearl Imada, Manuel Montes and Seiji Naya, for example, forecast rather modest economic effects for ASEAN cooperation – only a five to ten percent increase in intra-regional trade was expected. These low expectations reflected not only the unwillingness of the ASEAN governments to abandon their national interests but the already low level of ASEAN's intra-regional trade.[57]

The Creation of AFTA

At the political level there were several attempts to improve the PTA. The number of items covered by the PTA increased consistently up to the end of the 1980s, while getting items included on the exclusion list became more difficult.[58] However, owing to great upheavals in the world's politico-economic systems – the changes in Europe and the formation of NAFTA and APEC – ASEAN leaders realized that regional politico-economic cooperation required new and more profound efforts.

The decisive meeting for the creation of the ASEAN free trade area, AFTA, was the 23rd ASEAN Economic Ministers Meeting in Kuala Lumpur in October 1991. The meeting focused broadly on the politico-economic prospects of the ASEAN countries – the FTA was not the only proposal raised at that meeting. In fact, the Malaysian East Asian Economic Grouping (EAEG) proposal took the most visible role, owing to the Malaysian Prime Minister's assertive conduct at the meeting. Mahathir doubted rather openly the ability of ASEAN to create an operational free trade area. He put the priority on East Asian economic cooperation, meaning, first of all, the coordination of policies with East and Southeast Asian countries in global trade negotiations. His proposal emphasized regional economic group pressure in global trade negotiations rather than formal arrangements among regional countries.[59]

The Kuala Lumpur AEM meeting was preceded by the Thai Prime Minister's unyielding diplomacy to gain support for the FTA idea. This process followed the characteristic mode of ASEAN decision-making by which consensus is reached through low-profile exploration on various levels. When the Thais won over the ASEAN foreign ministers, they turned toward the ASEAN finance ministers – the most eager to defend national economic interests. The most remarkable change in the draft proposal, as it made its way through this consensus-forging process, came from the Indonesian government, which demanded that agriculture be left outside the FTA proposal.[60]

Besides the EAEG and the AFTA proposal, three other proposals were put forward at the Kuala Lumpur meeting. Indonesia proposed the Common Effective Preferential Tariff (CEPT) agreement among the ASEAN countries. The Philippine government had in mind an ASEAN Treaty of Economic Cooperation, and Singapore forwarded its concept of sub-regional growth triangles. All of these proposals were dealt with some months later at the Singapore ASEAN Summit in January 1992, and Thai Premier Anand Panyarachun's AFTA proposal, which included CEPT, clearly became the most important achievement of the summit.

The process that gave birth to AFTA largely followed the institutionalist procedures commonplace in the ASEAN organization, but added new elements. Two agreements formed the basis for the AFTA. In Singapore the ASEAN leaders of governments signed the Framework Agreement on Enhancing ASEAN Economic Cooperation, while the economic ministers signed the Agreement on a Common Effective Preferential Tariff Scheme for the Free Trade Area. Even though the agreement signed by the leaders was general and referred largely to the intent of the governments, when paired with the CEPT agreement, it provided more exact guidelines for economic cooperation than had previous ASEAN agreements. First, since the CEPT agreement began on a sector-by-sector basis, as opposed to the product-by-product approach of the PTA, national bargaining for exclusion became less possible. Second, the ministers agreed on an initial schedule for application. Still, the institutionalist practices used in ASEAN cooperation were reflected in the fact that the final schedule remained open, as did the details of implementing the sector approach – including how the exclusion lists were to be compiled. The agreements that created AFTA were, on the one hand, concrete enough to make AFTA internationally credible and, on the other hand, flexibly consistent enough with familiar ASEAN decision-making procedures to be acceptable to all the governments. Malaysian Mahathir failed to mention AFTA in his speeches and statements in the Singapore Summit and emphasized again the importance of EAEC.[61] Nevertheless, the Malaysian economy was one of the most developed of the ASEAN economies, so that the benefits of the free trade arrangements were obvious. Besides this, the Singapore Declaration launched at the Summit did mention EAEC and emphasized that "when the need arises, it could contribute to expanding cooperation among the region's economies, and the promotion of an open and free global trading system".[62]

The main instrument to reduce tariffs and to promote AFTA is the CEPT scheme. It differs in important ways from the PTA. First, its sector-by-sector approach limits national policies of favoring certain products and producers. Second, ASEAN could agree on an exact schedule for implementing tariff reductions partly because of a new organ of ASEAN, the AFTA Council, created for the implementation of AFTA. During the third AFTA Council meeting in December 1992, this schedule was published.

The CEPT scheme has a fast track and a normal track. The fast track includes 15 product groups.[63] For the items with tariffs above 20 percent, the tariffs will be reduced from zero to five percent in ten years. For the products that were already at 20 percent and below, tariffs will be reduced to the same level within seven years. In spite of the fact that all the ASEAN governments agreed to the fast track, only Malaysia and Singapore began tariff reductions immediately. Brunei, Indonesia and Thailand began cutting duties at 20 percent and below in 1995, and the Philippines in 1996. Tariffs on products on the normal track, including all those not on the fast track which were above 20 percent, will be brought down in eight years and reach the zero to five percent level by 2007. Products on the normal track which were already under the 20 percent tariff level will be brought down to zero to five percent in less than 10 years.[64]

From the point of view of free trade and effective regional allocation of products, the exclusion of agriculture from the AFTA arrangements severely limited the effects of the new FTA. Of course, compared to the old PTA, the CEPT scheme covers much more – the fifteen normal track production sectors account for nearly 40 percent of intra-ASEAN trade. Similarly, the more rigorously controlled exclusion list would be only temporary. AFTA applies the international Harmonized Commodity Description and Coding System (HS), a tariff classification and commodities coding system that makes the AFTA classification compatible with international trade standardization. HS nomenclature forms a six digit numbering system which places most developed and sophisticated products on higher levels. The AFTA exclusion list operates at the HS8–9 digit level, and the products would be there only temporarily.[65] The CEPT agreement specified that the products under CEPT meet the 40 percent domestic or ASEAN cumulative content requirement in order to enjoy the tariff reductions, while in the PTA the domestic content requirement is 60 percent. In this way AFTA tried to boost new production branches with a larger extra-ASEAN origin. This shift to the so-called AFTA-Plus illustrates ASEAN's aim to go beyond the traditional free trade area. Both the Singapore agreement for enhancing economic cooperation and the CEPT agreement paid attention to non-tariff barriers (NTB), including product standards and technical barriers.[66]

Whether the creation of AFTA moved ASEAN from a co-operative organization towards a supranational institution is a different question. The AFTA agreements hardly reinforce such a trend. The new institution, the AFTA Council, is a Ministerial body composed of representatives from each Member Country and the Secretary-General of ASEAN. In fact, a change in the role of the Secretary General, agreed to in Singapore 1992, did bring a supranational aspect to ASEAN economic and political cooperation. The Singapore Declaration said that "[t]he Secretary-General of the ASEAN Secretariat shall be redesignated as the Secretary-General of ASEAN with an enlarged mandate to initiate, advise, coordinate and implement ASEAN activities", emphasizing a more independent role for the Secretary General.[67] It would not be an exaggeration to say that the creation of AFTA, together with the change in the Secretary-General's role, illustrates an integrative tendency in Southeast Asian regionalism before and after the Singapore Summit.

AFTA and Southeast Asian Integration

Singaporean Prime Minister Goh Chok Tong remarked in December 1995 that AFTA "by today's standards ... is no longer bold". He added that "[i]n terms of economic integration, ASEAN is actually behind other regions".[68] Although the Prime Minister referred to the developments taking place in the other parts of the world, the key point was that from 1993 to 1995 intra-ASEAN trade had not increased as much as some ASEAN governments expected it would. During 1993–5 the total share of intra-ASEAN trade in overall ASEAN trade did not change remarkably.

Even though this failure could be understood in light of the fact that during the two years the schedule for the CEPT scheme had not progressed very far, Goh claimed that the signal sent to the external world by AFTA was not strong enough.[69] The judgment of the outside world was particularly important since other destinations keenly competed with ASEAN for capital and foreign direct investment (FDI). A very important aim of the free trade area was to assure foreign investors that the region offered a single marketplace; that assurance could not be delivered without the development of intra-regional trade. NAFTA and the MERCOSUR Customs Union on the other side of Pacific, not to mention the European Union, offered arrangements with faster trade liberalization schedules than AFTA and cut into ASEAN's competitiveness for FDIs. The vision of expanding ASEAN, and particularly the addition of a new member (Vietnam) in 1995, was, in this respect, a double-edged sword. Expansion worked against a faster liberalization process, although it might advance ASEAN's intra-regional investments. Referring clearly to this equation, Goh urged stronger measures to promote ASEAN economic integration under AFTA.[70]

The argument for *open regionalism* includes the idea of attracting extra-regional FDIs. The former ASEAN Deputy Secretary General defended strongly this rationale for AFTA.[71] Interestingly enough, during 1991–5 extra-ASEAN FDIs dropped remarkably, while intra-ASEAN FDIs clearly increased.[72] This pattern indicated, on the one hand, that foreign investors saw no better opportunities with AFTA in place than they had before AFTA; but, on the other hand, regional investors considered their opportunities enhanced. AFTA, as well as overall positive economic development, may have contributed to those enhanced opportunities. Thus, according to the advocates of stronger economic integration, the trade liberalization measures taken in AFTA were not enough to attract FDIs into the region. AFTA needed to be complemented with a freer investment environment under the ASEAN Investment Area (AIA).[73]

Owing to the structure of exports, the ASEAN economists argued that the growth of intra-ASEAN trade could not be the single tool in ASEAN economic cooperation. AFTA should be combined with other forms of economic cooperation and governance. Such a combination would increase ASEAN's value as an investment area as well as bring the added benefit of improved ASEAN political cooperation. With the establishment of the dispute settlement mechanism to cover agreements, the ASEAN members made a fairly small step toward a supranational institution as the ASEAN Secretariat got "the responsibility of monitoring and maintaining under surveillance the implementation of the SEOM's ruling and AEM's decision as the case may be."[74] Even this rather modest formulation recognized the need for more exact governance, and the discussion of economic integration facilitated by some supranational arrangements became more and more obvious in ASEAN economic cooperation.

From the point of view of economic integration, ASEAN efforts had concentrated mainly on trade; cooperation in finance, for example, was practically ignored. In March of 1997, on the eve of the Asian economic crisis, the ASEAN ministers of finance signed a "Ministerial Understanding on ASEAN Cooperation in Finance" in which the organization took its first and very tentative steps in this direction. Although the broad scope of this document ranged from banking to public finance and expressed the ASEAN finance ministers' aim of increasing transparency between member countries, the specifics focused mainly on information exchange.[75]

Because of the strong emphasis on national sovereignty in Southeast Asian regionalism, supra-nationalism has been taboo. However, in order to boost ASEAN economic integration, a Thai expert, Suthiphand Chirathivat, suggested that ASEAN should progress toward a common market. This move called for a much deeper integration process than the one taking place with AFTA. To accomplish his plan, Suthiphand suggested two-track implementation with the old ASEAN six moving in front and the new members following. Besides a free flow of goods, common markets also include cross-border flows of capital, labor and services. They demand, therefore, more "institutionalized" integration. The ASEAN countries, in their "ASEAN way" – that is, in their typical institutionalist decision-making mode – could pursue this process only partway. As one can understand from Suthiphand's discussion, in the end ASEAN would have to adopt more supranational institutions.[76]

In the discussion of the integration of intra-ASEAN trade after the Asian economic crisis, regional integration was not the main point. Members questioned to what extent ASEAN countries should boost intra-regional trade. Intra-ASEAN trade, measured by any method of calculation, did not exceed 25 per cent before 1997, and the economies and the economic structures of the ASEAN countries remained far from compatible. Why, then, shouldn't the ASEAN countries just forget economic cooperation and concentrate on global markets? Nevertheless, regionalism was still seen as a vehicle for national prosperity. For example, Mahathir, far from the loudest proponent of AFTA, argued that "[f]or AFTA to be meaningful, trade and investment between ASEAN nations must be substantially increased. I submit that earnest efforts in this direction must be made now so that ASEAN can quickly grow into a truly dynamic organization capable of meeting the challenges posed by the emergence of regional economic groupings in other parts of the world."[77] Here, intensifying regional trade and economic cooperation is rationalized as an effective response to the challenges of competition from other regional groupings, rather than valued on its own merits. Few instruments to support economic cooperation exist in the region other than the creation of institutions which increase the possibilities for enhanced intra-regional trade. Such institutions would call for effective cooperation in financial matters.

Although intra-ASEAN trade did not increase remarkably during 1993–7, ASEAN economic cooperation had constructed the concept of ASEAN as a united economic region. The power of this concept was proved during the Asian economic crisis, when economic decisions based on global and local market forces strictly followed the borders of ASEAN. In practice, South Korea, the main origin of the currency crises, was the only extra-ASEAN country powerfully hit by the currency dealers' selling and buying decisions.

Conclusion

The regionalist debate in the 1990s was divided into an economic and a political approach. In the economic debate, the ASEAN free trade area was the main concern. ASEAN's political approach focused on the expansion of the organization and aimed to include all Southeast Asian countries in the ASEAN organization. This expansion seemed consistent both with an institutionalist approach as well as with the member states' sovereign position vis-à-vis the regional organization.

The arguments supporting ASEAN's enlargement ranged from economic considerations to security questions, and finally the matter became an issue of ASEAN's independence from Western political powers, particularly from the US and the EU. Economic cooperation, investment possibilities and even economic integration were central themes in the early expansion phase, when Vietnam became a member, partly because of the coincidental debate on the formation of an ASEAN free trade area and partly because of the strong political and economic trends among the Vietnamese political leadership.

Economic arguments fell silent following the changes in Vietnamese politics and the diminishing enthusiasm for the possibilities of a free trade area among the ASEAN members. The institutionalist approach, which emphasizes ASEAN's role as a security system through common norms and rules, superseded the economic argument for cooperation. Contrary to economic cooperation, the intitutionalist argument emphasized that the enlargement process would be the easiest way to strengthen the organization. According to this logic, expansion would similarly strengthen ASEAN's decision-making system, as the new members were eager to accept the principle of consensus as the basis of the organization's decision-making.

While arguments regarding Vietnamese membership originated either from within Vietnam or from within the ASEAN members, the discussion regarding Myanmar's membership was dominated by the impact of the Western critique of Rangoon's human rights records. Bringing Myanmar into the organization helped forward ASEAN's long-standing goal of including all Southeast Asian countries as members as well as asserted ASEAN independence from the Western powers. In deciding to accept or reject Myanmar, the ASEAN countries had to choose whether they would support ASEAN unity or yield to pressure from external forces. Although the unanimity over the schedule of Myanmar's entrance into ASEAN stretched rather thin, the ASEAN way of reaching consensus contributed to Myanmar's joining in a tight schedule.

ASEAN's general discussion of its expansion as well as the high-level political decisions made about it, echo the main themes of *new regionalism*. The discussion of economic cooperation, however, obscures this view. That discourse strongly calls into question the central theme of new regionalism – that economic integration is part of *old regionalism* and not a significant phenomenon in *new regionalism*. The content of the expansion discussion, particularly as it concerned economic cooperation, suggests that economic integration is an important element of ASEAN regionalism.

3 Regionalism and Security in Southeast Asia

In the general literature on regionalism and regional integration, the concept of security has played an ambiguous role. The realist approach, which has a vague connection to regionalism, focuses the question of security on defense against military threat. As the main concern is national security, the regional solution becomes military alliances. However, from institutionalist or functionalist standpoints, the question of regional security is not so simple. Institutionalism also understands military action as the main threat against security, but it pays attention to the sources of war. Therefore from an institutionalist standpoint, the question of regional security becomes a matter of comprehensive and common security and involves economic, social and environmental problems. Superficially, functionalism seems to have little to say about security issues, let alone about defense questions. Originally, however, functionalist theories came into being as answers to the threat of war. It is only because of the strong position of strategic and defense studies in security issues that the functionalist approach is largely ignored. For functionalism, security threats come from military, political, economic and environmental problems which, if not solved, may catalyze war. The solution is regional cooperation, not seen as an end in itself but rather as a source of renewable forms of cooperation. The cooperative commitment of regional states to find solutions to concrete problems leads to socialization and integration in the region.

This situation prevails in European security studies as well as in Southeast Asian studies and reflects, of course, the fact that in European countries and European regionalism security correlates largely with defense policies, with problems being solved either independently by national means or cooperatively through military arrangements. In European integration, security issues – as far as defense policy is concerned – occupy the weakest sector in EU cooperation. It should come as no surprise, then, that ASEAN cooperation has failed to find a way to deal with security and defense issues at the political level.

THE CONCEPT OF SECURITY IN ASEAN

Despite the obscurity between security and defense in regionalist discourse in general and the silence on defense issues within ASEAN cooperation in particular, security has been one of the main concerns – if not the main issue – shaping ASEAN organization. Two factors emerge as important here: The Cold War constellation in the Asia – Pacific region in general and the need to stabilize post-colonial relations in Southeast Asia in particular.

Characteristically, the ASEAN documents have not specifically articulated these important motives. The Bangkok Declaration refers to the attempt to maintain "regional peace and stability" by adhering to the principles of the United Nations. Kuala Lumpur's ZOPFAN declaration asserts more specifically how this regional peace should be maintained. It emphasizes respect for the sovereignty and territorial integrity of all states, abstention from threat or use of force, peaceful settlement of disputes, equal rights and self-determination and non-interference in the affairs of states. The ZOPFAN declaration goes on to define the aim of ASEAN's external relations as the "neutralization" of Southeast Asia. Consequently, the organization's two first and basic documents set up the rules of conduct among the ASEAN states and define ASEAN as a security community having the important task of working as a conflict management mechanism among the member countries. The second, externally focused aim of "neutralization" was not realized during the Cold War period.

In emphasizing regional rules, norms and other means of confidence-building among the ASEAN members, the regional states aimed at common security. The ASEAN documents, read in isolation, evidence an institutionalist approach to security. However, the ASEAN leaders' statements – even from the organization's beginnings – emphasize the Cold War security environment. Official ASEAN documents do not mention the external security threat until the Bali treaties start to contemplate common action in external affairs whenever unanimous agreement exists. Against the background of the emergence of socialist Indochina in 1975, ASEAN's role in the defense of the members' collective and national security became very evident. During the Kampuchean question of 1979–91, ASEAN as an organization became an active player in the power game in East and Southeast Asia. ASEAN maintained that Southeast Asian security could be achieved through the strict enforcement of international law, realized by international diplomatic and economic pressure on Vietnam to withdraw its troops from Cambodia. The emphasis on international law in the Cambodian case highlighted the idea of collective security in ASEAN's external relations and reinforced an institutionalist posture in ASEAN cooperation.

Nevertheless, the ASEAN members' defense policies change the picture of the organization's role in regional security. Despite the emphasis on collective and common security within the ASEAN organization, the defense policies of the individual ASEAN members indicate that they charge to the organization no major national security role. The security postures and defense policies of the ASEAN members largely flow from the members' relationships with the superpowers and with each other – mutual relations within ASEAN being rather problematic during the period of the establishment of the organization. The concept of security that is used in ASEAN cooperation is, therefore, not the sum of its member's security postures. Quite the opposite.[1] The security approach taken by ASEAN reflects an institutionalist concern for ASEAN cooperation rather than the security interests of individual members.

Therefore, the main security role of ASEAN has focused on intra-ASEAN relations with regional security issues getting the most comprehensive coverage in ASEAN documents. Those basic documents comment on economic, social, political and military factors and see economic development and growth as the most important determinant of a regional security and peace based on the economic growth and social stability of member countries. When domestic security based on social stability is the main issue, the organization has emphasized the role of national sovereignty as the basic premise of ASEAN cooperation.

The emphasis on national sovereignty also united ASEAN against Vietnam's policy in Cambodia during the 1980s. The same resistance against external actors continued into the following decade in economic and political spheres. The emphasis on national sovereignty founded ASEAN's main security concept – constructive engagement – during the 1990s.

ASEAN doesn't hold a monopoly on the concept of constructive engagement. The concept has been in wide usage in at least two cases. Some Western countries used it to approach the South African white minority regime during the 1980s, a policy that Malaysian Mahathir Mohamad strongly condemned at that time.[2] The American foreign policy leadership also used the concept in defending the US rapprochement toward Communist China. The main content of the concept in American political vocabulary was, and still is, that promoting economic and political ties, while at the same time pressing American political values and open markets, is the most efficient way to change China and to establish peaceful cooperation. In ASEAN policy the concept makes use of the same elements, particularly the facet of positive cooperation. However, the ASEAN concept of constructive engagement does not seek to impose political values as American policy does. For ASEAN, the question is still on regional peace enforced by cooperation. Social and political changes within cooperative partners come as by-products, not main ends. ASEAN made full use of its version of the concept during its enlargement process, particularly in defending the membership of Myanmar. However, the concept has also proved useful in justifying the ASEAN members' policies of non-interference in the political and social upheavals taking place in Indonesia after the Asian economic crisis.

Despite the primary role of intra-ASEAN security, ASEAN's external security has been important too. First, the Cold War security environment was reflected in the position ASEAN took during the Kampuchean conflict. This conflict had an important impact on ASEAN in two respects – it presented a real military problem for one ASEAN member, Thailand, and it functioned as a glue holding the organization together for a decade. The conflict provided an opportunity for the ASEAN members to take common diplomatic action among international organizations and thereby assert the organization's identity and name. As an organization, ASEAN's position on the conflict did not deviate from its course of emphasizing comprehensive security. Nevertheless, to resolve the conflict ASEAN argued for strict respect for international law as far as national sovereignty was concerned, international sanctions and collective security.

It can be argued that the Cold War constellation shaped the ASEAN's basic axioms of security and its institutionalist approach toward intergovernmental cooperation. The defense aspect of security did not get a foothold in the organization, although some members did cooperate for defense purposes outside the ASEAN context. The military aspect played out differently. All the important ASEAN countries relied on US military power at least to some extent. They needed US forces to balance the growing military influence of the PRC.[3] Despite economic and political trends moving ASEAN countries toward East Asia, first of all toward Japan, the United States dominated militarily, not only because of its military presence, but also because it continued as the foremost supplier of weapons, especially the most sophisticated weapon systems.[4] Still, because of Southeast Asian experiences in the Vietnam War, ASEAN members could not place unwavering trust in the role of the US in maintaining stability in the region.[5] ASEAN still had a part to play in developing extended security.

Several realities motivated ASEAN efforts to develop extended security. First, intra-regional security could not guarantee political and social stability in Southeast Asia. Second, neither ASEAN as an organization nor the ASEAN members as a group of governments were powerful enough to maintain stability outside their borders. Third, the ASEAN countries had good reasons not to place unrestricted trust in US military, political and economic power. Finally, the changing regional structure – evolving from the Cold War constellation into a more open system – called for new measures. Vietnam's rapprochement to ASEAN, leading eventually to ASEAN enlargement, particularly brought into the Southeast Asian arena new security issues – first and foremost the heightening of Chinese interests.[6]

Some institutional practices supported the development of extended security. During the Cold War, ASEAN had opened dialogues with its external supporters on political, economic and security affairs. These dialogue relations, although they did not always take up security as the only or even most important issue, constructed a kind of security background for the ASEAN countries. When the Cold War ended, these dialogue relations came to the fore. The number of dialogue partners increased significantly, with India, the Soviet Union and the PRC joining the discussions. But the discussions, held bilaterally with the dialogue partners after the ASEAN Post Ministerial Conferences (PMC), started to scatter in various directions owing to different issues between partners. Moreover, in the post-Cold War situation bilateral talks could not adequately address multilateral issues – such as security problems in the vicinity of ASEAN.

Thus, the ASEAN security concerns went in two directions: In the first, ASEAN worked as a conflict management mechanism for intra-ASEAN relations. In the second, ASEAN focused on Asia-Pacific stability, since unsteadiness in the broader area would have ramifications on the Southeast Asian region. To work toward its first kind of security goals, ASEAN used the instrument of constructive engagement. For its second type of goal it sought some kind of broader ASEAN model for extended security.

EXTENDING THE ASEAN CONFLICT MANAGEMENT MECHANISM

In the Cold War two-bloc system the security role of ASEAN was limited to the members' efforts at devising a comprehensive strategy for economic growth and social stability; military-security was left to national defense and to the one superpower, the US. The comprehensive strategy, without any mention of military aspects, was written into ASEAN documents. The member nations' different approaches to foreign security alignments were, however, clearly reflected in their varying interpretations of the ZOPFAN concept of neutralization. In spite of the fact that ZOPFAN lost most of its relevance after the fall of the Soviet Union, differences remained among ASEAN member attitudes toward the US military presence in Southeast Asia. When Singapore openly admitted the balancing role of the US in the area, Malaysia, following her traditional neutralist line, emphasized the necessity for the absence of external military force. During Mahathir's era, the delineation of these differences has continued.[7] Particularly after the Gulf War, the Malaysian view became even more suspicious of the US. In the Gulf War the US showed its military supremacy in world affairs, and this impressed the Malaysians. On the other hand, they condemned the willingness of the US to intervene into the affairs of two Islamic countries.[8] Moreover, Mahathir charged the US with shaking Southeast Asian political stability by intervening in intra-ASEAN issues (Myanmar's membership) and by pursuing economic colonialism during the Asian economic crisis. In spite of these criticisms, however, Malaysia silently accepted the US military role. It has been pointed out that Malaysian political rhetoric on international issues differs from its actual operational policy.[9] The importance for Malaysia of the US security role was clearly proved during US Defense Secretary William Cohen's visit to Malaysia in January 1998, when Malaysian authorities were forced to admit the need for a "flexible and unrestricted" military presence of the US in the region.[10]

Nevertheless, in the Singapore Summit of 1992, the ASEAN leaders pronounced their common worry about unstable developments in the Asia – Pacific region and ramifications that instability might have in Southeast Asia. In a joint declaration the ASEAN Heads of States announced ASEAN's intention to move from purely intra-ASEAN security to enhanced security by increasing security cooperation with the other parties in the Asia – Pacific region.[11]

ASEAN soon moved in this second direction. Because of ASEAN's evolving relations with Vietnam, the question of the South China Sea became more important to the organization and introduced an even more serious Asia – Pacific security problem when Vietnam became an ASEAN member, because of the Vietnamese-Chinese territorial dispute there. In its Declaration on the South China Sea, 22 July 1992, ASEAN introduced "a code of international conduct over the South China Sea". The declaration pointed to several functionalist issues as motives for the code of conduct. However, the ASEAN foreign ministers who signed the declaration did not have functionalist cooperation in mind. They referred clearly to intergovernmental cooperation as the declaration's most important sentence urged "all parties concerned to apply the principles in the Treaty on Amity and Cooperation in Southeast Asia as the basis for establishing a code of international conduct".[12] Thus, the declaration included an idea for peaceful resolution of possible conflicts and initial rules governing the use of natural resources in the area rather than taking a step toward functional cooperation.

The ASEAN Declaration on the South China Sea indicated that the ASEAN governments had prepared themselves for broader security discussions than before. However, there was another concrete measure by which ASEAN intended to outline both the security dialogue and military developments. ASEAN's Treaty on the Southeast Asia Nuclear Weapon-Free Zone reflected the spirit of ZOPFAN but contained the same cleavages between spirit and implementation as the Kuala Lumpur declaration had. In a reflection of the different security positions of the various ASEAN countries, for example, the Treaty left the monitoring and control of visiting ships and aircraft to each state party. Each state, "on being notified, may decide for itself whether to allow visit by foreign ships and aircraft".[13]

The Singapore Summit Declaration of 1992 referred to ASEAN's interest in a broader dialogue for extended security. The ASEAN Regional Forum, the ARF, was established as a vehicle to promote that interest. Several initiatives on the architecture of Asia – Pacific security had been put forward before the ARF concept. The most important was Australian Foreign Minister Gareth Evans' proposal to establish a Conference on Security Cooperation in Asia (CSCA) based on the European model. The US and ASEAN rejected the proposal, but ASEAN presented a similar proposal less than a year later in Singapore.[14] As all the documents proved, the ASEAN leaders did not set any concrete aims for the ARF. The TAC treaty, the ASEAN Declaration on the South China Sea and the

Treaty on the Southeast Asia Nuclear Weapon-Free Zone marked the limits of ASEAN security dialogue.

The particularly ASEAN way of approaching the question – the two-track approach – followed the pattern established in ASEAN diplomacy. The ASEAN-ISIS discussion forum, however, was too limited for broader Asia – Pacific second-track security discussions. Interestingly enough, at a meeting in Seoul in November 1992, about 20 strategic and international studies centers in the Asia – Pacific region started to evolve second-track security dialogue using the same concept as ASEAN-ISIS cooperation. Later this process adopted the name "Council for Security Cooperation in the Asia Pacific (CSCAP)". With institutes covering the same countries of the Asia – Pacific region as would be joined together in the ARF, the CSCAP took as its task reinforcing the second-track discussion and thus supporting the forthcoming ARF process.

The CSCAP divided itself into four working groups – a confidence building measures working group, a comprehensive security working group, a maritime cooperation working group and a North Pacific working group. From the point of view of extended security, the most interesting task for the CSCAP was to develop the concept of comprehensive and cooperative security. Not surprisingly, the same concept was adopted in the ARF dialogue.[15] The task of the comprehensive security working group was to develop this concept.

Certainly the concept of *comprehensive* security has strong ASEAN origins.[16] The CSCAP and ARF dialogue added the facet of *cooperation* to the concept. This two-part concept challenged the old concepts of balance of power, collective security, international anarchy, etc. Accordingly, the concept of comprehensive security rests on the following premises: First, threats to both national and regional security take on a multi-dimensional nature. Second, the response to those threats must likewise be multi-dimensional. Third, a wide range of informal processes need to be put in place to achieve the security objective. The idea of comprehensive security was not a concept in the traditional scientific sense, then, but rather an academic and political approach. This approach – either including a military element or not – emphasizes a wide range of environmental, economic, and demographic issues which come together with other social factors to found comprehensive security.[17]

The *cooperation* part of the concept refers more pointedly to the political element of the process and in its action-oriented emphasis shows a strong functionalist tendency. The working group agreed that this part of the concept "focuses on the process by which security outcomes may be achieved" and founded its work "on a belief that multilateral cooperative activity is the most effective means of achieving security, whether comprehensive or otherwise".[18] Nevertheless, the working group distanced itself from functionalist security ideas as it asserted that the "cooperative security approach acknowledges the centrality of the state in security processes and the primacy of state interests in the achievement of security".[19]

The task of the second track is to sustain a security dialogue and thus to develop new initiatives for the first track. As one of the most important second track debaters, Indonesian Jusuf Wanadi put it, this second track has as its responsibility "the necessity to lay down a new strategic map for the Asia Pacific region. ...[G]overnments alone will not be capable of bringing this about, because the challenge is huge!"[20] While concrete cooperation takes place on the intergovernmental level between the states, the function of the non-governmental sector is to maintain second-track discussions that help construct and justify regional security systems.

Regardless of these preliminary understandings, the working group, for both political and academic reasons, encountered great difficulties in defining the two-part concept of comprehensive and cooperative security. Although the CSCAP is a second-track forum, national views clearly shaped participants' interpretations of comprehensive security.[21] States may easily apply the concept of comprehensive security on an individual basis, but on a broader sub-regional or regional level such application becomes more complex. Interestingly enough, the working group concluded that the comprehensive security concept called for common institutions founded on national states rather than on interstate systems. Regional security regimes are still too loose to produce the real outcomes necessary for comprehensive security.[22] The CSCAP concluded, however, that Asia-Pacific dialogue should reject formal European models of security such as the CSCE.[23] Taking into consideration "the special pragmatic Asian approach to issues," the Asian participants, including those from ASEAN countries, preferred loose structures and the slow institutionalization of present APEC arrangements and the forthcoming ARF. The chairman of the working group doubted, however, that these institutions would be able to deal with comprehensive security in its broadest sense.[24] Thus, non-Asian participants expressed doubts about the usefulness of the comprehensive security concept in Asia-Pacific security cooperation. These doubts, pointed implicitly at the ASEAN model of security both at the sub-regional and regional levels, remained a part of the ARF dialogue when participants criticized the ASEAN concept.

From the theoretical point of view, the CSCAP discussion on comprehensive and cooperative security focused on the debate between institutionalist and realist paradigms. Broadly speaking, in the CSCAP discussion, the dividing line of the debate geographically follows the line between Asia and the Western participants of the ARF. The Western participants were more critical toward the comprehensive security approach, but criticism also came from the Asian and ASEAN academics on the approach and the ARF role in Asia – Pacific security mechanisms.

Nonetheless, the concept of comprehensive security received serious consideration in the first ARF meeting in Bangkok, 25 July 1994, and was adopted in the second ARF Meeting in Brunei Darulsalam as a key concept for the ARF dialogue.[25] This adoption clearly reflected the primary position of ASEAN in the ARF process. In the second ARF meeting the ASEAN countries presented "a Concept Paper" which included the de facto agenda of the ARF. The concept paper was written in the spirit of the "ASEAN way" and emphasized the ASEAN model of maintaining regional peace.

The three challenges to regional security highlighted in the paper throw light on what ASEAN means by the concept of comprehensive security. Written at a time when Southeast Asian economic growth had continued for years and neither economic crisis nor depression was in sight, the paper pointed to uncontrolled economic growth as the first challenge since it would be accompanied "by significant shifts in power relations". In order to prevent possible conflict caused by these transitions, the task of ARF is to manage these changes and preserve the peace.

Second, the paper refers to the diversity of the region as a challenge to comprehensive security, and, despite modestly failing to mention concepts such as constructive engagement, makes clear that the ARF mechanism will not intervene in the internal affairs of regional countries. Instead, the ARF will "try to forge a consensual approach to security issues". Finally, the paper points to unresolved territorial disputes as security challenges and commissions the ARF "to gradually defuse these potential problems".[26]

In fact, the way the paper orders these challenges matches the way ASEAN has conceived of them. ASEAN has found it easier in a multilateral forum to discuss the first challenge of controlling the destabilizing potential of economic growth than it has the third challenge of helping to solve territorial disputes. Intra-ASEAN discussions have hardly touched on territorial questions. The concept paper concludes that all three challenges cannot be addressed simultaneously and that the ARF should adopt an "evolutionary approach".[27] The paper goes on to suggest a three-stage approach in which, in the first stage, the ARF would promote confidence-building measures (CBM), in the second stage would develop preventive diplomacy mechanisms, and in the third stage would devise conflict-resolution mechanisms. Confidence-building mechanisms start from two points of departure – the development of basic principles for regional interstate relations and the adoption of a comprehensive approach to security. Transparency in both broader security issues as well as in defense and military build-up serves as the enabling instrument in both instances.[28]

The concept paper suggests both conventional ASEAN methods, such as coordinating existing security study activities and increasing high level contacts on security matters, but also forwards new concrete initiatives. Despite the fact that the CSCE has been considered by ASEAN as an inappropriate model for Asia – Pacific security cooperation, the concrete measures urged by the paper do resemble those used in the CSCE – most obviously the presence of observers at military exercises. Nevertheless, remarkable differences arise in the area of obligations. In the ARF, nations invite observers on a voluntary basis. In the CSCE, the CBMs have also been mainly voluntary, but important obligations do exist: Member nations are obliged to provide prior notification of military maneuvers exceeding 25 000 troops, held within 250 kilometers from its borders.[29] Most major European military maneuvers and exercises fall within these parameters and thus warrant obligatory prior notification. In general, the CSCE process has produced, since Helsinki (1975), fairly detailed regulations, both on voluntary and obligatory observations. The ARF process, following "the ASEAN way" has not produced such a set of regulations.

As other ARF CBMs, the concept paper proposes that the ARF members participate in the UN conventional arms register and further explore a regional arms register. The paper also suggests the ARF establish maritime information databases and design measures to encourage personal contacts among military staff and institutions of the region.[30]

The section of the paper which deals with preventive diplomacy forcefully expressed ASEAN's approach to interstate relations. Annex A reiterats the principle of sovereignty in all its conventional prerogatives. Annex B suggests two concrete measures for engaging preventive diplomacy – first, the nomination of a Special Representative to undertake fact-finding missions in consultation with ARF members, and second, the exploration of the idea of a "Regional Risk Reducing Centre" to serve as a data base for the exchange of information. The Chairman's statements at each annual ARF meeting faithfully followed this ASEAN agenda. In this respect, the "ASEAN way" seemed to operate in a broader regional context.

The approach thus outlined in the concept paper established a minimal set of expectations for the ARF. The consensus of the members – and the agendas of the ARF meetings, in fact – went beyond this minimum. The discussions in the first and second track reflected the rather wide divides among ARF members and particularly between Western and Asian participants. This expression of contradictory views belongs in a natural way to the second track discussion. It is the task of the second track in this process to explore common interests and find topics and procedures which are acceptable to all members. However, rather different expectations prevailed, and conflicts – over which direction the ARF should take to enhance regional security and how concrete its work should be – rose to the first track discussions. As a consequence, it was suggested that security issues be dealt with in several security forums, as the issues were too wide to handle within a single regional framework.[31]

The questions raised by the Western members of the CSCAP and the ARF included the connection of human rights and democracy to extended security. In the ARF meetings, the United States and the EU raised some concrete issues, most prominently, the situation in Myanmar and its membership, first in ASEAN and then in the ARF. The Western members, particularly in the second track, called into question the universal principle of non-intervention and the absolute sovereignty of nations despite bad human rights records.[32] Remarkably, some Southeast Asian second track participants recommended common intervention in human rights issues, too, thus distancing themselves from the official ASEAN way.[33] In the first track, European and American diplomats repeatedly pointed out their negative attitude on Myanmar's membership and argued against the usefulness, in this instance, of constructive engagement. These conflicts carried over into the third ARF meeting in Jakarta, in July 1996, where the lack of consensus could not be concealed. Western participants denied the policy of constructive engagement in general and in the case of Myanmar in particular.[34] However, the Chairman produced a statement completely ignoring the Myanmar debate and announcing the criteria of participation, the most important of which was that all ASEAN members would automatically be participants in the ARF.[35]

Notwithstanding ASEAN's attempt to keep Asia-Pacific security dialogue under its control, two tendencies have eroded the organization's authority – first, the growing involvement of external powers in Southeast

Asian affairs, and, second, the globalization of the issues in the ARF. In spite of the fact that ASEAN has kept up the façade of consensus by playing the key role in the ARF and by making sure the Chairman's statements reflect supposedly common views, the obvious disagreements between the ARF participants – and particularly the Western political interest in becoming involved in some domestic questions in Southeast Asia – created concerns among ASEAN members.[36] The situation raises the question of whether or not ASEAN made a miscalculation in trying to incorporate extra-regional powers in its model of decision-making and conflict-management mechanism through AFTA. Miscalculation or no, the later developments in ASEAN, Chinese military operations in the South China Sea and particularly the Asian economic crisis, followed by political turbulence in Malaysia and Indonesia, remarkably reduced ASEAN's self-confident management of the ARF process.

The disintegration of Indonesia, in many respects, the most important ASEAN country, has changed the security constellation in Southeast Asia. The developments that led to the collapse of the Suharto regime in Indonesia raised severe doubts about the relevance of constructive engagement in inter-state relations in ASEAN. In Malaysia, the Mahathir administration's treatment of Malaysian former Deputy Prime Minister, Anwar Ibrahim, caused confusion and discord among the ASEAN governments. The Philippines, for example, broke the rules of constructive engagement when Manila openly criticized the Mahathir government about the Anwar Ibrahim affair. Similarly, certain ASEAN governments could hardly conceal their wish for Suharto's overthrow, and the Southeast Asian media, even in those countries where the media follows relatively closely the government's views, remained particularly open to the claims for the necessity of a regime change in Indonesia. Although Indonesian domestic developments where not placed on the ARF official agenda, the crisis critically decreased ASEAN's internal cohesion.

With the changes in the Indonesian government, ASEAN could no longer keep its internal affairs outside the ARF process. The situation in East Timor with the UN-arranged referendum on independence, the entry of UN troops into the area, and all the turbulence around the situation – broke down the concept of constructive engagement. The ASEAN governments had to acknowledge, now in the ARF chairman's statement,[37] the need for external involvement in Southeast Asian affairs, and particularly in this situation that neither Indonesia nor the ASEAN organization was able to handle. Its own inability to deal with East Timor and the concomitant and necessary involvement of external forces were particularly irksome to ASEAN.[38]

The globalization of the ARF originates from its structure. The reason for the rise of global issues in the ARF was not ASEAN's interests in all of them, but the fact that many of the ARF participants, such as the US, China, Russia and the EU have global political interests which go beyond the Asia-Pacific region – a fact evidenced in the ARF chairman's statements in the years of 1999 and 2000. Therefore, the character of the ARF as an Asia-Pacific dialogue process had broadened into a more global discussion forum.

Despite many critical views from both inside and outside Southeast Asia, neither the growing involvement of external powers in Southeast Asian affairs nor the globalization of the issues in ARF have necessarily reduced the rationality of ARF, although the bases for its rationality have changed. The main threat to extended security presented in the ARF Concept Paper, uncontrolled economic growth, has at least partly lost its relevance, but other reasons remain to link external powers to a Southeast Asian security system. As already mentioned, in Southeast Asia there has been a tendency to seek the help of external powers in stabilizing power constellations. Indonesia, which is a regional power, has expressed the strongest reservations against that tendency. The other states, including Malaysia, have silently accepted an external presence in Southeast Asia to balance the power of Indonesia. From the point of view of power politics, these states have swallowed their pride and accepted such an external presence. Now the question has become to what extent they are ready to accept the involvement of these external powers in their domestic affairs. Tolerance for this kind of involvement will, of course, vary. In every case, it is clear that the ASEAN countries accepted the UN intervention in East Timor in 1999 as the instability of Indonesia became a threat to regional security. On the other hand, the situation in the South China Sea has remained nearly unchanged during the ARF process; in this case ASEAN has an interest in keeping great powers involved in the area. As well as being useful in these practical ways, the globalization of ARF does not necessarily reduce its abstract value either. Quite the opposite. It is good that the ARF partners can speak about their global interests, on Kosovo,[39] for example, since these kinds of linkages always exist. For all these reasons, the ARF process seems legitimate from the institutionalist point of view.

REALISTS, THE ARF AND CHINA IN THE SOUTHEAST ASIAN POWER EQUATION

From the realist point of view, however, the ARF process looks very different. The realist standpoint examines regional security first of all with regard to the national defense of the regional states. In regard to regional affairs, it poses these questions: Which countries' military strategic security is increased and which are reduced? Which countries' military power and influence are increased and which are reduced?

The realists particularly point to growing military deployments and expenditures in the Asia – Pacific region as reflections of the changing security situation. During the 1990s, Chinese qualitative deployments have been a special concern to realists. Chinese military expenditures have not followed trends in its foreign policy but trends in its economic growth. China's claims on the South China Sea coupled with her increasing capacity to exert military power regionally have alarmed institutionalist ASEAN experts, too.[40]

ASEAN's diplomats and experts have good reason to be worried. None of the diplomatic and semi-diplomatic measures ASEAN has organized since the inaugural South China Sea workshop in Denpasar, Bali, in January 1990, has restrained Chinese territorial claims nor stopped the spread of its military occupation of the uninhabited reefs of the Spratly Islands. The question of the Spratly Islands is one of the most important territorial disputes in ASEAN owing to the fact that it presents both an intra-ASEAN problem as well as a broader regional dispute. Despite the Chinese claims (from both the PRC and Taiwan), four ASEAN countries – Brunei, Malaysia, Vietnam and the Philippines – have set their claims over these islands while Indonesia has made claims on the waters surrounding them. As the dispute over the Islands made a very visible contribution to the collision of Chino-Vietnamese relations already in the mid-1970s, it introduced a new – or perhaps intensified an old – security aspect in ASEAN. Two important motivations lay beneath the territorial claims – the largely unconfirmed likelihood of oil and gas deposits in the area, on the one hand, and the island group's strategic location, on the other.

The most important of ASEAN's diplomatic maneuvers followed the Chinese actions in the Spratlys. First, the ASEAN Declaration on the South China Sea, issued in Manila on 22 July 1992, criticized the new Chinese claims made in February of the same year. Then, in its March 1995 Statement on developments in the South China Sea, ASEAN protested the Chinese occupation of Mischief Reef in the Spratly archipelago claimed by the Philippines. ASEAN had some success in its diplomatic efforts. With them, ASEAN countries took a common stand against an external threat, and during the late 1990s ASEAN managed to arrange some multilateral talks with China on the South China Sea issue. However, no concrete issues in the South China Sea dispute have been resolved. At the same time, as realists have pointed out, neither the military deployments of ASEAN countries nor their military commitments prepared them for a crisis in the South China Sea. In Southeast Asian countries military deployments do correlate positively with economic growth. Deployments decreased during the Asian economic crisis, of 1997–1999 and have increased significantly in some countries since the crisis as these countries try to resume the procurement programs they canceled during the crisis. Despite this recently renewed interest in procurement and in contrast to the trends in China and Japan, military expenditures as a share of the GDP in the main ASEAN countries of Indonesia, Malaysia, the Philippines, and Thailand have gone down during the 1990s.[41]

With respect of China, the ARF's concern about the impact of economic growth on regional security and power relations seems to be justified. It is no surprise that the ARF's modest arms control measures have had no impact on arms deployments in the region. The statistics during the ARF process 1995–9 show that the only explanatory variable in the region has been the economic depression, which caused the decline in military spending during 1998 and 1999.

The realists refer to these quantitative facts, Chinese military maneuvers and their contradiction with the political parlance in the ARF. As the military capacity of a country is the main source of national security, they maintain that the ARF has not improved the Southeast Asian security environment because it has not tried to restrict Chinese military power. The realists argue that, despite its membership in the ARF, China has not restrained its policy in the South China Sea nor has it even engaged in real multilateral discussion, not to mention negotiations, on the dispute. In order to maintain its negotiation posture in this question, China has accepted only bilateral talks with the regional states. The realists assert that, through the ARF, the concept of comprehensive security and ostensible Asian opposition to the West over human rights questions have confused the ASEAN states and prevented them from realizing the Chinese threat to Southeast Asian security. The institutionalists point out, on the other hand, that the ARF process can be seen as a security-building measure, to a large extent, which cannot be gauged by quantitative means.[42]

Therefore, in the matter of Southeast Asian security, the latent contradiction between the national and ASEAN levels persists. It forms the context in which the security discourse on the different tracks of the ARF should be understood. Realist standpoints refer to national security and, to a certain extent, to Western views. The institutionalist approach emphasizes ASEAN cooperation and "Asian diplomatic practices." Functionalist aspects in the concept of cooperative security reflect original points of departure in ASEAN cooperation. In the ARF and CSCAP discussions, the different national security positions of the various ASEAN countries have surfaced. The internalization of ASEAN security discussion may provide a practical vehicle for dealing with the national/regional contradiction and help ASEAN intervene in members' affairs, a move impossible in normal ASEAN cooperation to date.

Part II
Regional Responses to Global Challenges

4 ASEAN in the Asia-Pacific Context

I have examined Southeast Asian regional development from the ASEAN point of view, particularly with respect to three regionalist approaches – functionalism, institutionalism and realism – and how the different elements in these approaches have been realized in practical regional co-operation. Despite the broader regional context of the ARF, my focus has been on intra-ASEAN relations. The point of view changes in this chapter. Since Southeast Asian countries have relatively limited political and economic power, they have to try to adopt and incorporate global political and economic influences into their regional systems, rather than imposing their own ideas on the world at large. The rather low degree of regional integration and the loose structure of the ASEAN organization make ASEAN's global relations different, in kind, from intra-ASEAN co-operation. Nevertheless, ASEAN is a response by the regional states to the challenges of global influences. Therefore it is difficult to assume that ASEAN's external policies are totally separate from the policies of regional co-operation.

Obviously the broader Asia-Pacific region provides the most important economic and political context for ASEAN, a fact I underscore in my discussion of ASEAN security in the previous chapter. Three powers – the USA, Japan and the Peoples' Republic of China – are particularly important in the political, economic and security relations of the ASEAN states. After the beginning of the GATT Uruguay round, Japanese direct investments rose dramatically in Southeast Asia. This increase was due to the arrangements between the US and Japan – the Plaza Accord – adopted in September 1985, which increased the value of the yen against the dollar. This also illustrated very well the restructuring of Japanese industry at the regional level. The ASEAN governments made this possible by opening their economies to FDIs for financing their future growth after the short recession of 1985–6. However, despite the decrease of the United States' role in Southeast Asian economies, the US markets were still of major significance for the ASEAN countries.[1] Therefore, they could not step aside from the US-led Asia-Pacific economic cooperation, although some ASEAN governments were rather critical of Washington's role.

In the ASEAN political parlance, functionalist, realist and institutionalist/constructivist arguments can be discerned. When dealing with ASEAN's external relations, the theoretical context of the new regionalism becomes important. Since this concept – or the more political version of *open regionalism* – has been largely developed to illustrate Asia-Pacific developments, it is no surprise that it fits well into the ASEAN debate on Asia-Pacific relations. When regionalism is analyzed through the concepts of functionalism and institutionalism, the focus falls on intra-regional relations, while the concepts of new regionalism and open regionalism emphasize the global environment and its change, with regional inter-state relations playing a minor role. Moreover, the new regionalism takes as its theoretical base political economy. The role of Asia-Pacific economic relations for ASEAN is so prominent that political economy infiltrates nearly all of the arguments surrounding ASEAN's relations toward Pacific co-operation.

Several important trends dominated Asia-Pacific developments during the 1980s and 1990s. Southeast Asia and the ASEAN states have not been immune to these trends and have tried to make both national and regional responses to them. The first of these trends is the rise of Japan as a global economic power. The second is the decrease of American economic and politico-military influence in Asia. The third is the modernization of China and its emergence as a major political power in East Asia. The fourth is the fall of the Soviet Union and the disintegration of its global bloc. The fifth is the emergence of regional groupings all over the world, combining global economic governance within the GATT (the General Agreement on Tariffs and Trade) and its successor, the WTO. The last is the economic growth of the Asia-Pacific region and Southeast Asia in particular. This trend played a crucial role in the Asia-Pacific debate during the 1990s. While these trends visibly influence the political stands of the ASEAN governments, they also shape the organization's external policy.

ASEAN AND EAST ASIA: THE EAEC AND BEYOND

The breakdown of Cold War international systems revealed the growing economic influence of Japan in the Southeast Asian region. Within ASEAN that influence became very obvious in the late 1980s, although it had begun much earlier, first with the Fukuda doctrine in the late 1970s and later with the early 1980s Malaysian "Look East" policy. Both economic and ideological factors underlay the ASEAN turn toward East Asia. On the economic side, Japan was attaining ever-growing economic influence, in many ASEAN countries assuming a position of dominance. On the political side, ideological factors such as anti-colonialist spirit and the Asian values discussion helped justify government policies in certain ASEAN states. Nonetheless, Japan's economic influence remained much more clear-cut among the ASEAN governments than its political influence, as the Malaysian East Asia Economic Group (EAEG) discussion made obvious.

Behind Mahathir Mohamad's East Asian Economic Group idea – later the East Asian Economic Caucus, EAEC – were well-founded politico-economic rationales. As Mahathir feared, in the early 1990s, ASEAN, even 10 members strong, could not assemble an integrated economic unit able to compete against global economic powers and equally influence the economic rules of world trade. The development of AFTA likewise proved the great difficulties involved in forging an integrated economic region in Southeast Asia, with its incompatible and competing economic structures typical of a small and geographically limited area. Mahathir proposed simply "closer economic co-operation involving the Pacific seaboard of Asia".[2] If the economic region were expanded, not along political lines but according to natural economic ties, ASEAN countries would associate with Japan, the PRC, Taiwan and South Korea. In the middle of the 1990s Japanese imports and exports to ASEAN alone – not to mention to the rest of East Asia – equaled European and US trade with ASEAN. The compatibilities between the Pacific seaboard nations would form a good basis for economic co-operation and integration.

The immediate context of the Malaysian proposal was the blockade in the GATT Uruguay round negotiations in early December 1990. Interestingly enough, the Malaysian proposal was not the only suggestion of its kind. Nearly two years earlier, Australian Prime Minister Bob Hawke called for the establishment of a Pacific Rim trading bloc as a response to EC reluctance to free agricultural products in world trade.[3] Hawke's short-lived proposal, which gave the US and Canada minor roles in an Asia-Pacific trade group composed of East and Southeast Asia together with Australia, soon evolved into the APEC process. The important difference between the Australian proposal and the Malaysian one was that the EAEG excluded Australia and the United States, claiming that, although most of the Asian countries (excluding Japan and South Korea) supported the USA and Australia against the EC on agricultural policy in the GATT, the United States and Asian countries pursued different economic interests.[4] These differences particularly concerned liberating textile products and opening world markets in services, including banking and insurance.[5]

The EAEG was to become an Asian response to the protectionist tendencies in world trade. How this response was to be realized, however, was obscure, since Mahathir and the Malaysian ministers did not divulge the explicit contents of the initiative. As a result, the debate on the EAEC concerned motives and intentions rather than real content. Mahathir himself steered the debate along this course. According to Mahathir's analysis, offered in a privately sponsored ASEAN conference in March, 1991, in Bali, the most important characteristic of the new post-Cold War situation was that old battlefields were turning into marketplaces. The economic giants, the US, Japan and the European Community, would accelerate their struggle for market shares. Since the fall of the Soviet Union, the Western economic powers no longer needed allies in the developing countries, and any privileges ASEAN might have previously enjoyed had disappeared with the Cold War. Now, Mahathir reasoned, the danger was that in this economic battle between giants ASEAN would be "caught in the cross-fire".[6]

In Bali, Mahathir explained to the other ASEAN leaders that ASEAN should choose its side. For him the choice was clear – the ASEAN countries should look neither to the EC nor to the United States for partnership. On the one hand, European ties had already lost their former significance for ASEAN – the European Community was turning inward toward East Europe and had little interest in Southeast Asia. On the other hand, the fall of the Soviet Union left a "sole American giant" to dominate world affairs. The world would continue to witness "a dramatic rise in the political, diplomatic and military clout of the US". Mahathir forecast that the US would increase its political, social and economic pressures and warned that even "military adventures cannot be excluded". Clearly, the motives for Mahathir's initiative were not purely economic: his proposal coincided with the Gulf War, which was fairly unpopular in Malaysia. Mahathir remarked that "the countries of Europe and America have a reputation for economic arm twisting" using human rights, environmental protection, democratic practices and all other possible excuses for "the suppression of the economic growth of potential competitors". All these reasons made them unreliable partners for the ASEAN countries.[7]

Even though the details of Mahathir's original blueprint remained obscure, the name change from a "group" to a "caucus" indicated that Malaysia had softened its position. Still, Europe had forged its own powerful regional group and NAFTA was concluded on the American continent. The Asian economies needed to join together in a pressure group of some kind. Mahathir argued that

> EAEG or EAEC should be neither a formal grouping like ASEAN, nor should it be a trade bloc like NAFTA or the European Community (EC). As it is dedicated to world free trade it cannot be protectionist and give its members preferential treatment in intra-regional trade. Its chief purpose is to provide a strong voice for the East Asian countries in trade negotiations with the rest of the world, particularly the EC and NAFTA.[8]

The EAEG/EAEC proposal received only half-hearted responses from the other ASEAN countries and a very elusive official reception by the Malaysian main target, Japan. Despite their lukewarm attitude, however, the other ASEAN countries never rejected the idea outright. Singapore was the first ASEAN country to accept Mahathir's idea;[9] the other ASEAN countries were more reserved. For example, Indonesia's Suharto ruled out support for any arrangement which resembled a trade bloc.[10] In response, Mahathir refined his definition of the proposal, stressing that the task of the EAEC was to ensure the terms of free trade in international trade negotiations against the protectionist tendencies of Europe and North America. It would not be a trade bloc itself, but would be "GATT and even APEC-compatible".[11] The heads of ASEAN governments discussed the EAEC at the Singapore Summit of 1992 and accepted it for ASEAN's agenda. The Singapore Declaration stated: "With respect to an EAEC, ASEAN recognizes that consultations on issues of common concern among East Asian economies, as and when the need arises, could contribute to expanding co-operation among the region's economies, and the promotion of an open and free global trading system."[12] Compatibility with APEC became a major issue. ASEAN fellow members tried to moderate the Malaysian formula to avoid confusion about the new Asia-Pacific economic co-operation in APEC.

In ASEAN diplomacy the question of the EAEC now turned outwards. No longer an intra-ASEAN issue, it became an instrument in ASEAN trade diplomacy. The ASEAN countries now tried to include the EAEC in the APEC process. In every case the strategy served as a tool, particularly in dealings with the US, to work for trade liberalization in the Asia-Pacific region.

The US and Australia made clear their unresponsive attitudes, stressing what they considered the pre-eminent role of APEC.[13] The Bush administration was very reluctant even to mention the concept by name. The US foreign policy leadership seemed to accept limited free trade areas, but Washington found the broader FTAs without US participation in the Pacific region unacceptable. Fear grew that the EAEG would lead to a "three region world" (Europe, the Americas and East Asia) instead of a "two region world" (Europe and the Pacific) – a very undesirable situation for the US, particularly with reference to world trade negotiations. Judging Mahathir's proposal as "very unwise,"[14] the Assistant Secretary of State, Richard Solomon, warned the ASEAN governments that "GATT-compatible regionalism, such as the ASEAN Free Trade Area, strengthens efforts to sustain and expand a global free trade regime. Closed, exclusionary groupings, however, would be very costly for trading partners on both sides of the Pacific."[15] ASEAN efforts to calm Americans failed, and fear of the EAEC as drawing a dividing line between the Eastern and the Western sides of the Pacific increased.

ASEAN put the concept on its agenda, and discussions with dialogue partners followed in the ASEAN Post-Ministerial Conferences. Reports of the dialogue sessions did not mention the details of the discussions. At the 27th Post-Ministerial Conference, ASEAN presented a detailed proposal on the EAEC which was also kept unpublished. Its main content was ASEAN's attempt to include the EAEC in the APEC process. Although detailed accounts of the concept had been kept out of print, the US attempt to evade the proposal finally failed. After the ASEAN conference, Assistant Secretary Winston Lord of the new Clinton administration had to comment on ASEAN's policy before the media. He refused to describe the proposal but did, nevertheless, make an exceptional top-level comment on US fears on the EAEC. He explained that the US was trying to be open-minded about the proposal but believed that "APEC is the most promising organization for freeing up trade and investment in the Asia-Pacific". Therefore "[w]e don't want to see anything develop that would have a dividing line down the Pacific". He emphasized that, despite the open US attitude, "we want to make sure that they (new regional proposals) don't in any way harm American interests".[16]

Japan's evasive attitude particularly annoyed Malaysia since in the Malaysian proposal Japan would take the lead in the new grouping. The timing of the proposal for Japan was disadvantageous. Japan's Prime Minister, Toshiki Kaifu, got it just before he postponed his ASEAN trip. Japan had committed to GATT principles and made its political commitments to APEC, which had been established just a year and half before. It was particularly important to Japan, at that moment when its interests were secured rather well, to leave the GATT undisturbed before the blockade of the Uruguay round. Moreover, the main focus of Kaifu's trip was to be the restoration of Indochina, in which Japan was taking a leading role, not the establishment of a new regional grouping.[17]

The continuing low Japanese profile indicated that the Japanese attitude reflected more than bad timing. In fact, in Japan, there had been much interest in Asian regional co-operation both on the governmental and the non-governmental level. In semi-official events and through government members, the Japanese had expressed their interest in closer economic co-operation in Asia on a regional basis.[18] In Japanese domestic political circles and among the Japanese public, Mahathir's proposal was even more popular.[19] Seemingly, American opposition to an organization fostering exclusive Asian economic co-operation under the leadership of Japan, together with the importance of Japanese export markets in the US, restricted Japan's policy.[20] Whether or not the official Japanese negative attitude was involuntary, the Malaysians did not hide their disappointment. They felt that, as the only non-Western member in the group of seven, Japan, as a matter of course, should take a leadership position in any regional arrangement in Asia. As Anwar Ibrahim, then the Deputy Prime Minister of Malaysia, put it, Japan's unwillingness to accept this role "and to become a voice of conscience in the world representing an Asian perspective is perplexing to many of us in Southeast Asia. Japan's ambivalence towards ASEAN's initiative to establish the East Asian Economic Caucus – EAEC – is indeed disappointing."[21] Although the Malaysians wanted to ensure that EAEC would not become an economic bloc, politically – at least on the symbolic level – they did not downplay its significance. This fact was one main element shaping the American rejection and the Japanese evasion.

The issue of the EAEC was the most visible element in ASEAN's stance toward East Asia. Its importance varied among different ASEAN countries. A serious weakness of the EAEC has been that, despite official ASEAN support, it has been looked upon as a Malaysian proposal. When it is connected to Mahathir's rhetoric, the US has been particularly unresponsive. The early Singaporean support did not necessarily contradict the Malaysian connection[22] since, together with Malaysia, Singapore had been the strongest proponent of common Asian values at the ideological level. In the views of the Americans and the Australians, then, the EAEC seemed to be a concrete politico-economic realization of Asian values, an Asian bloc. The support of the PRC for the EAEC, together with that of the new ASEAN member, Vietnam, probably did nothing to dispel American and Australian misgivings.[23]

The image of an ideological Asian bloc was further reinforced by the fact that the other old ASEAN members – Indonesia, the Philippines and Thailand – first gave only tepid support to the concept. They warmed slowly to the idea. It is supposed that the cool attitude of Indonesia resulted partly from the way Malaysia had introduced the concept without first consulting the other ASEAN countries. The Indonesian leadership felt itself disregarded in the matter. In addition to these ideological and status issues, the less-than-enthusiastic embrace of EAEC by some of the ASEAN countries had an economic base. Despite the growing importance of East Asia in the Southeast Asian economy, the United States was still the biggest single importer of Southeast Asian products. This factor was even more important for South Korea, who was not compelled to express its opinion on the EAEC. The openness of the US market for their exports was an immediate and abiding concern of these countries.

In spite of the fact that the EAEC was not realized during the 1990s, the underlying need for it still prevails. The composition of the Asian countries in the Asia-Europe meeting (ASEM) resembles that of the EAEC. Although ASEM has not had significant political and economic results, it offers a context for East Asian co-operation. And concrete East Asian economic co-operation has been emphasized in the debate surrounding the Asian economic crisis. Without dropping the EAEC from the agenda, ASEAN has adopted another form of co-operation, *ASEAN + 3*, which to a certain extent follows the EAEC idea.[24] Most importantly, it includes three prominent East Asian countries – the PRC, Japan and the Republic of Korea – and it has taken up a task similar to the one planned for the EAEC: to bring together the Asian states to discuss global trade and economic questions under the WTO. The first meeting of this kind took place in Bangkok in July, 1994. Politically, however, the *ASEAN + 3* is less radical than the EAEC: the co-operation takes place within the leadership of ASEAN and thus can be more regionally limited. This structure also guarantees the presence of the Republic of Korea, which would otherwise disregard the Japanese leadership in a regional organization. The first *ASEAN + 3* agenda was modest; rather than discussing East Asian political integration, it focused on boosting ASEAN economic integration.[25]

CHARACTERIZING ASEAN'S ROLE IN THE ASIA-PACIFIC CONTEXT

In the early 1990s, the debate on Asia-Pacific economic development and its connection to political culture – that is, the discussion on Asian values – became significant for Asia-Pacific regionalism. During the 1980,s the question of Asian political values had been merely academic; however, in the 1990s, three factors increased the importance of this debate. First Mahathir's concrete proposal on the EAEG focused attention on Asian co-operation. Second, important ASEAN leaders began to enter the debate. Mahathir Mohamad and Lee Kuan Yew, for example, took part in the discussion. Some prominent government members, such as Malaysian Deputy Prime Minister Anwar Ibrahim and a senior Singaporean foreign ministry official, Kishore Mahbubani, also contributed. Asian academic and expertise groups, as well as NGOs, continued the discussion. Third, the discussion spread to more politically significant issues, starting from the Tianamen incident in 1989 and moving on to the Burmese question as well as to some world trade issues. Despite the increasing importance of the debate on Asian values, however, other ASEAN countries have not actively taken part in this discussion at a high political level or shared the views of the advocates of Asian values and the Asian model. As a matter of fact, in the late 1990s, the new Thai government and the government of the Philippines rejected Asian values and the Asia model concepts. The future South Korean president, Kim Dae Jung, had rejected the Asian values concept in even stronger terms earlier.

In the ongoing discussions of political culture and economic development within Asia-Pacific economic and political regimes, the debate on economic and political liberalism dominates. Although the Southeast Asian approaches have tried to offer alternative models for social and economic development, economic and political liberalism have been the determinants of international relations both in academic discussion as well as in political debate.

In spite of the fact that the connection between Asian values and economic development has been discussed for years, in the United States this debate did not become intense until Samuel Huntington's *The Clash of Civilizations* was published in *Foreign Affairs* in 1993. During the 1980s and early 1990s the Asian model was examined on the economic and political levels. The concept of Asian values included in the model makes direct reference to Malaysian Prime Minister Mohamad Mahathir's "Look East" policy, but also works to justify politico-economic solutions in some ASEAN countries – in Indonesia, for example. Taking Japan as a model of economic and social development, the concept outlined the development of stronger economic and political relations to Japan. Then the experience of the newly industrialized Asian countries, NIC countries, broadened the scope of the idea and encouraged people to speak of the Asian model. With both Japan and the NIC countries as examples, some Southeast Asian leaders were encouraged to start the debate on a common Asian political and economic model.

The Asian model has thus been examined as a politico-cultural (ideological) phenomenon, as well as an economic model, an alternative both to the model offered by the developed countries as well as to the traditional model of developing countries based on primary production and agriculture. The model supposes that Asian economic development is founded on political stability, high saving rates, education, and investments in export-orientated industry and requires economic planning and control without a heavy public sector. Such conditions call for authoritarian governments, control over trade unions and limited rights to political participation in order to secure economic growth. Asian values, invested in hierarchical and authoritarian order, could justify the semi-totalitarian/semi-democratic political systems in developing countries. Before the Asian economic crisis, this model had attracted several influential advocates such as the IMF, the World Bank and the ADB, as well as prominent business leaders and academics.[26] Supporters made reference to governments determined to drive economic systems to more advanced levels, first in Japan, next in the Asian NICs and then in the second generation NICs (Thailand, Malaysia, the Philippines and Indonesia). Nevertheless, some critical views were presented before the crisis. The most famous of these is Paul Krugman's thesis. He claimed that the economic growth of the East and Southeast Asian countries was not based on any model but on the fact that growing inputs in an economy also produce growing outputs. Krugman argued that the high economic growth rate in Asia did not depend on the development of efficiency in production, but only on the growth of inputs, a fact critical to the Asian model. This analysis means that the Asian economies were facing decreasing efficiency of production.[27]

The debate on the Asian economic model and Asian values merged to include both the aspect of political and economic liberalization and the question of culturally based regionalism. The American and Asian debate concentrated mainly on the two broad issues of economic liberalization and political liberalism. In APEC economic liberalization has been the main question. Only after the Asian economic crises, has political liberalism in Asia-Pacific co-operation assumed real significance.

In this historical context, Huntington's thesis served as a springboard for the Asian values debate in the US and in Asia. First of all, Huntington's article gives a very good chance for Asian advocates of the Asian model to present their views. Particularly helpful in opening this opportunity was Huntington's point of departure – he asserted that the central question of a new emerging world order is the conflict between dominating cultures, not ideological or economic conflict.[28] This thesis defends the

Asian model against charges that it has been created to justify the alliance between repressive governments and big companies, arguing, instead, that Asian political systems are based on a deep cultural tradition. Although Huntington's arguments were not based on a solid scientific foundation, his article and the debate which followed it guided the discussion on the relationship between Asia and the West as well as the understanding of political choices both in the USA and in Southeast Asia. When Huntington asserted that "cultural commonality is a prerequisite for economic integration",[29] he underscored the central role of culture at the concrete level of politico-economic co-operation. The political ramifications of his analysis became clear in Huntington's political instructions for the Western governments – largely, divide and rule.[30] This advice has caused some concern in Asia.[31]

Huntington's article implies that political and economic liberalism is a culturally bound phenomenon and is more easily adopted in Western culture than in Asian cultures.[32] The questions raised by this assertion have prompted two kinds of answers. The rationalists do not deny the possibility that the opening of economies and democratization could progress in Southeast Asia. They claim, rather, that political and economic liberalism characterize a certain historical phase of social development. They deny only the fact that a totally free democratic system is possible in every society in every phase of development.[33] Unlike the rationalists, the advocates of Asian values at least partly accept Huntington's view that political and economic liberalism is culturally bound; they present an alternative model for Asian political and social development based primarily on technological development. So far as it is necessary, the government controls technological development, from which political development follows.[34] The division between these views is not always very clear – the Southeast Asian discussions often mix rational arguments with Asian values as well as with neo-colonial critique.[35]

Two primary oppositions emerge from this large debate: economic liberalism versus the Asian economic model and political liberalism versus Asian values. These oppositions shape ASEAN's orientation in Asia-Pacific co-operation, creating a common ideological base for ASEAN policies toward the external world and protecting the ASEAN countries from unlimited penetration by ideas of economic and political liberalism encountered through Asia-Pacific co-operation. In this context, the idea of the EAEC, kept alive by the ASEAN countries, provides important leverage for the ASEAN countries when they bargain with the United States about opening their economies and liberalizing Asia-Pacific trade.

APEC AND ASEAN

The original idea of Asia-Pacific economic co-operation emerged from non-governmental circles when academicians in the United States, Japan and Australia promoted the idea in forums such as the Pacific Basin Economic Council (PBEC) and the Pacific Economic Co-operation Council (PECC). Starting as a loose discussion focused on trade liberalization and the creation of common standards, APEC became politically more important when the US started to develop instruments to accelerate the slow progress in the GATT Uruguay round. Since its beginnings, the APEC organization has become institutionally stronger and politically more important.[36] In its own official jargon, APEC was established because of growing economic interdependence in the Asia-Pacific region. Nonetheless, its creation coincided with the difficult negotiations of the GATT Uruguay round. Obviously, one main motive behind the creation of APEC was to press the EC for trade liberalization. Despite the leading role of the USA, Australian Prime Minister Bob Hawke was the original initiator of the new Asia-Pacific co-operation. And, even though US and Australian interests were similar, particularly in the trade of agricultural products, his first proposal in early 1989 excluded the USA from a "core group" which would be formed by the ASEAN member states and Australia together with South Korea and Japan. When the Australian proposal gained modest support from Asian partners, the USA initiated active diplomacy in order to be included in the new Asia-Pacific group.[37]

The first ASEAN reactions to Hawke's proposal, both doubtful and suspicious, were based on justified fears about the impact new and broader regional groupings might have on ASEAN's role. After the ASEAN Post-Ministerial Conference in July 1989, however, ASEAN cautiously agreed to follow Hawke's proposal. Their reasoning was clear: more than 70 percent of ASEAN's external trade is within the Asia-Pacific region. Singapore, following the economic argument, took the most positive position toward the proposal. Both Indonesia and Malaysia, more concerned with political implications, remained cautious. Indonesia turned out to be more positive toward the proposal after the visit of Canberra's special envoy, Richard Woolcott, to Jakarta. Malaysia disliked both Australian and US participation and consented reluctantly in the name of ASEAN unity.[38] ASEAN's common stand was that APEC co-operation must not overlap with the tasks of ASEAN. The ASEAN foreign ministers declared

> that the APEC should continue to be a loose, exploratory and informal consultative process, that the APEC process should not dilute ASEAN's identity and that it should not be directed towards the establishment of an economic trading bloc, as this would be contrary to ASEAN's support for the establishment of a more fair and freer multilateral trading system. In pursuing this goal, ASEAN should take a pragmatic and gradual approach.[39]

The United States hoped that the new regional grouping would be an important instrument in global trade negotiations. The USA wanted to demonstrate to the EC that it had another option if the Europeans refused to open trade in agricultural products. It comes, therefore, as no surprise that before the Asian economic crisis, US policy in Asia concentrated on the liberalization of trade in the Asia-Pacific area. The focus was clearly on economic liberalization in a neo-classical spirit and not so much on political liberalism. US trade policy aimed at removing all the trade and investment barriers in the region, although the main target was the opening up of Japan's protected markets.

After the initial meeting in November 1989 in Canberra, some ASEAN members remained cautious toward APEC. They were afraid that APEC would cause redundancy in ASEAN and that the smaller economies of the ASEAN countries would be overwhelmed by the large economies, especially that of the USA. Despite their suspicion, however, they had to be present at the new grouping. At the Seoul Ministerial meeting in 1991, Korea managed to negotiate the entry of China, Hong Kong and Taiwan (Chinese Taipei). Now, when all of the important East Asian economies were members of the group, no ASEAN country could afford to stay away from APEC.

US concerns with Hawke's original exclusively Asian proposal proved that the US wanted to be an active member in Asia-Pacific trade liberalization. The US views with great caution East and Southeast Asian regionalism, especially ideas such as the EAEC including Japan, China, Asian NICs and ASEAN. US caution extends, as well, to politically more limited second-track projects like the Commission for a New Asia, which seeks an identity for Asian co-operation.[40] To the US, both projects represent the culturally determined regionalism of which Huntington warned.

Regionalism considered as a cultural entity gives rise to grave concerns in the US. Ideas like the EAEC have aroused fears that Asia means to exclude Americans from some important sector, of co-operation. In *Foreign Affairs* Robert Manning and Laura Stern illustrate these feelings by emphasizing that "the region's propensity to hedge against uncertainty has turned the EAEC into the beast that will not die."[41] "Uncertainty" means here the possible effects of US claims for creating an Asian-Pacific free trade area during the APEC process. Manning and Stern acknowledge the possibility that ASEAN might use the EAEC against Washington in trade liberalization, for example, opening the markets for services. Nevertheless, some American diplomats, such as the first executive director of the APEC secretariat, William Bodde Jr., were ready to accept the EAEC in APEC as "a caucus" after "obtaining some quiet assurances from Malaysia and other members of ASEAN that it would not become a 'we' against 'them' situation that could split APEC."[42]

Despite US distrust of culturally-based regionalism, the ASEAN organization has never provoked such fear as has, for example, its proposal, the EAEC. Several reasons make ASEAN less threatening. First, ASEAN was established during the Cold War by those Southeast Asian countries belonging to the Western Camp and was seen as a part of the mechanism blocking Communism in Southeast Asia. Second, ASEAN is regionally limited and economically weak; it includes neither the main Asian powers – Japan and China – nor the middle powers – Taiwan and South Korea. Third, intra-ASEAN trade policy, particularly AFTA (ASEAN Free Trade Area), supports the general aims of APEC. ASEAN's attempt to take steps to reduce tariffs and trade barriers ahead of the APEC schedule supports the United States' aims in Asia.

In its dealings in Asia, the United States has pursued bilateral relations, in the instance of Japan and South Korea, for example, or in the special relationship with China which originated in the triangle relationship of the USA, China and the Soviet Union. While the European Union has emphasized its relations with ASEAN as an important negotiating partner, Washington has given ASEAN only a minor role, emphasizing, instead, its bilateral relations with the Southeast Asian countries. Bilateral relations provide the US with opportunities to control the relations between Asian countries – as it has tried to do through its relations with Japan and China.[43] In much the same way, the United States has worked against the formation of the kind of constellation formed, for example, by the Asia-Europe Meeting (ASEM) which brings together East and Southeast Asian countries.

Despite its diplomatic efforts, however, the US has not managed to block the formation of an Asian front. Naturally, interest in opening up Japanese markets stimulated those Asian countries fearful of joining forces due to the vulnerability of their own markets and the United States' economic domination in Asia. Nearly all the ASEAN countries, except Singapore, expressed caution about institution building in APEC. This resistance, although effective, did not unite all the Asian member countries of APEC. Singapore, for example, joining the US, Australia, Canada and New Zealand, supported a more coherent APEC in order to urge Europe toward trade liberalization. Singapore's Senior Minister Lee Kuan Yew even supported the image of a two-bloc world – Europe and Asia-Pacific – in order to reduce Europe's weight in global trade negotiations.[44]

As the United States sought to develop APEC into a more permanent instrument capable of driving trade and investment liberalization in the Asia-Pacific area, the political element in APEC expanded and became more concrete. APEC should have a clear goal, the argument went, and that goal would make the group more solid. APEC's institutionalization started in the Bangkok Ministerial Meeting of 1992, when the ministers agreed to the establishment of the APEC secretariat in Singapore. The Clinton administration tried to help institution building by organizing the first APEC Leaders' Summit in Seattle. The main Asian powers, China and Japan, together with some other countries, particularly Malaysia, resisted this kind of development and emphasized APEC's role as more of a consultative body.[45] The transformation of APEC from a consultative body into a trading group began in the Seoul ministerial meeting, where the APEC members included on the agenda trade liberalization – the real goal of American institution building, rather than the coherence of APEC.[46] Although discussions asserted that the liberalization of trade should proceed on a voluntary basis, the speed of the US plans and particularly the firm attitude of the new Clinton administration two years later worried some Asian members.

The resistance mounted by the constellation of Asian countries culminated in Malaysia's public critique of the United States role in APEC. Malaysia demonstrated its position by boycotting the APEC Summit in Seattle in November 1993. The Summit was the first APEC leaders' meeting and important to the Clinton administration both externally and domestically. While other ASEAN countries attended the APEC Summit in Seattle, Mahathir stayed home and demonstrated support for the EAEC.[47] In the Seattle Summit, President Clinton clearly pointed out that US aims for APEC were not only economic; the US was ready to use the organization to promote American political ideas in Asia.[48]

In the APEC Bogor Summit in Indonesia the next year, two trends became clear. More and more, APEC was becoming a vehicle for trade liberalization. At the same time and for that reason, a gap had opened up between most of the Asian participants and the US. However, the Asian countries stopped short of making APEC into a negotiation forum for trade liberalization since, such a move could turn APEC "into a North-South confrontational type of thing".[49]

Despite the introduction of the EAEC, ASEAN could not take a unified position vis-à-vis these APEC issues. Different ASEAN countries had different interests[50] For many, trade liberalization under APEC was one thing; US political influence quite another. Malaysia, the most anxious to avoid political influence, supported trade liberalization. In fact, it surprised the other participants in the Bogor Summit by its willingness to host the APEC Summit of 1998, thus giving its support to overall economic co-operation under APEC.[51] On the other hand, the Philippines and Thailand, whose economies were vulnerable to free trade, opposed the fast track in Asia-Pacific trade liberalization but did not find APEC political concerns salient. Only institutionalist decision-making secured ASEAN unity on questions dealing with Asia-Pacific co-operation.

The opposition between the US and the Asian countries was effectively eased by Asian economic growth. Before the Asian economic crisis of 1997 it was estimated that by the year 2020 six Asian countries would rank among the world's ten largest economies. Moreover, the constantly increasing inter-Asian trade and investments would confirm the importance of the Asian countries for world trade. In light of these predictions, some Americans warned against pushing Asian governments too hard, lest the United States become isolated from the strengthening Asian powers. An exclusive and bold US policy would serve to increase those national and regional feelings already surfacing in the wake of Asian economic growth.[52]

Despite the US-Japanese trade dispute punctuated by the US Congress's critique of Japanese trade barriers, the trade liberalization discussions progressed in relative harmony. APEC wanted countries to commit themselves voluntarily to trade liberalization. The White House took advantage of the APEC process in order to push the European Community in the Uruguay Round.[53] Despite this atmosphere of equanimity, however, the Asian countries did manage in the Osaka Summit of 1995 to stop the institution building and block the establishment of APEC as a control mechanism. APEC could set voluntary limits for demolishing trade barriers, but not impose a fixed schedule. In the Manila Summit APEC failed even to agree on setting an agenda for a new round of trade negotiations under the WTO.[54] These events disappointed those countries wanting to follow a fast track in trade liberalization. It seemed very obvious that the spirit of the Osaka Summit would live into the next millennium.

Surprisingly enough, not even the Asian economic crisis drastically changed the situation in APEC. Trade liberalization continued to make very modest progress – and then only on a voluntary basis. Importantly, in the Vancouver Summit in November 1997, the Clinton administration was unable to press this issue because the Congress had refused to give the President so-called fast track authority.[55] On the other hand, the economic crisis impacted differently on the various ASEAN countries, and they were far from united. In the following years the APEC Summits were dominated by political issues – in Kuala Lumpur, the displacement and the jailing of the Deputy Prime Minister Anwar Ibrahim and in the Auckland Summit in September 1999, the crisis in East Timor.

On the political side, however, the Asian economic crisis confirmed the fears of the ASEAN governments – the USA would use APEC to interfere in regional affairs. Difficult political issues did not come to the fore in Vancouver, though, as the economic crisis had not yet destabilized the political systems of the Southeast Asian countries. In the Kuala Lumpur Summit, however, when many Southeast Asian governments were already wavering or had failed, the Asian/Western political values conflict occupied the very centre of the meeting. Nevertheless, the US foreign policy leadership's heavy support for and involvement in the pro-Anwar democracy movement garnered support only from the Philippines. No other APEC country supported it. Even Australia and New Zealand disapproved of Vice-President Al Gore's behavior in Kuala Lumpur. The statements by Al Gore and Secretary of State Madeleine Albright actually may have worked against the USA's intention to make APEC a more solid trade grouping.

It remains debatable exactly how well the concept of new regionalism or open regionalism fits into Asia-Pacific economic co-operation. The open regionalism concept refers to the absence of regional trade blocs and is, therefore, a policy instrument used particularly by the US. Although the concept is also accepted by ASEAN countries, it does not exactly illustrate ASEAN's policies in APEC. The politico-economic developments in the Asia-Pacific region have shown the concept's assumptions to be overoptimistic. In most instances the ASEAN countries have acted individually in APEC. On the other hand, the common policies ASEAN has managed to establish in APEC, the EAEC particularly, work as a bargaining game making use of politico-cultural arguments and anti-colonial rhetoric. They are most easily explained by politico-economic interests and a neorealist approach.

5 ASEAN and the EU: Politico-ideological Conflict and Economic Necessities

INTRODUCTION

Relations with Europe – first with the European Community and then with the European Union – make up another important external context shaping ASEAN as a regional organization. From the point of view of security, Europe's role has not been as relevant as the Asia-Pacific region's, and with respect to trade, Europe has played an even less prominent part. If, however, the economic world is divided into three regions – Europe, East Asia and the Americas – rather than a bipolar two, ASEAN cannot overlook Europe's importance. In fact, ASEAN has had important mutual and bilateral connections with its European counterpart from the middle of the 1970s. ASEAN's first interests with the EC were economic, beginning when ASEAN, in order to maintain Southeast Asian countries' access to the British markets, tried to secure its trade with the EC as the United Kingdom joined the Community. During the 1980s, owing to the Kampuchean issue, the political aspect of the bilateral relations became important too. At the end of 1980s and the beginning of 1990s, the economic and political aspects became inseparable. The various interests of ASEAN and the EC have been articulated at both bilateral and multilateral occasions – the GATT Uruguay round provided an important forum for the identification of the two regions' different economic interests. The politico-ideological issues got a firm foothold in the ASEAN – EC bilateral connections.

In these ways, the Post-Cold War period has rendered prominent the relations between ASEAN and the EC. The Cold War bloc structure not only neglected the examination of the regions as independent systems but also obscured the conflicting interests between them. There are well-founded reasons to examine these relations from the point of view of political economy. At first sight the traditional regionalist approaches seem to fail to explain very much about the politics between these two regions but rather illustrate the differing natures of the two regionalisms. On the other hand, an examination of the controversies between the EU and the East Asian countries during the GATT negotiations and in the WTO as well as in the bilateral EU – ASEAN negotiations makes very obvious the clash of economic interests. The politico-ideological conflicts between these two regional organizations, then, seem to be economically motivated. However, this "hidden agenda", as the economic motives behind politico-ideological issues are called, may not provide the whole answer to the question of EU-ASEAN relations. I am inclined to argue that despite the "hidden agenda," politico-ideological conflicts have very much to do with the dynamics of regional organization itself. Both ASEAN and the EU may have rather similar institutionalist backgrounds. The institutionalist approach to regionalism could, therefore, explain, at least partly, the politico-ideological issues at stake. The underlying idea here is that emerging regional systems try to develop their own politico-ideological cultures using the aspects of existing regional cultures. In this chapter, I discuss how these ideological elements have appeared in the agendas of these two regional organizations and how those ideological elements have manifested in the interactions between the two systems. I argue that the building of regional ideologies has an important role in shaping the dialogue between these two regional organizations.

SOUTHEAST ASIAN AND EUROPEAN INSTITUTIONALIST IDEAS IN AGENDA-SETTING

Norman Palmer's analysis of Asia-Pacific regional developments sheds light on European and Southeast Asian regional developments. It affords some tools for analyzing the differences between these two organizations. According to Palmer and to the other advocates of the concept of new regionalism, Europe represents the old, and the Asia-Pacific area the new. The old regionalism is characterized by the development of general integration, the deterioration of national sovereignty and the tendency toward federalism. However, in the Third World in general and in Southeast Asia in particular, the new regionalism promotes interdependence because of the globalization of markets and nationalism supported by the nation-building process still ongoing in several Southeast Asian countries.

The European Union and ASEAN seem to illustrate Palmer's theses well. European integration has progressed both vertically and horizontally, and after the Maastricht Treaty the federalist nature of the Union has strengthened. Likewise, the creation and the development of ASEAN generally fit Palmer's analysis. The basic declarations of ASEAN document global and regional interdependence as a starting point of regionalism, and, despite regional co-operation, national sovereignty is emphasized in every Southeast Asian country. Closely connected to the nation building of these countries, the concept of sovereignty engaged here differs from the traditionally understood concept.

Palmer's general analysis – as well as the analyses of the other advocates of new regionalism – covers important characteristics common to these two organizations. In spite of the fact that clear differences separate these organizations – supranational and functional tendencies of integration exert more force in the EU than in ASEAN, while national sovereignty figures more prominently in ASEAN than in the EU – similarities obviously exist. But the theories of new regionalism fail to see the strong intergovernmental aspect in both the EC and the EU. Because co-operation is clearly intergovernmental in the EU's common security and foreign policy, the institutionalist point of departure is emphasized in the EU's external relations.

From the institutionalist point of view, regional ideologies are an important force in building common values. In Southeast Asia, as well as in Europe, regional ideologies cluster together several ideas, in various arrangements and emphases in different countries. Thus regional ideologies focus on general trends widely accepted in these regions. In Southeast Asia the mosaic of regional ideas developed in a post-colonial world, where anti-colonialism, non-alignment and the two-bloc structure set the basic ideological patterns. Superimposed on this mosaic was a crucial new export-oriented economic model adopted from Japan, Taiwan and South Korea which distanced Southeast Asian regionalism from other Third World regional developments. Although these trends have been discussed earlier, some become particularly important in respect to ASEAN's relationship with the EU.

In Europe the main current of regional ideas developed in the Cold War two-bloc system. The EC was and the EU is greatly interested in creating common norms and values, formulating, alongside functionalist economic models, the political ideologies underlying integration. Western Europe and European integration stressed all the elements lacking in the Soviet Union's East-European satellites: democracy, the rule of law, human rights and fundamental freedoms. These elements were expressed through egalitarian principles, emphasizing economic, social, legal, as well as sexual equality. The articulation of these principles varied in different European countries, but generally they found expression as legitimate group interests or as different forms of welfare state ideas, especially in the Nordic countries. These egalitarian principles stand out in bold relief against the politico-economic model of the ASEAN countries, which emphasizes the primary objective of economic growth based on authoritarian governmental control of labor, wages and exchange rates. The important differences between the politico-ideological agendas of the EU and ASEAN have played a crucial role in the relations between these two organizations.

THE EU'S ASIA STRATEGY AND ASEAN

Norman Palmer's analysis of European integration as "old regionalism" leading in an increasingly federalist direction is less helpful in understanding the EU's common foreign and security policy (CFSP). During the Cold War era common foreign policy never became a primary issue in the Community's activities. Although European economic relations and legislation have, in certain respects, developed according to the neo-functional or even the federalist model, the Community's foreign policy did not follow these principles. Similarly, the EU's CFSP is still mainly the business of member country governments with the role of the Union's common institutions being peripheral. In order to unite foreign policy, the European Community members agreed on the foreign policy agenda documented in the Maastricht Treaty. The institutional weakness of common foreign policy decision-making highlighted the importance of the agenda in the EU's common foreign policy.

The European Union's policy toward ASEAN has to be examined from two points of view. From the standpoint of the political agenda written into the Maastricht Treaty, the central issue is the defense of common European values, including democracy, the rule of law, human rights and fundamental freedoms. The other important point of view driving the Union's ASEAN policy is the EU's attitude toward international trade and its commitments in the World Trade Organization (WTO). The multilateral context is important to the EU for articulating its economic interests and for achieving the broader political economic goal of synchronizing the economic interests of different regions. These economic considerations complement the ideologically motivated political agenda.

The European dialogue with ASEAN began in the early 1970s; economic matters formed the core of the relations up to the 1990s. Particularly in the 1970s, the dialogue included an attempt by the ASEAN countries to achieve a status similar to that of the Lomé countries, and when the ASEAN economies developed further, they intended to secure the free entry of their products into the Community's markets.[1] The Cold War prevented trade issues from turning into political questions. No particular political disagreements arose between these two organizations in the two-bloc structure, since the EC supported ASEAN's policy in the Kampuchean question and ASEAN supported the Western countries on the issue of Afghanistan.

However, this situation changed as the effects of post-Cold War international relations became obvious in the Asia-Pacific area. In the ASEAN Post-Ministerial Conference in Kuching in 1990, the differences between EU's and ASEAN's approaches to political and social questions, particularly involving human rights, stood out prominently – after the Tianamen Square massacre in China, ASEAN rejected the Community's policy of imposing sanctions against Beijing.

In contrast, the Community enforced the common approach to certain issues where human rights were the crucial denominator. In the Cold War situation, the EC had confronted human rights questions on several occasions. When the EC took its first common foreign policy steps with the EPC (European Political Co-operation), human rights issues figured prominently. In the case of relations with South Africa, human rights, particularly the abolition of apartheid, were emphasized and the use of economic sanctions was established as the Community's instrument in human rights questions.[2] The agenda of the EC concerning human rights and democracy issues as well as environmental questions emerged in the Kuala Lumpur Post-Ministerial Conference in 1991. There the EC's embrace of these issues was as clear as ASEAN's rejection of them. In the next conference in Manila it became obvious that, owing to the EC's agenda, a new co-operation agreement between the two organizations could not be achieved.

After the Maastricht Treaty, in spite of the fact that the European Union was very occupied with European integration and with Eastern Europe, the Union started to evaluate its global position. A very important part of this evaluation was the assessment of the Union's Asian strategy, in which the role of ASEAN was emphasized. The Commission delivered its new Asian-strategy to the European Parliament in 1994, which accepted it in 1995. A specific new EU–ASEAN strategy followed.

In the new Asian strategy, the Commission connected the EU's Asian policy to the common foreign and security policy. The strategy paper stated, "The European Union is entrusted with the task of developing a common foreign and security policy to enable it to protect its interests and values as well as playing a constructive role in world politics."[3] With the world economic growth being strongest in East and Southeast Asia, the Commission concluded that the political weight of Asia would also increase. However, the report made a fundamental and questionable delineation that linked Japan, South Korea and other East and Southeast Asian economies to the rest of the Asian countries, including Pakistan, Nepal, Bangladesh and Sri Lanka, excluding only the former Soviet Asian republics. This approach, much criticized both in Europe and in Asia, tended to deal with Asia as a unified area and emphasized its backwardness and instability.[4]

The Commission's new draft strategy paper on ASEAN relations, "Creating a New Dynamic in EU-ASEAN Relations," largely ignores this kind of interpretation and presents a much more appropriate geographical delineation. Nevertheless, the new strategy document was preceded by Asian and European criticism of the Union's Asian strategy. Issues of conditionality were particularly called into question.[5] The dialogue between the Union and ASEAN was in danger of becoming fruitless shadowboxing – one-sided views sparring with each other.

The EU's policy toward East Asia and Southeast Asia combined its political agenda – including the promotion of human rights, democracy, the rule of law and basic freedoms along with the claim for "fair trade" – with the economic interests of the EU and its member countries. The fair trade question involved not only such justified claims as international copyright protections, but also the much more questionable issue of the social clause. The social clause involved an EU demand that, before the trade agreement on equal treatment could be arrived at, the Southeast Asian countries change their social legislation and workers' conditions to better correspond with European standards. EU economic interests also include the need for some European countries to protect their labor-intensive production, as the EU's countermeasures against East and Southeast Asian imports show.[6] As these situations illustrate, it is sometimes difficult to separate political and economic interests when dealing with the EU's policy toward ASEAN.

The crucial questions in the EU's Asian strategy are the relationship to the social clause, conditionality and the EU's attempt to enforce its economic and political presence in Asia. These dualistic and contradictory elements clearly mark the Asian strategy and surfaced in the discussion of the European Parliament. Making clear the tension among the strategy's plural objectives, that discussion produced four documents – the Foreign Affairs Committee's (FAC) report on the Commission draft paper and the opinions of: the Committee on External Economic Relations (CEER); the Committee on the Environment, Public Health and Consumer Protection

(CEPHCP); and the Committee on Development and Co-operation (CDC). As they stress their particular goals, these four documents reveal the differing interests inside the Union.

The opinions of the CEPHCP and the CDC defended forcefully the introduction of the social clause into agreements made between the EU and ASEAN. Interestingly enough, but not surprisingly, their arguments approach the claims of fair trade. About the Asian economic model based on economic growth, the CEPHCP warned:

> such short-term policy should be avoided. The committee therefore calls on the Commission to ensure that the trade with the countries of Asia is fair trade. Neglecting public health and environmental interests and obtaining a price advantage over trading partners using 'environmentally-friendly' prices, i.e. prices which take into account effects on the environment (and public health), is unacceptable.[7]

The CEPHCP demanded a strict social and environmental clause. Such a position could be seen as a criticism of the Asian economic model and a defense of the European welfare state model. The Committee on Development and Co-operation shared the critical line of the CEPHCP. It defended the principle of conditionalising the development and co-operation agreements according to human rights and democracy records and criticized the Commission for neglecting the viewpoint of underdevelopment.[8] However, the FAC's report and CEER's opinion differed clearly from the CEPHCP's and CDC's critical delineations. In fact, the FAC warned of the dangers of the policy proposed by the CEPHCP and the CDC. The Foreign Affairs Committee and the CEER proposed that the Union should formulate several Asian strategies, owing to the differences among Asian regions and countries.[9] This suggestion, along with other ideas promoted by FAC and the CEER, such as the meeting of the heads of the governments of the EU and the Asian countries, was put into practice particularly in the EU's ASEAN strategy.

The EU's ASEAN strategy, which the Commission presented to the Parliament in July 1996, does not include as critical an emphasis as the Asian strategy does. Besides the different character of these strategies, political developments coming after the approval of the Asian strategy have possibly softened the EU's ASEAN strategy. Although the ASEAN strategy was officially a specific application of the broader Asian strategy, the differences between strategies were obvious. The discussion, which started after the Union's Asian strategy, pointed to the problematic questions of conditionality and fair trade. Politically, these questions had produced a state of deadlock in the ASEAN-EU negotiations for a new co-operation agreement. On the other hand, the political agenda of ASEAN was emphasized in the ASEAN-EU dialogue. In the EU's new strategy these two viewpoints were taken into consideration.

ASEAN'S REGIONALISM AND THE EU

ASEAN's political agenda is not documented in the way that the EU's agenda is in the Maastricht Treaty. Nor has ASEAN any comprehensive strategy for Europe as the EU has for Asia and ASEAN. Nevertheless, in ASEAN's dialogue with the EU certain of the Southeast Asian regionalistic ideas stand.

Contrary to the EC's early experience, foreign policy has always had an important place in intra-ASEAN co-operation. Because of the overall weak institutional structure of the ASEAN organization and the fact that presenting a common Southeast Asian front towards international issues was one of the primary aims of ASEAN, the organization emphasizes agenda-making through consensus. The basis of the agenda has been regional resilience through stability and the Asian economic model. This agenda includes emphasis on interdependence, sovereignty and unity. The agenda does not fix topics such as those adopted by the EU in the Maastricht Treaty. The issues within ASEAN's agenda do not come from any pre-set program but represent questions which pertain directly to the region's political and economic situation.

Although regionalism in Southeast Asia is characterized by the concepts of interdependence and sovereignty, integration is also playing an increasingly important role in this region. Despite slow consensus decision-making, the establishment of the ASEAN free trade area (AFTA) automatically integrated the economies in the area and made ASEAN a more coherent international actor. This integration, despite ASEAN's organizational weakness, forced the external powers, such as the European Union, to deal with ASEAN as a single unit.

In ASEAN's decision-making process the member country whose interests are most significantly involved determines the unanimity.[10] Thus, the concept of unity determines the issues on which ASEAN makes a common stand. In fact, ASEAN unity, although it is a leading principle of the organization's decision-making, has also been a question driving ASEAN's policy during the 1990s. The dismantling of the Cold War structure in Southeast Asia created the possibility of implementing the original ASEAN idea of gathering all ten Southeast Asian countries under the same organization. Therefore, unity works as both a principle and as an aim.

ASEAN's agenda toward the EC/EU developed partly as an answer to the European policy toward ASEAN. The agenda blends, therefore, into the general discussion of Asian values, democracy and economic efficiency. Some differences do exist, however, between the ASEAN – Europe discussions and the ASEAN – Pacific discussions. ASEAN – Europe discussions more pointedly emphasize issues of equity, social rights, the environment and fair trade versus economic efficiency, protectionism and colonial attitudes. The ASEAN – Pacific discussion contrasts political and economic freedoms with Asian values; that contrast has not had such an emphasis in the ASEAN – Europe discussion.

In brief, ASEAN's political agenda in the ASEAN-EU dialogue includes, on the one hand, recognition of mutual interdependence, and, on the other, an emphasis on ASEAN unity and sovereignty. Although interdependence and sovereignty together with ASEAN unity from time to time become contradictory, they do not form a clear dividing line separating the ASEAN countries. During the Kampuchean conflict, ASEAN unity was linked to the general condemnation of the violation of national sovereignty and territorial integrity of a neighboring country. In the dialogue with the EC, these concepts were linked to a rhetoric which places emphasis on the independence of the Southeast Asian countries from their old colonial masters. This kind of political language, clearly evident in Malaysian foreign policy, connects sovereignty and ASEAN unity but also democracy and human rights questions to the themes originating in old anti-colonial rhetoric, and occurs in the many Southeast Asian approaches.

The question of sovereignty first emerged in the EC-ASEAN dialogue when the Community attempted to introduce the social clause and conditionality. In the Community's and ASEAN's negotiations in 1991, the Malaysian Foreign Minister rejected, as being incompatible with the present stage of development, the European demand to introduce environmental issues, human rights and democratic values as a part of a new co-operation agreement. He particularly referred, in rather moderate terms, to the European colonial past in Southeast Asia:

> I wish to re-emphasize the ASEAN's strong conviction that these issues should not be viewed in isolation of our pressing need for promoting economic growth and sustainable development. Nor should it ignore other fundamental principles and factors such as historical experience, cultural diversity and socio-economic indicators. We

hope that the EC side will bear in mind our sensitivities and concerns on these issues.[11]

In its views on Southeast Asia, the European post-Cold War approach to human rights and democracy was connected to that of the US. These views pinpointed the West's intention to preserve its dominant position in a new world order by rejecting the Southeast Asian approach to national and regional development. In this discussion the differences between "Eastern" and "Western" approaches to democracy and human rights were apparent. The Asian way of development was articulated particularly by Malaysian and Singaporean leaders but reinforced by representatives from ASEAN think-tanks, including both academics and government officials. The arguments in this discussion defended the ASEAN countries' sovereign right to decide their own approach to development and underscored the differences between Western and Eastern views of democracy, human rights, basic freedoms and societal models. National sovereignty was broadened, particularly in the approach of the Malaysian Prime Minister, Mahathir Mohamad, to include the sovereignty of the whole region. Hence, Southeast Asia should defend its sovereignty to decide on regional affairs without interference from the West. This move links sovereignty to ASEAN unity. In fact, Mahathir's proposal for an East Asian Economic Caucus extends this idea to all East and Southeast Asia. Although the EAEC has not been the problem for the Europeans as it has been for the US, Mahathir's EAEC idea contained the same idea of sovereignty which has been obvious in the relations between the EU and ASEAN: "We on the Asian side of the Pacific are permanent neighbors. Surely the neighbors themselves should have more right than others to determine how they wish to relate to each other in economic, security and political matters, for now and for the future."[12]

Although the idea of the EAEC was not wholeheartedly supported by the other ASEAN governments, the general principle of sovereignty is shared throughout the region. This kind of discussion concentrated on the defense of the Southeast Asian development model with its primary emphasis on economic growth. Even more importantly, particularly among the Southeast Asian think-tanks, this response criticized the idea of transferring the Western model onto Asia. It denounced the Western model of democracy and its European application in the welfare society for their inefficiency and their demoralizing characteristics. Mahathir led this ideological attack, and numerous Southeast Asian politicians and academics have followed his lead.

In this debate, Southeast Asian arguments focus on the issues of democracy, human rights and Asian and European economic models. Southeast Asian spokesmen do not doubt the importance of democracy but rather doubt its form. They point out that several Southeast Asian countries have political systems based on free and regular elections. But these systems do not satisfy the advocates of Western-style democracy, who maintain that democracy includes both the absolute rights of individuals and minorities. The Asian approach differs from this Western approach in two respects. First, Asian values emphasize the primacy of society over the individual, while Western values advocate the primacy of individual rights over society. Some Southeast Asians have admitted, however, that neither of these paradigms makes democracy impossible. A much more severe and serious criticism attacked the West for overemphasizing minority protection and in doing so giving rise to problems of democracy and efficiency. As the Singaporean Foreign Ministry's Permanent Secretary, Kishore Mahbubani, has argued, minority protection and the particular interests of minority groups have led, in the United States, to a situation in which effective environmental legislation is blocked by a small but sufficiently powerful minority and, in the European Union, to a situation in which huge subsidies keep alive such unproductive economic sectors as agriculture.[13] Thus the question of democracy has led to a debate on the comparative merits and efficiencies of the Western and the Eastern economic-political models.

In his article in *Foreign Affairs,* Kishore Mahbubani raises this discussion to a concrete regional level. He argues that the regionalisms of the EU and ASEAN differ fundamentally. The European countries, at the same time as they expect non-European countries to adopt their political institutions and legal practices, are unable to co-operate with politico-cultural systems unlike their own. Thus "all the efforts to either deepen unification via the Maastricht Treaty or widen it by including similar European countries are tantamount to rearranging the living-room furniture while floodwaters are seeping in from the rising tides just outside the door". The EU is, as Mahbubani argues, using politico-cultural values and systems as a pretext for excluding outsiders from prosperity. The East and Southeast Asian approach stands out in bold relief from this European exclusivity, as "the impulse in East Asia is to draw societies into the region's dynamism, starting with Myanmar and Vietnam and eventually including even North Korea".[14] Therefore Mahbubani, like Lee Kuan Yew, preferred Asia – Pacific co-operation as a primary environment for ASEAN's globalization. Although the governments of the ASEAN countries accepted Myanmar into ASEAN, they did not necessarily accept the domestic situation in the country. The ASEAN countries try to attract new members into the economic dynamism of the region and thereby make their domestic situation easier. Mahbubani claims that European Union members are drawing a destabilizing geopolitical line between them and their neighbors, while such borders are gradually disappearing in Asia-Pacific regions.[15]

Be that as it may, there is, nonetheless, a latent contradiction between ASEAN's concept of interdependence and its concept of sovereignty, or, at least, there are different interpretations of interdependence. This contradiction has been most obvious in the resistance to the presence of outside powers in the area. The contradiction can also be seen in the discussion on politico-cultural values. While Third World countries may protect their national sovereignty against Western countries, that protection should not prevent them from seeing their own obvious evils. The Western claims for human rights, democracy and environmental protection should be studied seriously. It is in the interest of the Southeast Asian countries to initiate discussion on these matters. To fail to do so for the sake of overemphasized sovereignty would isolate the ASEAN countries and sever important ties of mutual interdependence.[16]

FROM THE EU-ASEAN DIALOGUE TO THE ASIA-EUROPE MEETING

The EU's – and the former European Community's – agenda has particularly clashed with that of ASEAN on two concrete issues. About the first of these issues – the East Timor question – Portugal especially has kept the Union's attention focused on human rights. In the second, the approach to Myanmar, the EU's policy has been to apply economic sanctions and isolate the Rangoon government for its bad human rights record and its suppression of the Myanmar opposition. On both of these issues, ASEAN has taken up the opposite policy. ASEAN considers the East Timor question a domestic matter under Indonesia's sovereign control. The case of Myanmar, for ASEAN, involves the organization's unity and invokes the concept of "One Southeast Asia," a position the ASEAN leaders have taken up with particularly unanimity.[17]

On a general level, then, two issues on the EU's agenda – human rights and democracy – square off against ASEAN's doctrines of regional unity and sovereignty. These oppositions seem to prevent enhanced political relations between the two organizations.

In a wider perspective, some common denominators support inter-regional co-operation. However, it is not always clear whether ASEAN interests coincide with EU interests. For example, the establishment of APEC was justified by the common interests of the US and Pacific Asia in the world's trade regime. From this point of view the US prefers the bipolar world, while the EU would prefer East Asia as a more independent actor. The APEC arrangement suggests that ASEAN favors Asia-Pacific co-operation over ASEAN-EU relations.

An examination of the trade disputes in the WTO dispute settlement mechanism does not support the contention that the US and Pacific Asia share common interests. Of course, such an examination gives only part of the picture – it does not describe the importance of the trade disputes, nor mention the politico-military relationship between the disputing parties. The WTO mechanism manages disputes throughout the world, and these disputes do not necessarily follow politico-security lines although, in the present world, these disputes may become more political, reflecting political and economic relations between regions. Out of the 184 WTO settled, inactive, or in-process dispute cases, disputes between the US and the EU or some EU member country number 42. Far fewer disputes are recorded between the EU or an EU country and East Asian countries – only 14 cases. At the same time, the US has 30 disputes with East Asian countries.[18] The US is the most active participant in disputes in the trade regime.

It seems, then, that there would be grounds for co-operation between the EU and East Asia in the world trade regime, too. Some of the disputes in the WTO between the EU and ASEAN are, however, more severe than individual trade disputes. The EU's attempt to include labor standards in the WTO's negotiations is one of the most important contested issues.[19] The EU is not standing alone in this effort; it has support from the US. The EU's attempt to start a new WTO negotiation round from the year 2000 received a rather divided response from the ASEAN countries.[20]

Whether the EU and the ASEAN governments share a common view on a tripolar global order based on relationships among the United States, East and Southeast Asia and Europe is another issue. Both regions understand that the relationship between the United States and Europe is strong, as are the ties between the USA and Asia, while the connection between East and Southeast Asia and Europe is much looser. Both the EU and ASEAN would obviously prefer a more balanced global order with enhanced relations with each other.

The EU and ASEAN can make use of several forums to harmonize their approaches – the EU-ASEAN annual meetings, the ASEAN Post-

Ministerial Conferences with Dialogue Partners, and the ASEAN Regional Forum (ARF). In addition, at the EU-ASEAN meeting in Karlsruhe in 1994, the two organizations decided to establish a group to accommodate their differing views. This "Eminent Persons Group" presented its report in June 1996 and its suggestions were used in the Union's report on a new ASEAN strategy.

Apart from these forums, even more important – from the point of view of a tripolar world – is the Asia-Europe Meeting (ASEM), first held in Bangkok in March, 1996. The ASEM is not purely the Union's and ASEAN's institution; rather it offers an arena for dialogue between the EU and East and Southeast Asian countries. ASEAN plays a particularly important role in the ASEM process. Singapore, its main initiator, and Thailand, the first host of the meeting, are both ASEAN countries. The basic idea of ASEM depends on one of the central concepts of ASEAN – mutual interdependence. In practical diplomacy, the ASEM process was closely associated with the EU-ASEAN dialogue when the EU-ASEAN ministerial meeting was synchronized with the ASEM ministerial meeting in Singapore in February 1997.

Nonetheless, the ASEM is officially a process between the European and Asian countries. The representation of the EU Commission in ASEM was justified only by the economic role played by the Union for the EU members. The EU's and ASEAN's interests met in the ASEM process in important respects. Apart from the economic interests of ASEAN in Europe, the political ties of mutual interdependencies were emphasized by several ASEAN governments. In this forum ASEAN, together with a broader East Asian group, has tried to find a context for discussion with the EU, in which disagreements are not the main issue. From the European point of view, the ASEM process offers the Union a new avenue of approach toward ASEAN and Asia.

Six months after the first ASEM summit in Bangkok in March of 1996, changes in the EU's ASEAN strategy became evident. ASEAN, as a loose organization, has not been a symmetrical partner with the Union. The EU has more ability to make important international treaties binding on its members while, in important interregional treaties, the ASEAN governments, not the organization itself, are in the crucial position. Internationally, besides acting in a unified way, the EU has tried to use treaties to arrange its relations with different countries and country groupings. Nevertheless, in the relationship between ASEAN and the EU, ASEAN has been more active in reaching a new agreement. It is an exaggeration to say that the European side has been passive about the agreement, but the institutions of the Union, particularly the Commission, have recognized the differing interests of its various member countries and realized the problems of setting up a comprehensive and effective agreement.[21]

Although the first ASEM summit emphasized the role of the leadership of the governments of the EU and the ASEAN member countries together with the East Asian governments, the political process of ASEM, following the Bangkok summit, adopted the familiar ASEAN two-track co-operation scheme. In this scheme, the first track includes the conventional diplomatic and political discussions between the national governments and the EU's institutions, while on the second track co-operation consists of important unofficial interaction among non-governmental organizations (NGOs), academic institutions and businesses from the two regions. One important purpose of this scheme is to transfer the difficult questions from the first track to the second track, where they can be dealt with in a more informal spirit, without engaging major politico-ideological matters of prestige.

In the Bangkok Summit, human rights and democracy questions were set aside, a decision interpreted as a political victory for ASEAN. In fact, two members of the EU had difficulty finding proper representatives for the Summit because of domestic disquiet over the human rights situation in some Asian countries.[22] The Summit focused mainly on the economic relations between Europe and East and Southeast Asia. Despite this focus, the final declaration, although it included some concrete economic projects and other forms of co-operation, had clear political meaning.

The Chairman's statement at the Bangkok meeting made an important appraisal of global developments and outlined the principles of Asian-European co-operation. While the statement confirmed the different stages of development in the two regional systems, it asserted that the two systems were mutually interdependent. The point of departure of the statement's appraisal of the international situation was that the relations among North America, Europe and East and Southeast Asia determine international relations and the global economy. Implicit in the statement is the idea that the weakness of Asian–European relations gives the United States an excessively strong position vis-à-vis these two regions. The statement concludes that Europe and Asia should increase mutual interdependence and interaction.[23] In Asian–European co-operation, common interests should be found and the elements which disrupt co-operation should be avoided. The concept of interdependence was the term used by the European leaders as they argued for co-operation; the concept was thus established as a basic principle of ASEM. This basic principle, of course, reflects the strong influence of ASEAN in the ASEM. ASEAN's influence could also be read in statements indicating the connection between the ASEAN-EU dialogue and the ASEM process. The statement did not deal with concrete human rights questions, an omission heavily criticized in the Western media. The statement did refer to treaties concerning human rights including, for example, the Vienna Declaration on Human Rights, which the ASEAN states had earlier criticized as being too Western.

Whether the ASEM process has managed to reinforce a tripolar world structure remains open to question. The political estimations in the ASEAN countries after the first ASEM declared that it had. The ASEAN countries particularly welcomed the European multilateral approach toward Asia and contrasted it to the US attempt to deal bilaterally with Asian countries. Similarly, the EU's policy for dealing with ASEAN as a negotiating partner was appreciated in Southeast Asia.[24]

The ASEM thus reflects the EU's new strategy toward Asia and particularly toward ASEAN at the same time as it reflects ASEAN's traditional way of binding the partners into mutual interdependencies. The new EU-ASEAN dialogue, however, could revive old questions such as Myanmar's new membership in ASEAN and the Rangoon government's opportunity to take part in ASEM. Even though the EU did accept Myanmar's coming membership as a *fait accompli* in June 1997, and despite the Commission's rather open position on the controversy,[25] not all the EU member governments were ready to take Myanmar into a closer EU-ASEAN dialogue. Evidence of the possible conflict could clearly be seen during British Foreign Secretary Robin Cook's tour in Asia in early September, where his comments on the possible rejection of Myanmar's attendance at ASEM by the EU evoked a quick and bitter response from the Malaysian Prime Minister.[26] With such issues inevitably arising, ideological tones may be impossible to avoid in the ASEM process.

The politico-ideological agenda was, however, left in the background at the next ASEM summit in April, 1998, in London where the Asian financial crisis cast a shadow over the conference. The ASEAN countries took few initiatives, owing to their weak economic domestic and international position, and the EU countries did not raise the politico-ideological agenda. It seemed that the EU intended to emphasize a tripolar world order by reinforcing the economic agenda of ASEM rather than the ideological one. The sensitive issues such as human rights issues were not publicly discussed, and in the political realm the focus fell on the enlargement of ASEM. On this topic no consensus was reached.

The expansion of ASEM was first discussed in the ASEM Bangkok Summit, with enlargement on the Asian side limited only to East and

Southeast Asia, a policy particularly forwarded by the ASEAN countries.[27] The enlargement of ASEM was further discussed in ASEM III in Seoul in November 2000, when 20 countries applied to join ASEM. The most important and the most contested applicants were India, Myanmar, Australia and New Zealand. India's membership had already been discussed at length in London when the host, Britain, had tried to gain membership for India. Some of the Asian participants, including some Southeast Asian countries, were reluctant to include India in ASEM. The EU rejected Burmese membership. Interestingly enough, the membership of Australia and New Zealand was broadly accepted, the only problem being whether should they be counted on the Asian or the European side. Malaysia announced in the Seoul Summit that it would accept those countries only if they came in on the European side.[28]

Politically, the most concrete and perhaps most important issue in ASEM II was the creation of the ASEM Asian Financial Crises Response Trust Fund to provide support for the East Asian crisis countries. Britain sponsored the initiative, and the European Commission became the largest contributor. Contributions also came from the national governments of European countries and from China.[29] From the point of view of economic realities, this fund, which functioned in association with the World Bank, was largely symbolic. A similar fund established under the World Bank by the Japanese government – the Japanese Social Development Fund, set up to target the developing countries and particularly the Asian countries – has doubled the ASEM Fund's resources of $45 million. The symbolic importance of the ASEM fund should not be underestimated, however, since the US had torpedoed other plans to create within the global economic regime special financial institutions aimed at alleviating the Asian economic crisis. From the European point of view, the value of the ASEM fund lay in its implicit reiteration of a tripolar world order. Following the same reason, the EU authorities expressed no consternation over the connection between ASEM and EAEC.[30] In October 2000, the EU external relations Commissioner, Chris Patten, suggested, just before the third ASEM in Seoul, that *ASEAN+3* and other forms of "greater Asian regional integration can only be welcomed", thus taking an approach quite different from the one taken by the US.[31]

The third ASEM clearly demonstrated the willingness of the EU as well as ASEM's Asian countries to tie discussions to global economic governance. There the participants committed to trade liberalization under the WTO and devised action plans, one on trade facilitation and another on investment promotion, to complement this commitment.[32]

Even before the first ASEM, some ASEAN countries hoped to use the organization as a vehicle for trade liberalization,[33] but Malaysia and Indonesia had opposed timetables and new institutional forms.[34]

Politico-ideological agendas have played an important role in the interaction between these two organizations – a fact which underscores their institutionalist character. The building of each one's own regional culture has had a crucial impact on its external policies. For both organizations, then, the tension between the politico-ideological agenda and politico-economic interests is significant. After the Asian economic crisis, however, this tension has relaxed. The role of politico-ideological agendas has been remarkably reduced, and the importance of global politico-economic issues correspondingly increased.

ASEAN's organizational structure as well as the weakness of the EU's CFSP leaves plenty of room for individual members to dialogue, but, in the long run and in light of the global economy, the importance of relations between the two organizations is evident. This emphasis forces the organizations to step back from politico-ideological issues and to choose, rather, concrete political and economic priorities. The approach of the EU to the idea of the EAEC, for example, proves the EU's willingness to see East Asia as a more independent force in the global scale, with ASEAN taking a particularly important role. At the same time, ASEAN has shown growing patience with the EU's claims on human rights and social clauses in order to maintain the EU as a counterbalance to the US in a global economic regime.

Part III
Southeast Asian Regionalism After the Asian Economic Crisis

6 The Asian Economic Crisis, the Southeast Asian Countries and ASEAN

THE EAST ASIAN MIRACLE AND SOUTHEAST ASIAN REGIONALISM

The general literature on East and Southeast Asian regionalism binds the success of regionalism to the rapid economic growth of the region. The same holds true for ASEAN. Both the academic literature and ASEAN's official speeches make the connection between regionalism and economic success. This connection makes sense. Four out of five of the original ASEAN countries – Indonesia, Malaysia, Singapore and Thailand – enjoyed rapid and continuous economic growth (over five percent per year for over 20 years) – quite a distinctive accomplishment compared to other developing countries. Only the Philippines, burdened by violent and unstable domestic political development, lacked this growth. Without doubt, the economic success of the majority of the ASEAN countries remarkably strengthened the emergence of the concept of *new* regionalism. This concept, in turn, connects to the so-called East Asian (economic) *miracle* studies.

East and Southeast Asian *miracle* studies, however, find their point of departure elsewhere. These studies begin with the central concept of the Asian economic model, not regional inter-state relations. The original miracle studies deal with five East Asian economies – Japan, Taiwan, South Korea, Singapore and Hong Kong. The model for the miracle is Japan. These countries' miracle status lies not only in the economic growth they were able to sustain, but in the fact that their economies were able to grow even though the countries lack natural resources and, as Jon Woronoff put it, "for decades, or more exactly, centuries, they showed no particular predisposition for economic progress".[1]

Several studies like Woronoff's emerged. The most authoritative of them, made by the World Bank research team, was titled *The East Asian Miracle – Economic Growth and Public Policy* and connected Indonesia,

Malaysia and Thailand to "the high performing Asian economies" (HPAE).[2] In this study, the World Bank deviated from its earlier neo-liberal economic thinking and free-market capitalism, positions that have determined the World Bank's policies. The study began when one of the Bank's main donors, Japan, wanted recognition for its economic policy. The Japanese government was favourably disposed to launch the study and apparently funded it.[3]

The study emphasized, of course, the role of the Asian economic model, according to which economic growth and political stability take priority over the development of democratic and legal institutions. In this model the economy is based on export-oriented industry, and the interdependence of global markets is emphasized. Although free global markets is one of the prerequisites of the model, regional governments have undertaken economic planning, specifically for industrialization in key sectors, and have been able to protect these sectors against international competition.

This model, whether or not real, seemed to function well for over 20 years according to statistical parameters. In the early 1990s the speed of economic growth accelerated further. If Brunei and the Philippines are excluded, the GDP growth rates of the ASEAN countries during the period 1992–5 varied between 6.2 and 9.5 percent. The Philippines too, reached a relatively high growth rate of 5.8 percent in the year 1996. In 1994 the total weighted ASEAN growth rate, including Brunei and the Philippines, was 7.8 percent; in 1995, 7.9 percent and in 1996, 7 percent.[4] Both investments and industrial output grew rapidly. Similarly, the external interaction of the Southeast Asian countries grew steadily. From the middle of the 1970s the economic structure developed and the direction of foreign trade shifted more and more toward East Asia. In the middle of the 1990s intra-ASEAN trade, including Singapore's entrepot trade, accounted for over 20 percent of total trade, while trade with Japan accounted for another 20 percent. If the trade with Korea, Taiwan and the PRC is figured in, the share of ASEAN's total trade with East and Southeast Asia came to nearly 50 percent. Although the absolute trade of ASEAN with the US and Europe had increased, it lagged behind the trade with Japan; Europe's share was about 13 percent, the US's share about 17 percent. The development of foreign direct investments (FDI) followed the development of trade. In the middle of the 1990s Japanese investments in Southeast Asia surpassed US and European FDIs. The role of Japanese investments is particularly significant in Malaysia, but also in other Southeast Asian countries, such as in the Philippines, Indonesia and Thailand. Although no official connection or co-operation exists among

Southeast Asian currencies, the importance of the Japanese economy has bound those currencies to the Japanese yen. The strengthening of yen during the 1980s and 1990s brought a corresponding strengthening of some regional currencies against the US dollar, although the trade was based, of course, on the dollar.

With its exclusive focus on the Asian model, the World Bank study, along with other miracle studies, failed to take into account the role of regionalism in the orchestration of the miracle. In another World Bank study of 1993, Arvind Panagariya's working paper, East Asian regionalism became a special focus. Panagariya did not, however, equate East Asian economic growth with regionalism. Quite the contrary, he saw sub-regional arrangements as undesirable and claimed, accordingly, that AFTA would be counterproductive. AFTA would need to include Japan to be productive. A broader East Asian trade bloc – he is too ashamed to mention the EAEC – would not be feasible, however, because it would provoke retaliatory actions from the US. Panagariya concluded that, because of the official US rejection of the idea of an exclusive East Asian trade bloc, only non-discriminatory, open regionalism (read: APEC) could work.[5]

The World Bank, when scrutinizing East Asia's miracle, concentrated only on the domestic prerequisites of economic growth. Its study is concerned with public policy, macroeconomic stability, the role of institutions, the accumulation of human capital and the allocation of resources.[6] Despite Paul Krugman's critique of the Asian miracle model, the global financial institutions continued to support its feasibility. The Asian Development Bank (ADB) study carried out by Hilton L. Root rejected Krugman's thesis that the economic growth of the East and Southeast Asian countries is based, not on an Asian model, but on the fact that growing inputs to the economy also produce growing outputs. Root claimed that Krugman ignored "the role of institutional and organizational innovation" and this oversight "leads him to underestimate the region's achievement" and its principle source of growth.[7] This study also failed to discuss the relationship between regionalism and growth.

One of the last miracle studies, the ADB's *Emerging Asia – Changes and Challenges*, does mention the role of regionalism in a positive light, first of all, as it works to integrate Asia into the global economy. The study mentioned ASEAN along with APEC but forecast no important regional economic role for AFTA. The ADB's study noted that "ASEAN has helped to deepen the dialogue between these countries on a wide range of issues and may act as an additional stimulus toward trade reform in some countries".[8]

Whether regionalism has contributed to economic growth in East and Southeast Asia in purely economic terms is an open question, but the East Asian economic crisis proved that regionalism did matter in economic terms. Starting in Northeast Asia – South Korea – the crisis closely followed the borders of ASEAN, hitting with differing intensities the economies and political systems of each ASEAN member. This movement proved that the market forces, at least, considered ASEAN as a single economic region.

FROM CURRENCY CRISIS TO POLITICAL CRISES

Although the floating of the Thai baht on 2 July 1997, woke the media up to the critical economic situation in Southeast Asia, the first signs of the crisis had occurred at the beginning of the year. Statistics showed that the rate of Thai GDP growth had gone down from 8.6 percent in 1995 to 5.5 percent in 1996. Such a drop would have been acceptable except for another negative indicator, the huge number of unsettled loans in Thai banks. Similar signs also appeared in other Southeast and East Asian economies, particularly in the economy of South Korea. In January and February the problems of both South Korea's and Thailand's economies became evident. Foreign investors had lost their confidence in Thai companies' ability to settle their debts, and this lack of confidence led to sales of both Thai currency and stocks. Coincidentally, two huge Korean industrial conglomerates, *chaebols*, Hanbo and Sammi, encountered financial difficulties that led to dramatic bankruptcies. In Korea during this particular year, eight of the top 30 *chaebols* followed suit. Although open panic on the Southeast Asian stock market was avoided during the spring of 1997, in all Southeast Asian stock exchanges stocks showed a downward trend. In April a headline in the *Far Eastern Economic Review*, "West Beats East," referred to the strange situation on the Asian stock markets where no profits were expected.[9] Together with the bankruptcies of some major Thai banks, the media publicized the huge number of unsettled loans not only in Thai banks but also in Indonesian and Malaysian banks.

When speculation began that Japan might devalue the yen, the globally operating investors, both in Southeast Asia and overseas, started to sell their Southeast Asian stocks and the weakest Southeast Asian currencies, beginning with the Thai baht. The Thai central bank's attempt to defend the baht exacerbated the crisis as it consumed almost all of its foreign currency reserves. The government could not help but float the baht, and it was devalued by 15–20 percent.

After the devaluation of the baht, the pressure shifted to the other Southeast Asian currencies, first to the Philippines peso and the Malaysian ringgit and then, surprisingly, to the Singaporean dollar, which was basically very strong. The Indonesian rupiah, which was not hit until the beginning of August, fell most dramatically. Its value dropped about 80 percent against the US dollar. In other Southeast Asian countries the decrease in the value of currencies was not so dramatic – the peso went down about 33 percent, the ringgit about 36 and the baht 39 percent. The Singaporean dollar continued to be strong, losing only temporarily about 17 percent of its value against the US dollar.

It should be noted, however, that changes in the currency rates against the US dollar do not give the whole picture of the strength or weakness of Southeast Asian currencies, although the dollar – as a central currency – tells much about Southeast Asian countries' position in the global economy. Simultaneously with the devaluation of the Southeast Asian currencies, the US dollar strengthened against all other central currencies, such as the French franc, the German mark and the Japanese yen, by at least 13 percent. The Singaporean dollar ended up only a few percent weaker than these currencies, while the Australian and the New Zealand dollars, for example, fell lower than the Singaporean dollar.

The crisis which started as a currency crisis turned into a financial crisis and spread to the stock and property markets. Thus in Singapore, for example, where the currency stayed relatively strong, the value of properties went down about 30 percent from 1996 prices. Stock values fell even lower. In Singapore for example, the Singaporean Straits Times index fell bout 46.4 percent from the beginning of 1997 to June 1998. The situation was much worse in the other Southeast Asian countries and in South Korea, where the changes in the currency and interest rates led to unemployment and a series of bankruptcies. The financial situation of Southeast Asian enterprises weakened essentially when foreign investments were withdrawn from the region, especially from Thailand, Malaysia and Indonesia. Japanese capital in particular was withdrawn from the Asian markets – as early as the beginning of 1998 about 1.17 billion dollars of Japanese funds had been moved from the Asian markets. This withdrawal hit Malaysia particularly hard. The Kuala Lumpur stock exchange's index fell about 60 percent in a year.

Several economic indicators reflected the changes in the currency rates and the economic depression that followed. The decrease in the value of regional currencies alone increased the foreign debt of the local banks. The burden of debt in proportion to the GDP increased in relation to the fall in the value of the currencies. Economic growth became negative in nearly all Southeast Asian countries, and inflation was very severe particularly in Indonesia, but also in Thailand.

These economic phenomena were part of the first wave of the Southeast Asian economic crisis which became relatively severe in all Southeast Asian countries. The second wave impacted differently on each country in the region and fragmented the entire regional system. At the economic level unemployment was its most obvious indicator; at the social level the crisis was marked by the return of migrant labor, impoverishment and even famine; and in politics social, political and ethnic unrest as well as the fall of governments and regimes resulted. The most extreme developments took place in Indonesia, where the collapse of the rupiah destroyed people's purchasing power and caused severe disruptions in the country's food supply. Even Singapore suffered some social evils although she escaped the second wave relatively easily and the most obvious signs of depression disappeared in 1999.

From the standpoint of the development of the GDPs, 1998 was the only bad year for Southeast Asian countries. In that year GDP growth was negative in all the old ASEAN countries except for Singapore, which managed a 0.4 percent positive growth. In the following year, 1999, the GDPs of all the Southeast Asian countries grew, although more moderately than in the pre-crisis period.[10]

Despite its short-lived effect on GDPs, the economic crisis brought about more permanent changes on both regional and domestic levels. The first domestic changes in Southeast Asia took place in Thailand. The government in power at the beginning of the crisis – the Chavalit Yongchaiyudh government – was forced to resign on 6 November 1997. Thailand managed to maintain its democratic institutions, contrary to its earlier experiences, and new general elections brought Chuan Leekpai's coalition to power. In this way the political crisis, followed by the financial crisis, was resolved very quickly in Thailand. A similar development took place in South Korea, where the general elections brought to power the most important opposition leader, Kim Dae Jung. Together with Thailand, the Philippines, Singapore and the less developed new ASEAN members survived the economic depression without major political crisis. However, the political crisis that broke out in Malaysia, and particularly in Indonesia, had much more serious consequences.

The argument can be made that the political crisis in Malaysia had nothing to do with the economic crisis but was rather a domestic power struggle. Malaysia's recent political history and the political backgrounds of Prime Minister Mohamad Mahathir and his Deputy, Finance Minister Anwar Ibrahim, in part support this claim. But the political struggle which occurred between Mahathir and Anwar and resulted in Anwar's dismissal and incarceration cannot be understood without factoring in the economic crisis and its impacts. Mahathir triumphed by managing to turn the economic crisis into a domestic political issue.

Mahathir and Anwar represented different political routes to recovery from the economic crisis. These paths described important political choices in Malaysian domestic and ethnic policies. Mahathir's economic policy had very much to do with ethnic relations. Therefore external economic intervention – either financially or economically grounded – would have deep political consequences.

Very soon after the outbreak of the economic crisis, the conflict between Anwar and Mahathir surfaced. In Malaysia the ethnic Malaysian and other indigenous population, *bumiputras,* constitute about 59 percent of the total population. The Chinese, economically the most important group, make up about 31 percent of the population, and the Indians account for the other 10 percent. The main task of Malaysian governments during the last 30 years – since the race riots of 1969 – has been to control these ethnic divisions. Since 1981 Prime Minister Mahathir Mohamad has followed in the footsteps of his predecessors and given a central role to the *New Economic Policy* (NEP) and its restatement in *Vision 2020* (1990). Through these policies, he has aimed to increase the *bumiputras* contribution to the Malaysian economy.

During the 1980s that goal was achieved when the government initiated the privatization of state enterprises and gave them to *bumiputras*. This action created a new business class, particularly strong in certain service sectors – such as telecommunications, mass traffic and transportation – and in certain industrial sectors considered nationally important. The privatization coincided with a period of economic growth and made the new owners multi-millionaires. Circles close to the leadership of the governing coalition, in particular the UMNO (United Malays National Organization), and the government, including the Prime Minister's own family, seemed to take advantage of this privatization. The economic boom tempted these young enterprises into a kind of growth which inevitably caused them to run into debt. During the favorable economic situation many foreign and short-term dollar loans were taken.[11]

The financial crisis hit these enterprises particularly hard. The conflict between Mahathir and Anwar focused largely on this issue. In order to keep *bumiputra capitalism* alive, Mahathir's administration tried to hold interest rates as low as possible. Mahathir blamed foreign currency traders for the crisis and argued that *bumiputra* business should not be punished. In spite of the fact that Finance Minister Anwar Ibrahim accepted Mahathir's view at least partly,[12] he was ready for stronger measures to restructure the Malaysian economy. He preferred to let market forces determine interest rates, although such a move would shift ownership of the *bumiputra* enterprises either to the ethnic Chinese or to foreigners. Mahathir seemed to prefer the latter choice when his administration increased the foreign ownership in Malaysian enterprises from 49 percent to 70 percent.[13]

Mahathir represented the Asian economic crisis as a form of neo-colonialism, caused by the currency traders and supported by the international economic regimes and some Western governments. Anwar did not share Mahathir's anti-colonialist model; rather his policy followed the line of the IMF and had its blessing.[14] His policy also garnered support inside the UMNO. Encouraged by the fall of Suharto, the UMNO youth wing started to demand reforms in the government and the disclosure of the government's relations with business. In a move particularly irksome to Mahathir, Anwar subscribed to these demands.[15] Mahathir then published a list that proved that the businesses of Anwar supporters, including the business of UMNO youth chief Datuk Ahmad Zahid Hamidi, had also benefited from the government's privatization projects.[16]

With this forceful counter-attack, Mahathir succeeded in taking a firm hold on the party in the UMNO's General Assembly in June 1998. Turning the controversy into an intra-party or even intra-Malay issue, Mahathir charged Anwar with homosexuality, a crime in Malaysia. He thus managed to limit Anwar's support to his traditional Islamic following and a few reform groups. Despite the pro-Anwar movement, which organized demonstrations very unusual in Malaysia, Mahathir's power was not really in danger. The foreign support that Anwar got actually worked to Mahathir's advantage. The Anwar affair, however, created mixed reactions among Malaysia's ASEAN partners and revealed the different political approaches inside ASEAN. The support for Anwar in governmental circles in some ASEAN countries indicated that the Malaysian situation had called into question some basic ASEAN axioms.

Of all the Southeast Asian countries, Indonesia suffered the most dramatic political consequences from the economic crisis. The crisis hit Suharto's administration, the Indonesian political system and national unity very hard. The Indonesian political crisis in turn paralyzed the whole ASEAN organization. As had the Malaysian political crisis, the Indonesian situation forced other ASEAN countries to reconsider the basic axioms of ASEAN co-operation in order to make the organization operative.

According to the Bretton Woods institutions, the IMF and the World Bank, Indonesian macro-economic policy was sound. Despite strong economic growth, it had a balanced budget and moderate monetary policy. However, structural politico-economic problems, unacknowledged by these institutions, threatened the country's stability. The central bank, Bank Indonesia, exerted no control over private lending, nor did it collect exact information on the huge private debt. This limited role of the central bank was reflected in the degenerated politico-economic relations of the long-standing Suharto regime. Foreign investors realized this dangerous situation when economic bubbles began to burst in other Southeast Asian countries. The withdrawal of foreign investment in Indonesia started a much deeper depression than in neighboring countries and launched the kind of political conflicts that had earlier been absorbed or suppressed by the Suharto administration.

The political situation in Indonesia was far from normal even before the financial crisis. Indonesia was hit by a series of riots, a new wave that started from the Jakarta riots of July 1996 and spread over the huge island state. Typically of Indonesian disturbances, the riots were a mix of political, ethnic and social unrest caused by the national policies of the central government and the corruption of local authorities. In some regions the riots turned into religious violence. The General Elections of 1997 and the Presidential Elections of 1998 exacerbated the violence because of the repression of opposition during the electoral campaigns.[17] This political unrest, together with the separatist and independence movements in different parts of Indonesia, culminated in Suharto's loss of control.

On the stage set by this internal unrest, external actors – first the IMF and then the US – played crucial roles in the economic developments in Indonesia and in the reshuffling of its political leadership. The Suharto government was forced to ask the IMF for aid in the fall of 1997, but the IMF's help was not fully implemented because of disagreements about loan conditions. The stalemate between the IMF and the Suharto regime, together with partial adherence to the IMF's conditions, resulted in a jump in food prices and disturbances in the food supply. The EU and especially the US pressed Suharto to accept the IMF conditions, and in March 1998 the former vice-president of the IMF suggested that Suharto leave his post. The diminishing foreign support for Suharto weakened support for the leader and for the Indonesian political elite even inside the ruling Golgar party.

The legitimacy of Suharto's power had rested on economic growth and the support of the Indonesian armed forces. It was, in fact, the approval of the armed forces that confirmed the transfer of power from Suharto to his old minister, Bacharuddin Jusuf Habibie, in May 1998, when the Indonesian political elite abandoned its ruler. The transfer of power to Habibie did not, however, calm the political, ethnic and separatist conflicts in Indonesia. The most difficult conflict the new administration faced was the East Timor question because it directly concerned the unity of the nation. The independence movements in Irian Irian Jaya and Aceh as well as other separatist phenomena in Maluku and South Sulawesi posed difficult problems for Habibie and for the administration that followed his. Although these regions contribute only 17 percent of the country's GDP and contain an even smaller share of the population, they cover one third of the total land area and include important but largely unexploited natural resources, such as oil, gas, timber, copper and gold. After losing East Timor, Indonesia especially needed to hold Aceh because the gradual separation of these provinces would mean the end of the country in its present form.

Habibie's flaw lay in the fact that he came from the Suharto administration. It soon became clear that he could not gain the confidence of the opposition – most importantly Megawati Sukarnoputri's supporters and the Islamic groups. Two specific issues – the separation of East Timor and the Bali bank scandal – forced him to resign from the presidency. Abdurrahman Wahid, a moderate Muslim leader who also goes by the name Gus Dur, became the president and offered a compromise between the old regime and new political forces. The competing opposition politician, Megawati Sukarnoputri, was elected vice-president in order to appease the political opposition.

THE ASIAN CRISIS, REGIONALISM AND THE SOUTHEAST ASIAN MODEL

The plunge of the Southeast Asian economies soon revealed both the ideological and politico-economic competition in the Asia and Pacific region. The Western attack against the Asian model and the politico-economic values implicit in it suddenly took on fresh strength. A series of "what-went-wrong" books and articles appeared, all evincing very similar explanations. Works like *The Trouble with Tigers – The Rise and Fall of Southeast Asia*,[18] offered the popular explanation that the crisis was due to the Asian economic model and the corruption of the value system. According to this argument, these values were not what their supporters claimed them to be but rather a system of justifications for self-serving, bureaucratic, corrupt and anti-democratic politico-economic practices carried on by the ruling political elite and the business class. Similarly, the Asian model was not at all as efficient as had been reported, Rather Southeast Asia had profited from a mistaken belief in its efficiency that prompted ignorant foreigners to invest in inefficient factories, mega-projects, properties and consumption. Such mistakes were made possible only by the lack of transparency, the absence of true competition and the control over certain economic and industrial sectors that governments in the region exerted. [19] The IMF accepted this view and paid particular attention in its loan conditions to transparency, the abolition of state subsidies and trade liberalization that extended into financial and insurance sectors. The popular argument further asserted that the Southeast Asian economic depression, while restoring normal parameters to the development of the 'little tigers', destroyed the basic glue of ASEAN – Asian values.[20] The Western media and Western NGOs enthusiastically adopted this view, particularly during the political upheavals following the financial crisis.

This indictment of the Asian model and values was of course important since the model had been used to justify power structures in several ASEAN countries and had also been incorporated into the structure of ASEAN co-operation. It could be argued, though, that the Asian values debate accounted for only a small part of ASEAN value building; that debate may have more significance for the justification of some individual ASEAN members' domestic policies. On the other hand, some prominent leaders advocated the Asian value model, even though it has no uniform content. The two prominent spokesmen for Asian values, Singaporean Lee Kuan Yew and Malaysian Mahathir Mohamad argued for different economic models and political values. In the Asian model debate Lee Kuan Yew began with an emphasis on Confucian values, whereas Mahathir's ideas originate in the anti-Western nationalism developed from anti-colonial communalism. Ideas similar to Mahathir's can be found in the early thinking of the Singaporean People's Action Party's (PAP) which were prominent before Singapore's independence;[21] in fact, Lee Kuan Yew's political thinking also draws strength from these anti-colonial roots.[22]

Anti-colonialism forms the base of Indonesian political thinking and Filipino leftist nationalism too. In fact, Mahathir has not emphasized the genuineness of Asian values, but has copied the Western values of orderliness, discipline and firm social organization that gave to the West superiority over the East. He argues that the East should not allow the same kind of rejection of those successful values as occurred in the West.[23] On the one hand, the Asian politico-economic model as a justification of authoritarian capitalist rule and the belief in economic superiority were not dominating ideas of the ASEAN organization. On the other hand, anti-colonialism, which Mahathir skillfully incorporated into the Asian values discussion, was broadly shared by the Asian NGOs.[24]

Nevertheless, the role of the economy makes a solid foundation for ASEAN's thinking as well as for the construction of regionalism in Southeast Asia whether that construction emphasises institutionalist, realist or functionalist tendencies. These three tendencies together form a system that I call the Southeast Asian regionalist model. It is not, of course, a model as such, but a concordance of different regionalist ideas and therefore includes contradictory elements. ASEAN's official texts and speeches define the institutionalist approach. Realism emerges particularly when the ASEAN leaders reflect on the global environment. Earlier only ASEAN's expertise groups espoused functionalism, but during and after the crisis political leaders have increasingly adopted it.

From the institutionalist point of view, the fall of the Southeast Asian economies was most dramatic, though not catastrophic. Since the Asian model has significance for the institutionalist construction of regionalism, the economic depression and its particular indictment of Asian values seriously challenged this approach. This challenge, however, was not fatal although it undermined Southeast Asians' confidence.[25] According to the institutionalist argument, regional peace and co-operation will create conditions for the development of member societies – regional co-operation is not expected to create extra wealth for its members. Therefore the regional organization has done its part if it has secured peace during hard times such as the economic crisis period of 1997–1999.

This institutionalist regionalist approach was, indeed, put to the test during the crisis period although even before the crisis it was already clear that this approach would be incapable of offering any real economic solution to a regional crisis. So far the approach has demonstrated its efficiency in the area of political co-operation. ASEAN could handle some of the political issues that faced it – such as the joining of new members – while other more serious issues – such as the political crises in Malaysia and in Indonesia – ASEAN was not even expected to deal with. The way the Indonesian crises – both economic and political – paralysed the organization clearly showed, however, the limits of institutionalism in ASEAN co-operation.

As it sought solutions to the economic crisis and the political crises that followed it, the Southeast Asian regionalist debate, predictably, leaned on realism and functionalism. Realist and functionalist arguments flavour Southeast Asian anti-colonial parlance and political rhetoric, both of which emphasise the role of economic power. On the other hand, the Southeast Asian political elite did put forward suggestions for supranational solutions in order to cope with the economic crisis, a phenomenon that would have seemed quite strange in the pre-crisis period.

Economic Crisis, Realism and Anti-colonialism

In a very interesting and fascinating way, Southeast Asian realist parlance confuses values, anti-colonialist rhetoric and realist standpoints. Both Mahathir and Lee Kuan Yew share the view that the political struggle in the post-Cold War period continues in the economic arena. The two spokesmen may choose different starting points for their arguments, with Mahathir believing that politics leads economics and Lee Kuan Yew believing that economic leads politics. They may also understand the nature of the enemy differently – Lee Kuan Yew seems to see the West as a combination of autonomous players, seeking economic gain, where Mahathir sees in the developed West a concerted effort on the part of the political parties, trade unions, media and the NGOs to work toward keeping the East behind the West.[26] They both, however, emphasise the instrumental roles of both economics and values.

This essential sameness notwithstanding, their various approaches toward the Asian economic crisis revealed different emphases. They occupied different positions, of course. First, the much stronger economic fundamentals in Singapore allowed it to resist the crisis more successfully than Malaysia could. Second, the Singaporeans accepted the rules of the game of international trade and finance better than the Malaysians did because MNCs (multinational companies) have been more important in the Singaporean economy than they have been in the Malaysian economy. Third, Mahathir was a leader in charge, whereas Lee Kuan Yew did not enjoy – officially at least – a similar position.

Officially the Singaporean leadership accepted the analysis of the IMF and the World Bank that the crisis was due to over-borrowing and reckless investments. Similarly, they accepted the reforms offered by the IMF.[27] However, as Lee remarked, the pre-crisis optimism that prevailed among Southeast Asians and foreign investors was also well founded –

high growth was accompanied by low inflation, the governments' balanced budgets and high savings rates. Owing to these fundamentals, from the beginning of the 1990s, investors from G 7 countries started to offer new capital. Coincidentally with the financial liberalisation in the Southeast Asian countries required particularly by the IMF, the World Bank and the WTO, new short-term capital inflows came into the region. The financial liberalisation included foreign exchange control liberalisation in Thailand while in Indonesia the central bank did not really have foreign currency exchange control. The governments had no control over private lending.[28] According to Lee, then, the crisis can be seen as a sum of mistakes made both by the governments in financial liberalisation and by private sector business. Acknowledging these other contributing factors, Lee Kuan Yew rejected the idea that the Asian model and Asian values had anything to do with the crisis. Quite the contrary, he argued that Confucian values, first of all dedication to hard work, would offer the way out of the crisis.[29]

As the Singaporean diagnosis of the Asian economic crisis followed the main lines of the international financial institutions, the Singaporean government quite naturally used the same measures to rebuild its economy as the IMF and the World Bank required for their loans. It suggested the same measures to the other Southeast Asian countries. Because the consequence of the currency crises was the flight of foreign investments, the most urgent task of Southeast Asian countries was to attract those investments once again. Southeast Asian countries should do everything possible to liberate trade in order to get foreign investors interested in Southeast Asia as an investment area. Lee Kuan Yew saw the possibility for common action within ASEAN. Thus the Singaporean leadership took the Asian crisis as a natural phenomenon of the global economic system. Individual countries had to accept it and to try to adapt to the rules of the system. Regional efforts should not work against globalism but make the ASEAN region even more attractive to global actors.[30]

Superficially, Mahathir took a totally different approach. His anti-colonial rhetoric, although sympathetically received in Southeast Asia in both governmental and non-governmental circles, deviated from that of the other old ASEAN members. Although Mahathir's power was criticised, several different NGOs shared the view that the Western powers were behind the crisis. Mahathir also argued that Malaysia had voluntarily fulfilled most of the conditions set by the IMF although it never negotiated for the IMF's bailout. From 1997 to August 1998 Mahathir's rhetoric was balanced by the approach of his Deputy, Anwar Ibrahim. Mahathir presented his analysis of the causes of the crisis in the boldest form at the World Bank's seminar in Hong Kong, 20 September 1997. The crucial message of his speech was that the Southeast Asian economic crisis had been intentionally caused. Although he identified currency traders as the main actors in the crisis, he implied that more politically motivated actors were the primary cause. At the very beginning of the speech he made a reference to the East Asian Economic Caucus, giving the impression that the crisis was engineered to strike a blow at economic co-operation in East Asia. His analysis, which was heavily based on power politics, suggested that the old power centres would try to crush the emerging regions in an effort to deny them the political power that would inevitably increase with economic development. More specifically, he suggested that Malaysia had achieved a higher development level by not following the conventional advice of the developed countries and could thus be seen as a dangerous example for other developing countries. Mahathir did not name the particular country behind the crisis, but one can easily imagine that the target was the US, the international economic institutions that the US dominates and possibly the US Western allies.[31]

After suggesting that the crisis served the interests of the US and the European powers, Mahathir claimed that they based their analysis on a different conception than did the Asians. While ASEAN and East Asian countries saw their prosperity as benefiting all regional countries and the world, the Western analysis grew out of a zero sum game where one country's or region's gain was another's loss.[32] For Mahathir the crisis had nothing to do with Asian values, but rather with the immorality of the currency traders and the Western leaders who lauded currency manipulation as an integral part of the free trade system.[33]

According to Mahathir, the crisis was due to the Western leaders, who wanted to restore Southeast Asian tigers to the position of developing countries, and to foreign investors who use their economic power to exploit weak countries whenever possible. Considering his point of view, the measures that he advocated to cope with crisis are understandable. First, at the global level, he challenged the necessity of the currency trade. If trade could not be closed, he called for broad international measures to control it. Second, he asked for regional measures in the ASEAN context that would better protect regional countries against the effects of global economic forces. At the national level, despite following the main guidelines of the IMF, he insisted the Malaysian government keep the interest rate low; in September 1998 it launched broad finance and capital control, fixing the ringgit rate at 3.8 against the US dollar.

Mahathir did not make his stand against the West alone. His suggestions and his policies gained foreign sympathy and support. ASEAN closed ranks particularly around his attack on the currency traders.[34] Interestingly enough, his proposal for the control of international currency trade gained support from some EU countries, first of all from France. The regional initiatives were discussed in the ASEAN meetings, and Malaysian's unilateral capital and currency control was widely understood in Asia.

It should be remembered, however, that, at the same time as Mahathir was accusing the West of manufacturing the economic crisis, Malaysia was implementing the suggestions of the global financial institutions. In fact the political struggle in Malaysia helped him make these implementations. Anwar Ibrahim, who supported a stricter financial policy, made a suitable scapegoat for the *bumiputra* business interests. Anwar's scapegoating became evident in the UMNO General Assembly in June 1998, when the veteran politicians and the provincial leaders supported Mahathir. Anwar's reforms were undoubtedly necessary for Malaysian survival, nevertheless, he could be blamed for them and Mahathir could once again enjoy the support of the *bumibutra*.

Mahathir's realism surfaced on two sides. At the global level he presented the crisis as a product of power politics between the developed West and the developing countries. His regional initiatives can be seen from this perspective. His anti-colonial rhetoric also served his domestic political struggle. Although anti-colonialism was not the concept which mobilised political masses in Malaysia, with it he gathered around himself the political elite's support. Lee Kuan Yew's realism originated from the recognition of external realities and thus followed the basic axioms of the realist school. He saw the role of regional organization as helping member countries adapt to these external conditions. This adaptation, however, could include measures unfamiliar to realist thinking.

ASEAN's Economic Initiatives

At the level of regional co-operation the seriousness of the economic situation in ASEAN was underestimated at the beginning of the currency crisis. Even three and a half months after the outbreak of the crisis, the ASEAN Economic Ministers were confident "that ASEAN will continue its high rate of growth and will remain a dynamic region". They compared the present crisis to the 1985 economic recession and reasoned that, just as had that recession twelve years earlier, "the current economic situation will provide ASEAN with the opportunity to eliminate inherent weakness, readjust and strengthen the foundation of their economies".[35]

The economic ministers believed in the old ASEAN axiom that national resilience, itself a product of strong economic fundamentals, would bear the Southeast Asian countries over the crisis. Their faith proved overoptimistic. Even if they had correctly forecast the seriousness of the situation, the ASEAN Economic Ministers could have done nothing about it. They had no common instruments with which to combat the crisis since the national governments had refused to deliver those kinds of resources or decision-making powers to the ASEAN organization.

The old ASEAN vocabulary of national and regional resilience was soon forgotten when it became clear that the region faced, not a short-term recession, but economic and financial turbulence that could turn into a long-lasting economic depression. As the crisis expanded, so did the realisation that the global economic players' roles would be more crucial. The ASEAN countries needed support from the international economic regime, first of all from the IMF, and that need put them in a new situation. The conditions of the IMF support packages, particularly for Indonesia and Malaysia, included measures that the governments considered impingments on their national sovereignty. Therefore the idea of regional measures, much stronger than ever before presented in ASEAN, gained surprisingly broad support.

Just before the crisis ASEAN had created a forum where common actions against such situations as the economic crisis could be considered. The ASEAN Financial Ministers had their first annual ministerial meeting in Phuket, Thailand in March 1997. At that meeting the Ministers stated that "ASEAN shall move towards greater economic integration by building on existing economic co-operation activities, initiating new areas of co-operation, and promoting closer co-operation in international fora".[36] Although no concrete aims were set, the task of the meetings was to follow the changes in international economies by consultative meetings. However, when the Financial Ministers gathered for their first special meeting on 1 December 1997, they sought not only to exchange views but also to consider common actions they might take to escape the crisis that was trying the whole region's resilience.

Despite ASEAN's modest regional approach in the early stage of the crisis, two instruments were proposed during the fall of 1997. The first suggested an increase in intra-ASEAN trade in order to effect a decrease in the expensive dollar-based trade. This strategy would boost the regional economies as expensive currency would not be needed. To this end, the measures adopted in AFTA should be reconsidered. The second instrument suggested was financial. The financial authorities in the

ASEAN countries and particularly in the Philippines proposed a separate Asian fund to balance economic swings and absorb their bad effects.

The background of the Asian fund was not only economic. In creating the Asian fund, ASEAN was originally attempting to create a fund independent of control by the IMF and its big donors. Since the conditions attached to the IMF bailout included much broader measures than were needed for economic restoration, the IMF's help was also seen as an attempt to curb the sovereignty of the needy. Several types of arrangements were proposed for the Asian Fund. In a Thai suggestion the East and Southeast Asian nations would organize an OECD-type of arrangement which would co-ordinate the macro-economic policies of the regional countries. The Thai authorities discussed not only ways the possible new crisis could be averted, but also the concrete mechanism which could provide co-ordinated policies and economic capacities to form a united front against the attacks on currency. To support such a mechanism a regionally controlled fund was needed. $50 billion was proposed as a preliminary figure for the fund. But, because of the economic turmoil, the Southeast Asian countries were not able to contribute that much to the fund; Japanese financial muscle was needed.[37]

The fund enjoyed broad support among the ASEAN countries even though, as one Thai official warned, there were "geopolitical issues" that "could interfere with the goals of establishing an Asian Fund".[38] This warning was not inappropriate. Soon it became clear that the IMF, with the US and some other Western powers in the background, opposed the establishment of an independent Asian Fund. The forces opposed to the fund feared that the conditions of the IMF would lose their significance if an Asian financial system could offer support free from IMF-like requirements.[39]

In the special ASEAN Finance Ministers Meeting in Kuala Lumpur in December 1997, the Ministers abandoned the Asian Fund idea, owing to the resistance of the IMF and the US. In fact, the ASEAN countries had outlined several different models of the fund, one even supplemented the financial resources from the IMF and thus followed its general guidelines. But the IMF and the US rejected all arrangements which would replace the IMF. Despite the positive attitude of Japan toward the Fund, in all likelihood, it could not provide enough funds for the system to be effective. At the Kuala Lumpur meeting the ASEAN Finance Ministers developed a much more modest plan, a surveillance mechanism to better monitor the financial developments of the regional countries. The problem in ASEAN, however, has been the heavy emphasis on national sovereignty and the policy of non-interference. Such traditions would, of course, hamper effective surveillance of a regional body. Although the need for a supranational institution was acknowledged in practical policy, the ASEAN governments were unwilling to renounce their control. Putting the ASEAN Secretariat in charge of the monitoring[40] would clearly increase supra-nationalism in the organization.

Despite the problem of sovereignty, ASEAN continued to study the surveillance mechanism. In the discussion with the ASEAN's Central Banks' Governors in late February 1998, the general roles of the IMF and the ADB were accepted.[41] During the Europe – Asia Meeting, ASEM II in London, a regional "watchdog" was discussed.[42] Not surprisingly, the ASEAN Finance Ministers finally created a compromise watchdog mechanism that neither made dramatic inroads into member sovereignty nor pushed ASEAN toward supra-nationalism. Following the consensus agreement of the Ministers, made in Washington in October 1998, the ASEAN surveillance process would be seen as part of IMF-conducted global surveillance. Elements of the process would emphasise the regional organization's role in the surveillance, however, so the system would have both inter-governmental and supranational characteristics. Inter-governmentalism was emphasised by the leading role of the ASEAN Finance Ministers' Meeting (AFMM). The core of the surveillance process would be formulated at the ASEAN Senior Finance Officials Meeting (ASFOM) and the ASEAN Central Bank Forum. Through this watchdog mechanism, new institutions were created. The ASEAN Surveillance Co-ordinating Unit (ASCU) was established in the ASEAN Secretariat as well as the ASEAN Surveillance Technical Support Unit (ASTSU) which would be based at the ADB in Manila.[43]

Despite the basically supportive role played by the ASCU, several of the tasks it undertakes strengthen the role of the Secretariat. Among these, the most important is the preparation, co-ordination, review and consolidation of inputs and information from member states. The ASEAN Surveillance Process does not include the surveillance of short-term capital flows, which the ASEAN countries started to discuss with Japan, China and the Republic of Korea at the Finance and Central Banks Deputies meeting in Hanoi. These arrangements took place in a general East Asian context, and this fact was perhaps more significant from the point of view of regional financial control than the arrangements themselves.[44] This East Asian context indicated the fairly broad understanding in ASEAN of the necessity to increase East Asian co-operation and the willingness to deal with financial problems among the Asian countries without interference from the IMF.

An even more ambitious proposal than the Asian Fund proposal came with the initiatives in currency co-operation. Starting with the modest suggestion of using local currencies in regional trade and ending with an immodest proposal for the creation of an ASEAN currency, this discussion reflected both the perceived need to defend the regional economies against currency traders as well as important changes in the thinking of the ASEAN political elite. Since currency remains such an important symbol of national independence and sovereignty, the fact that ASEAN could critically examine a proposal – however utopian – for a regional ASEAN currency demonstrated the depth of this change.

The debate on an ASEAN currency moved in two different directions – toward broader East Asian financial co-operation on the one hand, and, on the other, toward a more limited Southeast Asian context in which financial issues were tied to intra-ASEAN trade. The broader context intersects with the regional context as the limits of the Southeast Asian fund proposal became clear. The initiative for currency co-operation originated from the initiative to increase intra-ASEAN trade, as the devaluation of regional currencies made dollar-based extra-regional trade too expensive for the ASEAN countries.

The trade and finance issues merged in early 1998, when the mainly Malaysian-initiated debate contemplated the possibility of using only local currencies in regional trade. In fact, it is rather obscure how serious an effort ASEAN made to achieve currency co-operation, but, in any case, the debate surrounding the issue was held at a fairly high level. From the very beginning it became clear that Singapore, who had the strongest currency, was not interested in this discussion. Singapore's lack of interest left only three ASEAN countries actively involved – Malaysia, Thailand and the Philippines. The Indochinese countries still remained rather isolated from the ASEAN trade, and instability of the Indonesian rupiah eliminated it from the discussion.

The simplest proposal suggested that the regional trading countries should use the currency of the seller's country in their bilateral trade. The plan – evolved by the Central Bank's Governors and supported by the ASEAN Finance Ministers in their second official meeting in Jakarta on 28 February 1998 – included a Bilateral Payments Agreement (BPA), a mechanism which would have involved high-tech clearing houses to keep track of the daily balances of the various currencies. Malaysia, the Philippines and Thailand would have been the first to begin trading with their own currencies; the other ASEAN members had an option to join whenever they were able. The voluntary character of these arrangements reflected traditional ASEAN decision-making, but at the same time revealed the basic weakness of the mechanism, the freedom of the participants either to maintain the arrangements or to abandon them.[45]

In a more ambitious plan the ASEAN countries would use their own currency unit (ACU) at least in intra-ASEAN trade. Both the Japanese yen and the Singapore dollar were suggested as basic currencies for this purpose. Japan refused politely, referring to its own economic situation, and Singapore unconditionally refused the use of its currency to support weak Southeast Asian currencies.[46]

In any case, the ASEAN experts doubted that a common currency would have much effect on regional trade because of the very limited scope of trade among the participating countries. The share of the trade among Indonesia, Thailand and the Philippines amounted to less than 5 percent of their total trade. At the political level, the difficulties were even greater than the practical problems. In the absence of two important ASEAN countries, Singapore and Indonesia, ASEAN was trying to develop a supra-national mechanism – a regional currency – using traditional institutionalist decision-making procedures. The desperation of the undertaking only highlighted its economic insignificance. Therefore ASEAN's discussion on a common currency can be seen more accurately as a political manifestation of growing regional unity than a real economic possibility.

The other approach concentrated more clearly on intra-ASEAN trade and urged that ASEAN should make every effort to restore investor confidence in the region.[47] To move toward this goal the proposal called for an acceleration of the AFTA process. These financial and trade efforts were not mutually exclusive, although the restoration of investor confidence involved the already in-place concept of regional trade liberalisation, whereas effective financial co-operation called for measures the governments were not really ready for.

The concentration on the AFTA process would mean accelerating the implementation of the free trade area, enforcing its inclusivity – in particular strengthening the rules and disciplines of the CEPT agreement – and increasing customs co-operation. In the Hanoi Summit in December 1998 the ASEAN leaders agreed to accelerate the implementation of AFTA by one year, from 2003 to 2002, by which date the original six members will accomplish trade liberalisation. By the year 2002 all the items on the inclusion list will have 0–5 percent tariffs. The strengthening of the CEPT agreement was made by agreeing in October 1998 on the notification procedures concerning actions that may nullify existing benefits enjoyed by other AFTA members. The co-ordinated customs policy was enforced by the ASEAN Customs Policy Implementation and Work Programme (PIWP).

As it tried to deal with the economic crisis, ASEAN obviously managed to make concrete advances in trade issues but not in finance issues. A number of factors helped facilitate the progress made in trade issues. In general, it became easier for the ASEAN governments to agree on trade liberalisation once the IMF had forced both Thailand and Indonesia to do so. Second, after the Hanoi Summit some ASEAN countries had made provisos concerning certain sectors in the AFTA implementation scheme, and these provisos smoothed the way for their participation. Finally, all the ASEAN agreements gave the participants the option to retract what had been agreed on whenever their interests called for it. Because of this institutional weakness of ASEAN, foreign investor confidence would be difficult to regain; that confidence would come, not as a result of the regional measures ASEAN struggled to enact, but as a result of development in the individual countries.

7 Global Governance and Regionalist Solutions

ECONOMIC REGIMES AND SOUTHEAST ASIAN COUNTRIES

The penetration of economic issues into ASEAN cooperation illustrates well changes in the international system since the establishment of the organization. The point of departure in establishing ASEAN was intergovernmental cooperation in regional relations as well as dealing with other international issues which were important to regional security. The Cold War context limited cooperation to the capitalist Southeast Asian countries which were politically closely linked to the Western security system. The dramatic effects of the destruction of the Cold War two-bloc system was expressed in Lee Kuan Yew's statement on the need to find new uniting factors in the organization and that one important factor would be competition in the world's economic regimes.[1]

Without mentioning any particular regime, most probably he had the global trade regime, the GATT, in mind. Indeed, the GATT Uruguay round negotiations tested and united ASEAN's cooperation with the external world and produced several common efforts in the GATT and in its successor, the WTO, as well as in another trade cooperation scheme, APEC. In APEC, ASEAN's vehicle to unite itself has been the EAEC. ASEAN's active policy in these organizations and its demand for trade liberalization, as well as the measures of some ASEAN countries to liberate their own economies, redeemed the use of the concept of *open regionalism* when referring to ASEAN.

In the early post-Cold War situation the global trade regime was the most important economic regime for ASEAN cooperation. However, during and after the Southeast Asian economic crisis the most apparent economic regime has been the world's financial regime, first of all, the other two Bretton Woods institutions – the IMF and the World Bank – and their role in facilitating and controlling the region's economic development. In economic terms the IMF has had a more important role, but in broader social and political terms, the World Bank's role has also been visible.

ASEAN and the World Trade Regime

Like many other global economic actors and trading groups, ASEAN's point of departure has been to defend trade liberalization in the world's trade regime. However, like other actors, the ASEAN member countries have had their own interests protecting some domestic sectors from free international competition. Hence ASEAN's policy was often determined according to common parlance among developing countries emphasizing the need for protection against the economic power of the developed countries.

The ASEAN countries had accepted and supported the idea and the formation of the World Trade Organization. Due to heavy dependence on foreign trade, the general rules of global trade benefit all ASEAN members. Although the ASEAN economies have been more competitive than complementary, common interest in global trade has been much easier to find than in regional trade. Therefore, ASEAN has found a common front in the WTO on several important issues, such as the environment as well as issues of labor standards and trade. The problem for ASEAN is, however, that the WTO is not the sole mechanism regulating world trade, but there have appeared several governmental and non-governmental organizations also forming a part of the World trade regime.

From the point of view of governmental organizations, APEC is most important to the Southeast Asian countries, as one of the main motives behind it was to affect the GATT negotiations. However, the use of APEC to promote ASEAN's interests in the WTO has often run counter to the different interests of the United States and Japan, as evident in the APEC Kuala Lumpur meeting in November 1999.[2] Besides APEC, some more specific trade organizations, such as the International Timber Trade Organization, ITTO, are important to the ASEAN countries. Non-governmental mechanisms, which increasingly have gained power in world trade, are a recent phenomenon in the global trade regime. Some of these new mechanisms are working through governmental organizations; for example, trade unions and many non-governmental organizations have put pressures particularly on Western governments. Nevertheless, some of these mechanisms are functioning more independently, such as product standardization schemes. These new mechanisms have been a challenge for ASEAN, as the traditional ASEAN diplomacy is no longer valid for them.

The role of the WTO is, of course, crucial. Despite it being established in 1995, the world's multilateral trading system under the GATT is much older. The GATT originated from one of the Bretton Woods institutions, the International Trade Organization (ITO), but as the US Congress did not ratify the ITO, a more flexible substitution was adopted. The system took shape during a series of trade negotiations. The first GATT rounds focused on tariff reductions, but later the negotiations broadened their scope to areas such as anti-dumping and non-tariff measures.[3] Owing to the general aim of lowering trade barriers, the WTO has been reluctant to establish trade rules restricting commerce, such as social, labor and environmental standards, within the multilateral trading system.

The system as such is effective. The heart of it is comprised of the agreements negotiated and signed by a large majority of the states of the world and ratified by their national institutions. Therefore, they are legally binding in both international trade and commerce as well as for internal trade policies, within agreed limits. When the WTO was established, this all was further institutionalized. The tasks of the WTO were to administer trade agreements, act as a forum for further trade negotiations, settle trade disputes and review and assist in formulating trade policies. This trade regime is dynamic in the sense that the trade negotiations did not end when the WTO was established and the new trade rules are continuously taking shape. Because of this, certain non-governmental pressures can influence the WTO rules.

ASEAN's interests in the WTO have been in the WTO's strict attitude against non-tariff trade barriers. During the Uruguay round 1986–1993, the ASEAN countries supported trade liberalization under United States leadership. Particularly in issues of agricultural trade, they form the nucleus of U.S. policy supporters. Under the leadership of Australia, Indonesia, Malaysia, the Philippines and Thailand formed, together with other nine Pacific countries, a group of "fair trading nations" which put their weight behind the U.S. campaign for the reform of global agricultural trade.[4] This cooperation was in the background when Australia proposed the formation of APEC in 1989. During the APEC ministerial meeting in Seoul in November 1991, the ASEAN countries backed strongly the liberalization of agricultural trade and called on the EC to give up its agricultural subsidies. Although some reference was made to Japan's policy of protecting its agricultural production, the main target was the European Community.[5]

The support of the ASEAN countries for the US in the WTO has not been, however, all that extensive. The ASEAN countries have tried to protect certain sectors from free competition, such as the car industry in Malaysia and Indonesia and the service sector in nearly all the ASEAN countries except Singapore. The Asian economic crisis forced the ASEAN countries to accept most of the measures required by the developed countries and a clear impression was that the US was taking advantage of the Asian crisis when arguing for service liberalization in the WTO.[6] There were severe clashes between Malaysia and the US on the liberalization of the insurance sector in the WTO negotiations, which ended in a formal stalemate between the US and Malaysia. Accordingly, the US left in place the same restrictions on Malaysian financial service business as Malaysia left in order to protect its own financial service sector.

ASEAN's interest in the WTO was also other trade issues in which the NTBs were involved. The advantage of the WTO for the ASEAN countries has been that the trade organization has adopted labor, social and environmental issues rather reluctantly into the trade negotiations. Similarly it has taken a relatively critical attitude toward product standardization and eco-labeling. Therefore, ASEAN's point of departure has been that these issues could be discussed only in the WTO contexts.[7] The willingness of the ASEAN countries to deal with trade-related environmental issues in the WTO has been particularly due to the WTO's negative attitude toward trade barriers linked with environmental protection. In its trade-related environmental disputes, the WTO has always taken actions for the benefit of a complainant and against the country intending environmental protection.[8]

Notwithstanding ASEAN's hope for WTO-regulated international trade, new non-governmental mechanisms particularly in environmental issues have taken on an ever-growing role in world trade in some sectors which are important for the ASEAN countries. The most important sector has been tropical forestry and the timber trade. Therefore, the world trade regime is not expressed only in the WTO, but the WTO and several other organizations. ASEAN has resisted this development. In the end it or a given member country must, in many cases, give up its original position.

The consumer-led ecological movements in the developed Western countries have been difficult for the ASEAN governments. In eco-labeling the certification bodies try to sell their labels to consumers and the effect of certification depends on the extent to which the consumers have accepted the certification. Owing to environmental organizations and the green movement, the products with environmental certification have become increasingly popular in the Western developed countries during the 1990s. ASEAN's traditional diplomatic means in dealing with the environment-trade link have gained some success, particularly in the WTO. Sometimes these environmental movements try to exert direct influence on the domestic governments. As, for example, in the early

1990s, when the Austrian government started to prepare measures for protecting tropical timber. It started to consider eco-labeling when timber producers, mainly in Southeast Asian countries, had complained to the ITTO and the GATT about Austrian attempts to restrict the use of tropical timber. After giving up efforts to increase tariffs on tropical timber products, Austria started to prepare eco-labeling legislation concerning also tropical products, including timber. The ASEAN economic ministers protested against it and the case was brought to the GATT.[9] The expected negative attitude of the GATT caused the Austrian government to postpone its legislative measures.[10]

However, owing to the fact that product standardization, including eco-labeling, is increasingly being taken charge of by non-governmental bodies, ASEAN had to comply with the new developments. Therefore, the multilateral forum of the WTO was not the only solution. While domestic consumers in importing countries are increasingly demanding products with sustainable producing methods, the multilateral institution's decisions have not affected such consumer habits. Therefore, ASEAN tried to adapt to the situation and started to negotiate for a common certification system with the respective governments. This took place when the environmental standards were taken into the agenda of ASEAN and the CER (Closer Economic Relations between Australia and New Zealand) meetings.

The ASEAN – CER discussions were conducted on the basis of a politically rather neutral ISO 14000 environmental certification system.[11] However, even more irksome for the ASEAN countries have been the negotiations with purely non-governmental Western certification bodies with rather strong political criteria. ISO 14000 criteria have taken into account proper forestry practices and sustainable development. However, there have emerged certification bodies that pay attention to the social issues and political rights of the indigenous people living in the area where the cuts are made. These bodies have no connection to national legislation or governmental bodies in any country, but they are associations of consumer, business, environmental and other expertise circles which permit their certification to be used in the different standardization schemes.

In the rhetoric of ASEAN, the Western environmental organizations support their governments in setting new NTBs and particularly the Malaysian Prime Minister Mahathir Mohamad accused these organizations of promoting a new form of colonialism. In his view, these organizations are serving the rich North in keeping the poor South underdeveloped.[12] Therefore the issue of forest certification between Malaysian authorities and an environmental standardization body, the Forest Stewardship Council, (FSC) was troublesome for the Malaysian government.

This forced also the Southeast Asian authorities to develop national certification systems. However, for several reasons, for example the critical attitude of Western media, Western consumers did not acknowledge the Southeast Asian national forest certification systems. Instead of this, in the late 1990s, the FSC's certification gained growing acceptance among Western consumers. When Californian authorities decided to purchase timber only with the FSC's certification, Malaysia undertook diplomatic action in order to annul the Californian decision, as the FSC's criteria called for prioritizing the social and political rights of the indigenous people against Malaysia's sovereignty. The publicity which followed did not help Malaysia. In the end Malaysian authorities had to start negotiations with the FSC leadership in order to gain the FSC's acceptance of the Malaysian timber certification.

These new global actors do not as such mean a dramatic shift in the World trade regime, because only an extensive regime can change the terms of global trade. This can be done only inside the WTO's system. So far the ASEAN countries could sell their certified products to Western markets and uncertified ones to the East Asian countries, particularly on growing Chinese markets. However, all this put new pressure on the WTO's trade negotiations and demonstrates to the ASEAN countries that traditional diplomacy, in which the organization was rather successful during the 1980's, has partly lost its significance. On the other hand, the power of a rather new certification body implied a change in the trade regime and a decrease of ASEAN's and its members' prestige after the Southeast Asian economic crisis.

The IMF, the World Bank and the ASEAN Countries

The relationship between world financial authorities and the ASEAN countries changed dramatically during the Asian economic crisis 1997–1998. In general, both the IMF and the World Bank roles in the region were less visible in the 1980s and in the early 1990s than during and after the crisis. On the other hand, the ASEAN countries, with their export-oriented economic infrastructure, with their well-controlled public spending, as well as their opening of foreign capital inflows during the late 1980s and early 1990s, were the IMF's model pupils in the Third World.[13] Its sister organization, the World Bank, would have its reservations on social and political development in Southeast Asia.

Nevertheless, the political reasons for the Japanese to possibly emphasize their developmental model among the developing countries, made the World Bank neglect these aspects and praise the Asian economic model.

Originally the IMF was created to promote a liberal world order by acting as a medium between unregulated global capitalism and national protectionist policies. However, the rapid growth of international capital markets reduced its significance in industrialized countries. Therefore the role of the IMF since its creation has developed toward a financial rescue organization for the developing countries and its aid has been regarded as a result of false economic management.

Thus the relationship between the ASEAN countries and the IMF had not been emphasized among the regional countries before the crisis, although the Philippines and Thailand had received their aid packages and carried out their recovery programs during the 1980s. During his visit to Southeast Asia just before the collapse of regional finance sectors, the IMF director Michel Camdessus did not see anything especially wrong in the ASEAN economies when he met the ASEAN finance ministers in their first meeting in Phuket in Thailand in March 1997. Even more than a week later, when the Thai government published the $3.9 billion bad property debt in Thai banks, he did not see any reason for the further development of the crisis.

The IMF offered emergency aid to the Philippines in July 1997, because it already had an on-going recovery program with the IMF. In early August Thailand called for help from the IMF, but Indonesia did not turn to the IMF until October 1997. Malaysia did not ask help from the IMF, but presented a belt-tightening budget, which largely involved similar measures that appeared in the IMF's loan conditions.

The IMF did not get involved in the economic affairs of the ASEAN countries without the given government's invitation. The role of the IMF emerges when the country in need of financial help turns to the IMF. The IMF provides temporary financial assistance to its member countries having difficulties in paying for imports or taking care of their foreign debt. In return, the countries have to agree to undertake policy reforms to correct the problems which the IMF sees as underlying their balance of payments difficulties. The issues that the IMF considers to be behind the economic and financial problems refer to the normative role of this world organization. This normative role has never been precisely uniform, but it has usually referred to the idea of solving economic difficulties with free markets and non-discrimination between nationals and foreigners, which means the complete openness of national economies. These are normative in the sense that these funding conditions do not necessarily have anything to do with the actual economic problems.[14]

Despite the fact that the IMF is treated as an independent actor, it is an intergovernmental institution, not a supranational organization. However, its decision-making differs from typical intergovernmental institutions that normally base their decisions on consensus. In the IMF, the decisions are based on the voting power of the member governments, which are related to the funds they provide to the IMF. In the end of 2000 the share of US votes was 17.29 percent, Japan's 6.20, Germany's 6.06 and France and United Kingdom had both 5.01 percent of the total votes.[15] This distribution is reflected in the fact that the economic policy norms represent those of Western developed countries.[16]

Those ASEAN countries which were forced to apply IMF aid were particularly reluctant to accept some of the IMF's loan conditions. Some ASEAN governments as well as many economic experts both inside and outside Southeast Asia, including the World Bank chief economist Joseph Stiglitz and the former IMF employee, professor Jeffrey Sachs, were inclined to think that the IMF's long-standing claim to liberate financial markets was the reason for the crisis. Therefore the IMF's conditions have nothing to do with economic recovery in this case.[17] Accordingly, the IMF is now only realizing its agenda by taking advantage of the miserable economic situation of the petitioners. The obvious claim of opening the rest of Southeast Asian markets to foreign companies and capital emphasized the political aspects of loan conditions. Therefore there exists a strong tendency to think that the IMF's policy was coincident with the interests of the US to open Asian markets for its business in a situation in which the Asian countries, including Japan, are more or less defenseless.

This reasonable suspicion did not, however, burst into the open anti-US or anti-Western sentiment at the governmental level, although some outbursts of it during Indonesian political unrest took place. On the high political level only the Malaysian government criticized the US role behind the IMF. On the unofficial level and in the media the US passive policy in hiding behind the IMF was criticized more openly.[18] Even the main Singaporean newspaper, *the Straits Times,* criticized the US and the IMF roles of inflaming the economic crisis into political crises in the region.[19] More open criticism was still made by Southeast Asian experts and NGOs, such as the Just World Trust and the Focus on Global South.

When the IMF's explanation of the crisis was the lost confidence of the foreign investors in the regional economies due to problems in economic management,[20] the alternative explanation pointed back to the

IMF's own policy. Accordingly, Southeast Asian economies have been vulnerable owing to the fact that FDIs dominate their economies too much. The flow of FDI led to strong financial interests which led, on the one hand, to currency appreciation and declining exports and economic growth. On the other hand, it further stimulated both financial liberalization and international capital inflows, heating up stock markets and short-term foreign borrowings. The short term borrowings particularly appeared to be fateful for Southeast Asian economies. The IMF had not realized that its own policy of liberalizing finance markets could lead to a problem – to the over-borrowing of the private markets.[21]

Therefore, the IMF's agenda, the continuation of economic liberalization, which in its loan conditions was expressed in removing all the barriers around the domestic financial and service sectors and cutting down all the state subsidies including those in the industrial, agriculture and transport sectors, seemed to escalate the crisis. These measures affected particularly the social aspects of the crisis. Interestingly enough, the Philippines, which has undergone the IMF's program already from the mid 1980s and now was again caught in a financial crisis, did not change the IMF's recovery program. Thailand, which was forced to beg for IMF help in early August 1997, has had to adopt *an austerity program*, which was geared toward the public sector. It included an increase in the value-added tax, a surplus of the public budget, a cut in fiscal spending, a clean-up of the finance sector and the discontinuation of subsidizing ailing finance companies. Thus the public sector was chastised although it was rather innocent of causing the crisis. Similar measures were adopted in Indonesia when it accepted the IMF's conditions, which included also tariff reductions connected to the WTO negotiations. This concerned particularly the Indonesian attempt to protect its national car industry, a case which the US had brought to the WTO.[22]

However, the final resistance of the Suharto regime postponed the implementation of the IMF loan. Suharto turned negative toward IMF conditions after he was re-elected in March of 1998. He claimed that these conditions would not be compatible with Indonesia's constitution. Moreover, Suharto presented the idea of pegging the rupiah to the US dollar instead of letting it float.[23] The Suharto regime's resistance led to unprecedented international pressure during which it became obscure whether the IMF was an instrument for political reforms or a vehicle for economic recovery. In fact, during the spring it became clear that the Western powers had withdrawn their support from Suharto and the IMF help package became available only after Suharto resigned.

Malaysia followed the IMF agenda partly, although it avoided requesting the IMF's help. In December 1997 it published its belt-tightening budget, the architect of which was the Finance Minister and Deputy Prime Minister Anwar Ibrahim. It also included cuts in budget spending and market liberalization, but also measures strictly contrary to the IMF's agenda and, finally, Mahathir changed unilaterally the rules of foreign exchange markets. The different signals of the Prime Minister and his Deputy obscured the line which Malaysia was taking, but the line was cleared when Anwar was sacked: To attract private investments back and the keep Malaysian sovereignty over decisions on some crucial sectors.

Mahathir's rhetoric on defending Malaysia's sovereignty was not baseless, when politico-economic ethnic aspects were taken into consideration. In this respect, Malaysian defense of its insurance sector in the WTO negotiations on financial services reflects this fact. On the other hand, the purposefulness with which Malaysia undertook its budgetary cuts and further opened its markets was remarked on the IMF.[24]

Surely the financial controls which Malaysia undertook a year after the outbreak of the crisis were against the economic doctrine of the IMF. Although Malaysia's economic fundamentals were much better than Indonesia's and Thailand's economic bases, the value of the ringgit remained very unstable. This was maybe partly due to Mahathir's indiscreet rhetoric, which made the investors nervous. However, the currency traders also took advantage of the unstable situation by short-borrowing and selling huge amounts of ringgit, which devaluated the currency. Thus these currency traders made big profits when they bought their ringgit loans back.

In spite of the fact that Malaysian financial controls were imposed simultaneously with Anwar's sacking, these two things did not apparently have a direct connection with each other. According to Mahathir, Anwar – when still in the government – had accepted the financial controls as a last resort a month before the measures were taken.[25] Anwar said in early May 1998 that Malaysia could not agree with all the recommendations given by the IMF.[26] On the other hand, Mahathir's bold move against the norms of the world's economic regime enforced his position against the attacks of the pro-Anwar Reformasi movement, particularly when the controls also seemed to work.[27]

Malaysian capital controls included simply two measures. First, the government stopped the ringgit trade by fixing the ringgit exchange rate at 3.80 to one US dollar. Second, the government adopted restrictions on the Kuala Lumpur Stock Exchange (KLSE) in order to stop speculation with share prices and short- selling activities, mainly from the Singaporean-based Central Limited Order Book (CLOB). The CLOB traded Malaysian shares without the approval of the KLSE by using the companies who were registered in the KLSE. The right of trading of these companies in the KLSE was now abolished.

Both of these measures were against the textbooks accepted by the IMF. Malaysia's establishment of a fixed exchange rate was exactly the same as Suharto tried to execute and failed due to the resistance of the IMF.[28] Therefore the IMF and several global financial institutions, including the US Federal Bank and private institutions, reacted critically.[29] The Malaysian measures created mixed feelings also in her ASEAN and Asian partners. The most critical views came from the Thai and the Philippine governments, who had accepted the IMF's loan conditions. Similarly the Singaporean leadership had some reservations over Mahathir's measures, although Senior Minister Lee Kuan Yew had some sympathy for Mahathir's cold-blooded move.[30] From the point of view of ASEAN, Malaysian controls did not harm any agreement made in ASEAN, as ASEAN financial cooperation was in its initial stages. With the same tune as Lee Kuan Yew, some other ASEAN leaders, together with Chinese and Japanese officials, understood Malaysian policy to stabilize its financial situation.[31]

Despite various individual comments, ASEAN – as an organization – did not challenge the IMF's economic doctrine. The ASEAN countries learned in November 1997 that the IMF would firmly protect its authority when it kept ASEAN and Japan from establishing the Asian Fund. Instead of this, some ASEAN countries individually opposed the IMF, particularly when the IMF's policy seemed to shake the political stability in the area. In the case of Indonesia during the Suharto regime's last months, both Malaysia and Singapore started economically supporting Indonesia when the IMF lingered with its bailout. The reason for Singaporean and Malaysian policy was obviously not the IMF's loan conditions, but the threat that the IMF's delay would throw Indonesia into political chaos which would undermine the whole regional system.

The IMF did not admit that its policy before and in the beginning of the crisis went wrong in Southeast Asia. Contrary to the IMF, its sister organization, the World Bank, reflected on its own past policy critically and openly. This has, however, something to do with the different political role of the World Bank. Like the IMF's bailouts, the World Bank's loans – since the Bank started with policy-based program lending followed by the Structural Adjusted Loans (SAL) in the early 1980s – are conditioned. However, the overlapping roles of the IMF and the World Bank created continuous, both latent and open, tensions. In general, the IMF should deal with exchange rates and adjustment for temporary balance of payments problems, while the Bank has to deal with development programs and projects and to set development priorities. Nevertheless, there are overlapping areas dealing with financial issues such as institutions, capital markets and domestic savings. These overlapping and obscure areas, which affect both the IMF's and the World Bank's sectors, reflect differences in the policy priorities of these organizations. During the 1980s the World Bank tried to reduce this tension by binding the SAL to the IMF's stabilization programs. This made, of course, the Bank's loans more strictly conditioned on the economic doctrine of the IMF.[32]

There exists, however, a clear difference between putting into practice the Fund's versus the Bank's conditionality. The IMF's conditions are precise, since reference is made to macroeconomic indicators. Thus if the IMF's client fails to meet the aims of the Fund's conditions, the results are clear and serious, resulting in the interruption of lending. The World Bank's conditions, owing to the Bank's main role of funding developmental programs, are more relative and sometimes highly qualitative. The aims and the realized results are difficult to judge and therefore the conditions are usually negotiable. This difference may be very confusing to the government that is part of both the IMF's stabilization program and is simultaneously receiving a Bank loan as well, as is usually the case.[33]

In Southeast Asia the World Bank had been involved – in the footsteps of the IMF – both in the Philippines' and in Thailand's economic development in the 1980s. Interestingly enough, the World Bank's SAL program in the Philippines before the fall of Marcos aimed to repair the errors of the IMF's earlier policy which had led to the overvaluation of the peso. The conditions set by the Bank dealt very much with dissolving the barriers erected by the Marcos administration in order to protect the interests of the Marcos family and its circles. These barriers had made the Filipino economy ineffective. The IMF woke up to these problems not until the US withdrew its support from Marcos after the assassination of Benigno Aquino, the husband of the subsequent president.[34] The Bank's loan conditions in Thailand were partly the same as in the Philippines, focusing on internal economic liberalization and export promotion. Obviously, the Bank's and the IMF's policies in Thailand were better synchronized than in the Philippines.[35]

In the early 1990s, the World Bank accepted broadly the Asian model as expressed in the *East Asian Miracle* study and also, in some respects, the close relations between government and business. The World Bank's self-reflection was focused mainly on this.[36] This did not mean that the Bank would have denied the model entirely,[37] but self-criticism concerned now the political sidelines of the model.

Politically, if not economically, the World Bank's deviation from the Asian or Japanese model is significant. Although the apparent target was the Suharto regime and the post-Suharto political disturbances, the World Bank's new orientation was targeted also against the proponents of the Asian model, Malaysia and Singapore, and obviously, indirectly against Japan. The Bank introduced a new guiding principle of *democracy and market economy*, attacking the need for authoritarian governance in certain phases of development. In the World Bank's conference in Seoul in February 1999, one of the Bank's directors, Vinod Thomas, stated that democracy and markets are two wheels of a cart. Accordingly, this means "a paradigm shift in thinking about development strategy" because it signals "an end to a mentality revealed by such sequencing as 'grow first, take care of social/structural problems later' or 'liberalize first, regulate later' or 'markets first, democracy later'". This means that the World Bank would pay attention to issues like corruption and emphasis on participation both in business management and political governance.[38] The Asian crisis has, as pointed out by the World Bank President, encouraged "a healthy and participatory civil society" and rooting out corruption and cronyism.[39]

An equation sign was made between political and private business governance. The World Bank report estimated that the East Asian crisis particularly showed the importance of corporate governance. The concept refers to the rules and incentives which direct and control a company's management by shareholders "while taking into account the interests of other legitimate stakeholders". For this, the World Bank introduced a loan to support corporate governance reform and during 1998 it was granted to South Korea and three ASEAN countries, Indonesia, Malaysia and Thailand, to facilitate escaping the crisis. The amount of the loan varied from $2.48 billion (South Korea) to $300 (Malaysia).[40]

The Bank's case in point was South Korea, where the newly elected President Kim Dae Jung's attempt to renew the political system and restructure *cheabols* were positively remarked on. One cannot help but take account of ideological aspects in this. Kim Dae Jung, already in 1994, when he was the most prominent opposition figure, responded to Lee Kuan Yew in his discussion with Fareed Zakaria on Asian values in *Foreign Affairs*.[41] In his *Foreign Affairs* article, Kim denied the Asian model and concept of Asian values and emphasized the inevitabilily of democracy in modern development.[42] Together with his visible role as a long-standing opposition leader against previous repressive governments and by winning democratic elections, he fits perfectly in this role.[43]

In ASEAN two countries have had the potential to be models in terms of World Bank approaches – Thailand and the Philippines. The developments roughly similar to those in South Korea took place in Thailand, and Joseph Estrada, who won the presidency in the Philippines in 1998 tried also to take this role in ASEAN. Nevertheless, due to their more modest records, the support of the World Bank for both the Thai and Filipino governments has not been as visible as that for the Kim Dae Jung administration.

The intervention of global economic regimes, first of all the IMF and the World Bank, showed the incoherence of the ASEAN countries both economically and politically and obviously, further split ASEAN cooperation. These global organizations dealt with the regional countries bilaterally, ignoring the regional organization and sometimes, as the case of the Asian Fund showed, rejecting regional cooperation in their field. It showed that the institutionalist approach has little to offer when a global actor with such economic power penetrates regional economies. Of course, on the other side of the coin the ASEAN countries were rather incapable of arranging concrete regional cooperation when the crisis hit Southeast Asia.

SOUTHEAST ASIAN POLITICAL CRISES, GLOBAL INTERVENTIONS AND REGIONAL APPROACHES

The Asian economic crisis thus launched several political crises in Southeast Asia. These crises created a challenge to the whole regional organization. Traditionally, domestic issues of the member countries have been outside ASEAN cooperation. However, the economic crisis brought along a double-sided problem: on the one hand, it created domestic political conflicts which would spill over the region and on the other hand, this would lead to the further intervention of external powers into regional affairs.

The following pages examine how the ASEAN members have tried to react to the political crises that followed the economic recession, particularly to those of Indonesia and Malaysia. At the same time, they follow how the rhetoric at the high political level developed during the crisis period. Therefore, before the examination of the two country cases, the chapter discusses the attempt to renew ASEAN so that it would better handle these kinds of crisis situations.

The Relevance of Constructive Engagement

The fact that the most important ASEAN country, Indonesia, sunk into economic and political crises, paralyzed the whole organization. The organizational structure and the institutionalist decision-making system did not make the intervention into regional problems easier. The "ASEAN way", that is, the respect for each other's sovereignty and non-intervention in domestic affairs, together with the concept of constructive engagement, effectively kept the ASEAN members from cooperating in addressing Indonesia's problems. However, the resistance of ASEAN to deal with its members' affairs threatened now one of the main functions of the organization: to keep outside powers from intervening in the regional affairs of ASEAN. Thus the crisis showed that ASEAN had no organizational shelters when national resilience failed.

The concepts that seemed to be workable in a situation of constant economic growth and following the principle of ASEAN's interstate relations – national and regional resilience and *constructive engagement* – appeared to be more or less insignificant in a situation of regional crises caused by economic recession. However, the critical enquiry against the principle of *constructive engagement* did not originate from the economic crisis. Regional NGOs and human right groups had already joined Western critics of the principle when addressing the human rights situation in Myanmar and in the country's joining of ASEAN. At the top political level, critical examination of the principle started when Anwar Ibrahim, then acting prime minister of Malaysia, introduced the concept of *constructive intervention* in cases in which the domestic situation of one regional country would undermine the whole regional system.

The background for Anwar Ibrahim's contemplation was Cambodia's political struggle in the summer of 1997, which blocked the country's entry into ASEAN. In fact the new concept of constructive intervention was nothing new in the case of Cambodia, because the organization had actively been involved in the internal affairs of the country since the early 1980s. Nevertheless, Anwar's idea, which he presented in a column in *Newsweek* in July 1997, was a new one, because he wanted to extend the concept to deal with ASEAN´s policy toward Myanmar. This means that the organization would intervene in the domestic affairs of a *member* country in certain circumstances. Anwar suggested that the ASEAN countries would start to discuss a new concept and ASEAN rights to interfere in a situation "where the threat of spillovers of domestic economic, social and political upheavals can seriously undermine the stability of the entire region". Therefore ASEAN's active interference into the Cambodian political situation would be a case of example rather than exception. Therefore ASEAN should, as Anwar suggested, move in the same direction also with the Rangoon government.[44]

Constructive intervention would include, following the experience of the Cambodian agreement made in Paris in 1991, "direct assistance to firm up electoral processes" and "an increased commitment to legal and administrative reforms". Because "there are core humanitarian values" that bind the people, constructive intervention includes the promotion of "the development of human capital and the general strengthening of civil society and the rule of law". It does not, according to Anwar, deviate from ASEAN's principle of unity in diversity, but "each country must find its own path to civil society". The time of absolute non-interference is, however, over because "all of us in the region are our brother's keepers."[45]

Did Anwar's contemplation mean also deviation from institutionalist decision-making? This was obviously not the case. What Anwar suggested was a mechanism for intergovernmental cooperation, when ASEAN was faced with a domestic crisis that could spillover into the region. In fact, ASEAN developed a new institution – the ASEAN Troika – to reach the political settlements in Cambodia, when ASEAN postponed Cambodian membership owing to domestic political problems. The statement that the troika made in Bangkok in April 1998 included those components which Anwar introduced in constructive intervention.[46] In the ASEAN Third Informal Summit in Manila in November 1999, the Filipino President Joseph Estrada strongly promoted the further use of the troika model which is composed of the previous, present and future chairmen of the ASEAN Standing Committee. The ASEAN leaders, according to Estrada, went to suggest that the Troika should make "constructive efforts to meet the challenges posed by its expansion and issues concerning 'human rights, governance and the environment'".[47]

In the ASEAN informal meeting in Manila, the foreign ministers agreed to develop the troika model. They did not mention, however, such areas of concern as Estrada did, but decided that the troika would be constituted as an ad hoc body which should support and assist the ASEAN foreign ministers. The purpose of it is "to enable ASEAN to address in a timely manner urgent and important regional political and security issues and situations of common concerns likely to disturb regional peace and harmony". It should work on the basic ASEAN principles, in accordance with the TAC, "and in particular the core principles of consensus and non-interference". Therefore it should be part of an institutionalist decision-making system. Nevertheless, the establishment of the Troika reflected the problems of an intergovernmental decision-making system in situations like the Asian crisis.[48]

Whether all the ASEAN leaders backed Anwar's ideas or Estrada's attempt to develop the ASEAN Troika towards an ASEAN instrument of intervening in its members' problems was doubtful. There appeared a short-lived group inside ASEAN, including Anwar, Thai Foreign Minister Surin Pitsuwan, Filipino President Joseph Estrada, together with his cabinet, and Suharto's successor B.J. Habibie, who all advanced the idea of renewing ASEAN basic rules of behavior. The fact that Mahathir's cabinet did not share Anwar's ideas and that Habibie was more concerned with Indonesian internal problems, effectively limited the power of this group. These reformists, with the Thai Foreign Minister and his Filipino colleague Domingo L. Siazon at the head, attempted to renew basic principles at the ASEAN Ministerial Meeting in July 1998 in Manila. At the meeting, the reformers avoided the issue of constructive engagement publicly, but they demanded stronger political integration of the organization in order to meet future challenges.[49] This effort was clearly defeated by the ASEAN "conservatives", Singapore and Malaysia. At the closing ceremony, Singaporean Foreign Minister S. Jayakumar did not try to cover the triumph of the conservatives and argued that the present economic and political crises have proved the value of the principles of non-intervention and decision-making by consensus.[50]

The reformist group was further weakened when Anwar was ousted from Mahathir's cabinet in the fall of 1998 and Habibie had to give up power one year later. In spite of the fact that the reformists had failed to reform ASEAN principles and decision-making, the emergence of the reformists at the top political level suggested that the ASEAN expertise groups' ideas for stronger political integration among ASEAN countries had found their way to the top political level. This conflict also reflected, however, the disagreement among the members on the way in which to develop the organization and disunity in a situation in which the organization had expanded but cooperation in serious matters had only slightly advanced.[51]

ASEAN Member Responses to Indonesia's Regime Crisis and Disintegration

Owing to the differences on how to develop the organization, it was rather clear that no serious attempt by ASEAN to get involved in Indonesia's political crisis was made. When the attempts to establish the Asia Fund were rejected as a substitution for the IMF's help, no other serious common ASEAN initiative was proposed. The proposals for a common currency or to use local currencies in regional trade were interesting and showed that further ASEAN integration was needed, but the actual state of affairs proved them to be unrealistic. For example, when Mahathir promoted his common currency plans and even when Indonesia responded positively, Suharto simultaneously tried to peg the rupiah to the US dollar.

On the political side, the ASEAN members' approaches were even more inconsistent. Traditionally ASEAN policy has been of both strict non-interference in the members' internal affairs and to support regional countries against external pressure. Despite a growing number of common statements, the organization was rather unable to formulate a common line in important political questions, not even to speak about common political action. In the question of non-interference, the growing anxiety on the regional ramifications of Indonesia's economic and political crises made the other ASEAN members deviate from the traditional line.

One explanation of ASEAN's inability in taking political action is, of course, that the crisis hit all the ASEAN members and two others of them were in the same position as Indonesia to beg for the IMF's help. Thailand's new government accepted the IMF's loan conditions without public protest and became a promoter of its policy in Southeast Asia. Similarly, the Philippines had accepted the IMF's conditions and Singapore, the interests of which coincide with financial and trade liberalization, followed the IMF's lines. Of the original ASEAN members, only Malaysia was ready to support Indonesia against the demands of international financial regimes.

This is not to say that the ASEAN members found the IMF's medicine to be the best way of handling the crisis. Quite the contrary, the liberalization of financial markets was broadly accepted as a basic cause of the crisis and although the Singaporean government favored liberalization, not all the IMF's demands for trade and financial liberalization were seen as a proper way of handling Indonesia's crisis. This did not, however, prevent Prime Minister Goh Chock Tong from persuading Suharto to accept the IMF's conditions. Nevertheless, the impasse between the Suharto regime and the IMF tried the Singaporeans' patience and the state-controlled media started to suggest that Suharto leave. However, even stronger interference from the Singaporean side took place, when Senior Minister Lee Kuan Yew doubted the ability of the new leader, B.J. Habibie, to handle the crisis. During the Habibie administration Singaporean-Indonesian relations remained cool, normalizing only after Abdurrahman Wahid came to power.[52]

However, the Asian economic crisis made irrevocable changes in ASEAN interstate relations. Despite the fact that the authorities tried in general to refrain from criticizing the domestic affairs of its neighbors, the role of the media and the expertise community had changed from an earlier more cautious line. This became clearly evident in both Indonesia's separatist conflicts and in the Malaysian domestic political struggle.

The principle of non-interference in ASEAN's interstate relations has concerned both the issues of dealing with political opposition as well as different ethnic and regional issues. One of the main purposes of ASEAN has been to deal with indistinct territorial issues that have originated from the colonial period. Therefore the territorial issues connected with the possibility of internal disintegration have been an absolute tabu in ASEAN regionalism. Concerning separatist tendencies, ASEAN's policy of non-intervening has been even more categorical – Indonesia, Malaysia and the Philippines all have regional minorities who may have claims for autonomy.

Therefore, since Indonesia's annexation of East Timor after the fall of Portuguese rule in 1975, Indonesia's policy was broadly accepted in ASEAN. Only Singapore had reservations against it, but the only symptom of Singapore's dissenting opinion was its abstentions in UN voting on East Timor. Singapore abandoned this separate line in the 34th UN session in 1979 in order to unite ASEAN against Vietnam in the UN votes on the Kampuchean issue.[53]

It comes, therefore, as no surprise that Singapore's media was quite active and took initiative in these questions. Also the Thai and the Filipino media followed this line. In the case of East Timor, regional NGOs had already showed their influence. This influence, which the NGOs had gained rapidly during the 1990s, was particularly important in Thailand and in the Philippines and they had taken advantage of international summits like APEC and ASEM in order to promote their cause. The views of the regional NGOs were particularly well-published in the Thai English language newspapers, but the news was reported perhaps more selectively in other regional newspapers.[54]

Interestingly enough, some activities of NGOs were increasingly regional. This was not only the case with political and human rights issues, but also with the NGOs concentrating on social and environmental issues.[55] However, the human rights meetings had particularly much publicity. In several meetings on East Timor the NGOs got rather a lot of media coverage. In the Philippines the Ramos administration tried to reject a regional meeting on East Timor due to pressure from Indonesia, but failed. In Kuala Lumpur the Asia Pacific Conference on East Timor in November 1996 was broken up by Malaysian ruling party activists orchestrated by the Malaysian authorities, but the case was reported widely. Due to these activities, the East Timorese separatist movement enjoyed sympathy in the region.

The Habibie administration faced pressures on the East Timor question from many sides. During the crisis, the activities of the East Timorese independence movement had force partly owing to the publicity it had gained both in the region and in the West during the 1990's. The East Timorese Nobel laureates – Archbishop Carlos Belo and Jose Ramos Horta – of course, helped in this. Second, it became obvious that the Western powers took advantage of Indonesia's desperate situation and linked the East Timorese situation to funding by the IMF and the World Bank.[56] Third, the United Nations strengthened its activities owing to the worsening human rights situation in East Timor.

When the East Timorese leaders had rejected all plans for partial autonomy, Habibie said in January 1999 that Indonesia might consider independence for East Timor. Habibie's announcement was followed by negotiations between the UN Secretary General's Personal Representative and high-level representatives of the Indonesian and Portuguese foreign ministries. On 5 May 1999, the Indonesian government promised in the agreement made under the UN to accept a "popular consultation" on East Timor's independence. In the referendum arranged and organized by the world organization in late August the same year, the pro-independence position got 78.5 percent of the votes.

ASEAN, or the ASEAN countries, were aside from these developments. Only after the violence accelerated after the referendum, the ASEAN countries took clearer stands. In the UN Security Council debate Singapore took an unusually strict attitude toward Indonesia in urging it to follow the UN's policy in East Timor, when it became obvious that pro-Indonesia groups were mainly responsible for the violence. Similar voices were not heard from other representatives of the ASEAN countries.[57] Despite different behavior among the ASEAN members,

ASEAN as an organization hardly mentioned East Timor in its documents. However, some voices were heard that ASEAN should take a more active political role in East Timor.[58] Several ASEAN countries, Malaysia, the Philippines, Singapore and Thailand, took part in the peacekeeping force which was part of the UN transitional administration in East Timor (UNTAET) and which was established in September 1999. The participation of ASEAN countries was possible only after Indonesia specially requested their participation. The unofficial ASEAN link became evident when the position of force commander of the UN troops was given to a Thai general.

For ASEAN, the UN context was the best way to solve the East Timor issue. The organization had no mechanism to take charge of it and this was not seriously considered. On the other hand, the UN context prevented the direct involvement of great powers in the region, although Australia's visible role was criticized particularly in Indonesia and Malaysia. When the independence of East Timor became obvious, East Timor was invited to engage in ASEAN cooperation. Unofficial sources in the Habibie administration announced its willingness to accept East Timor into ASEAN already before the referendum. However, the East Timorese leadership turned down this offer. Jose Ramos Horta said in August 1999 that ASEAN would not be the international context for East Timor, but rather the South Pacific Forum and Australia and New Zealand. Accordingly the "East Timorese are much more at home in Fiji, Papua New Guinea and Vanuatu than with Thailand or Indonesia", but he expected that the Philippines and Singapore will be "important future partners" of an independent East Timor.[59] ASEAN gave an official invitation to the Transitional Administration in East Timor to attend the 33rd AMM in Bangkok July 22, but the East Timorese delegation was not in attendance.

The recognition of East Timor's independence meant that ASEAN acknowledged a *de facto* situation rather than adopting an active policy. This emphatically showed the meaning and importance of non-interference in ASEAN's inter-state relations. Although the individual members deviated from this policy, the regional organization could not be the context in which any intervention could be made. Contrary to this, ASEAN expressed its support for the territorial unity of Indonesia, curbing down all the expectations that ASEAN would possibly allow more separatism in Indonesia. This was proved at the Bangkok Ministerial Meeting in July 2000, where ASEAN rejected all the support from the separatist movements in Aceh and Irian Jaya.[60]

The ASEAN Member States and the Malaysian Power Struggle

Indonesia's developments pointed out the differences between the policy of ASEAN and the policies of its members. If the intensity and social influences of the Indonesian and Malaysian crises are compared, one cannot help wondering at the reactions of Malaysia's neighbors and some more distant powers. In general the issue was on the power struggle inside Malaysia's semi-authoritarian government. Therefore ASEAN did not react. Still, the displacement of Anwar Ibrahim from Mahathir's government and the consequent trial and imprisonment got unusual attention and reactions from the neighbors. Because ASEAN's cooperation is intergovernmental this, of course, weakened ASEAN as a regional actor.

Despite the domestic political nature of the Anwar case, it cannot be understood without the Asian economic crisis and international intervention in it. Malaysian domestic policy, particularly ethnic *bumiputra* policy, played a role. Another catalyst was also the different political origins of Mahathir and Anwar. Mahathir had established his power in the Malaysian main political coalition, the UMNO, during his nearly 20 years of leadership. Anwar had to suffer his position as a student leader of a Muslim organization and was jailed under the Malaysian internal security act during the 1980s. However, Mahathir pardoned him politically and took him into his cabinet, where he was promoted at the end to Finance Minister and Deputy Prime Minister. He was thus expected to be a succeeding Prime Minister. The profiles of Anwar's supporters in the UMNO are distinct from the Party mainstream; they combined both reformers and religious groups. Therefore he got solid adversaries in the UMNO mainstream and the circles which had benefited from *bumiputra* policy.

During the Asian crisis an interesting political profile of Anwar took shape. On the one hand, he was to his supporters a modern Muslim leader and, on the other hand, he was, to the outside world, a political and economic liberal without similar nationalistic colors as his Prime Minister and the cabinet. Therefore Anwar was a popular person among the IMF and other financial institutions. Similarly there emerged in the region a reformist group, discussed earlier, having a similar outlook on the economic reforms and regional matters. As a central person in this group, he had prestige not only with reformist, but also with Muslim activists across the region, particularly in Indonesia.

However, Anwar was ousted by his opponents using rumors of homosexuality which were circulated during the UMNO circles already in the summer of 1997. According to Malaysian law, homosexuality is a crime. Mahathir referred to these rumors when he ousted Anwar from the government as unsuitable for being in charge of such a high position. When Anwar and his supporters started to fight for Anwar's political future, he was jailed and put on trial, which became farcical with changes of prosecution, testimonies and the cancellation of witnesses. In the end, he was convicted of corruption.

Anwar's treatment created an unexpectedly strong reaction in the region. Two figures of the reformer group, Habibie and Estrada, reacted strongly. The leaders met together in order to discuss the Anwar case. Even Singapore's Lee Kuan Yew condemned Anwar's treatment when it became evident that he was maltreated during his arrest.[61] Anwar's arrests took place just before the APEC's leaders meeting in Kuala Lumpur and there existed a possibility that some leaders would cancel their visits to Kuala Lumpur. Although the ASEAN leaders made no cancellations, at least some bilateral visits were cancelled, for example, between Habibie and Mahathir and the Filipino – Malaysian meeting on border issues.[62]

The publicity of the APEC summit focused on Malaysia's internal situation, which would be a total catastrophe to the host if not for the overkill of the US authorities. Although Anwar's treatment was not accepted, Vice President Al Gore's speech and demonstrative exit in the middle of lunch was condemned by the other participants, even by the Australian Prime Minister. Only Estrada supported Gore's speech, which hailed Anwar's supporters, "the brave People of Malaysia".[63] However, even the West and particularly the US made much stronger public interference into Malaysian domestic affairs than in the Indonesian case; in the latter case the US and the rest of Western powers were rather powerless. This is particularly due to the fact that they were not able to use such instruments as in the Indonesian case – the IMF and the World Bank – to shake up the government or to persuade the Mahathir government to keep to the correct political line.

Anwar's detention cooled Malaysian relations with the Philippines and Indonesia, but Malaysian newspapers attacked also the Singapore media on reporting Anwar's case.[64] Coincidentally with this, Malaysian relations with the Singaporean authorities were strained. Together with Singaporean media reports, the Senior Minister Lee Kuan Yew's memoirs published in September were attacked by Malaysians. Similarly, Malaysian currency controls harmed Singaporean interests.[65] The strained relations turned into political measures when Malaysia curbed airspace earlier allowed to be used by Singapore Air Force planes.[66]

Although the Malaysian political struggle caused discord between the ASEAN members, it was not as severe for ASEAN cooperation as the Indonesian political turmoil. In the Malaysian crisis there was no possibility for such external interference into regional affairs as in the Indonesian case. Despite strained relations between Malaysia and its neighbors, this did not reflect directly on ASEAN's cooperation. The ASEAN leaders met at the Sixth ASEAN Summit in Hanoi in December 1998 and no reform of ASEAN's basic principles was presented. Quite the contrary, this kind of attempt was watered down for a long time to come when the host, Vietnam, managed to secure the entry of Cambodia into the organization. This proved the fact that enlargement was a more convenient way to develop the organization than to develop organizational coherence.

8 Southeast Asian Regionalist Trends in the Beginning of the New Millennium

THE LEGACY OF THE 1990s

In the late 1990s, when ASEAN reformers raised the idea of shifting the basis of ASEAN's decision-making from non-interference to intervention, the reformers were more likely responding to actual political issues than attempting serious change in the organization. While claiming a desire to reform ASEAN's decision-making in order to establish supra-regional institutions, the reformers instead articulated their political stands, highlighting their differences with the traditionalists. The likelihood they could develop common institutions that would bind national decisions and legal systems of the ASEAN members were slim. The expansion of ASEAN in the early and middle of 1990s only confirmed this reality. Therefore, one could argue that the priority to expand the organization instead of deepening regional organization in the early and mid-1990s is now dictating ASEAN's development in the beginning of the new millennium, since deepening is even more difficult to carry out in the expanded organization.

This decision to expand ASEAN, rather than to make it a more autonomous player, confirmed one of the ASEAN's original roles to provide a conflict management system for the regional states. In this role ASEAN has been successful – no major conflict has occurred between the regional states – not even during economic and political crises. This record justifies ASEAN's policies and organizational structure. ASEAN might not have achieved this coherence and success if it had moved away from its basic principle of non-interference and asserted its right to intervene – in certain circumstances – into the domestic affairs of its members. In such a situation, in which the member countries face huge economic and political differences and do not have an authorized common body to decide for intervention, a decision by ASEAN governments to intervene would be fateful for the organization.

The debate on limited or *constructive intervention* among ASEAN touched on another of the organization's important motives: to prevent outside powers from intervening into regional affairs. To avert the danger of foreign interference, ASEAN has relied on the instruments of national and regional resilience and economic growth leading to political and social stability. The Asian economic crisis proved clearly the weakness of this formula. ASEAN members, in particular Indonesia, suffered from severe political instability, and fears about outsiders controlling Southeast Asian developments proved well-founded. Avoiding outsider control will require more profound structural changes, both in domestic political systems as well as in regional organization.

ASEAN's goals to maintain its members' sovereignty, uphold a principle of non-interference and prevent outside powers from intervening into regional affairs contradict each other, to some extent. Therefore the crucial notion of a contradiction between regional coherence and national sovereignty is of great significance in gaining insight into regional developments. This contradiction forms an important analytical scheme for examining both the attempts to develop the organization and for following political debate on the organization. National preferences, political and economic interests all come into play. Some of these factors follow national boundaries, while others follow domestic and political interests of each member country. Still others involve tensions between the experts, NGOs and politicians.

How to solve this particular contradiction is not, however, the only problem regional countries must address. The organization has to deal with other issues that go back to the 1990s. Of course, the primary tension between supra-nationalism and national sovereignty also figures into the formulation of these other questions to a more or less obvious degree. ASEAN needs to create effective institutions, particularly to deal with questions of economic co-operation and environmental protection. On the other hand, there are areas in which supra-national regionalism has not gone very far at all, not even in Europe, where common foreign and security issues have been intergovernmental and strictly under the control of national institutions. Finally, new phenomena have emerged that transcend the debate between supra-nationalism and inter-governmentalism. Regional NGOs have developed in Southeast Asia with particular interests in human rights, social and environmental affairs and in trade issues. They form a new kind of regionalism – regionalism "from below" – and are shaping new co-operative regional forms outside governmental and ASEAN contexts.

POST-CRISIS INSTITUTIONALISM AND FUNCTIONALISM

During the economic crisis several initiatives emerged from the top political level. These initiatives concerned financial co-operation, particularly currency co-operation. Their implementation would have required common authoritative institutions, and such institutions would have changed the nature of ASEAN as an intergovernmental organization. The difficult political issues which affected the whole region called for new mechanisms such as the ASEAN Troika. Whether these new initiatives and mechanisms grow out of the ASEAN institutionalist approach or emerge as part of ASEAN neo-functionalism is not always easy to discern, since both approaches overlap. But the crisis made one thing clear – more political and economic integration is needed in ASEAN regionalism.

Integration, per se, does not necessitate the abandonment of the "ASEAN way" of consensus-based decision-making. It does mean, however, that the need for procedures that lead to consensus are significantly decreased. In fact, ASEAN had increasingly adopted a *10-x mechanism* into its decision-making in the late 1990s. This means that the country, or countries, which cannot accept a particular decision, simply step aside. This kind of procedure cannot be used for important solutions. However, the ability to create institutions which decrease the need for consensus decision-making would remarkably increase the organization's efficiency, while permanent institutions and organs continue to direct and control the execution of ASEAN policies. Such institutions, of course, do limit the power of the member governments, but they do not imply that institutionalist and inter-governmental decision-making must disappear. Accordingly, in contrast to the European academic discussion, the debate among ASEAN experts about these issues makes no clear distinctions between functionalism and institutionalism,

The post-crisis debate on ASEAN focuses particularly on the inefficiency of the organization – a failing that became obvious during the crisis – and has led to two conclusions: Western watchers and Southeast Asian realists argue that the organization has only marginal importance, and, therefore, claim that attention should be paid to national measures. From this point of view, ASEAN is merely a pressure group relied on when its members need to defend their own interests globally. As such, it should retain its basic principle of non-interference.

In contrast, others suggest a need for change in the organization, they divide into camps supporting either neo-functionalist or institutionalist measures. These approaches are difficult to separate because both promote the same method of ASEAN co-operation – enhancing integration, first in economic issues, then in political ones. The Asian economic crisis as such was not necessarily negative for ASEAN's economic co-operation.[1] The IMF's conditions helped to hasten AFTA's schedule. At the Hanoi Summit ASEAN made decisions resulting in changing the target year of its complementation to 2002 for the six original signatories. Although Malaysia voiced some reservations concerning the protection of its national car production, trade, as well as other measures, were advanced despite the domestic problems of some members. It is therefore no surprise that both functionalist and neo-functionalist emphases emerged in the field of economic co-operation. Interestingly enough, this kind of emphasis – where economic co-operation and political integration are connected – is commonplace within the organization – from ASEAN's employees to the governmental circles of the member countries. In spite of the fact that supra-nationalism is officially taboo in the ASEAN vocabulary, a strong tendency exists to create common organizations to direct ASEAN's integration.[2]

Only a few concrete suggestions, however, about how to proceed with this integration process have been put forward, either by decision-makers or by second-track experts. Although most of the suggestions from either quarter include notable critiques of ASEAN's efficiency, they remain abstract, carefully avoiding the issue of the sovereignty of the member nations. Only a few concrete approaches have been put forth. In the *ASEAN Economic Bulletin,* a group of Thai economists examined the state of economic integration in ASEAN and came to the same conclusion as many other experts – the organization's institutional framework is not consistent with its present state of economic integration. They suggested developing ASEAN's legislative and institutional framework, making particular use of the ASEAN Inter-parliamentary Organization, AIPO, which has played only a secondary role in the region. Established in 1977 to encourage co-operation between the ASEAN member countries' parliaments, the AIPO was given no particular road map for doing so, and, because parliaments in many ASEAN countries have little power, the mission of the AIPO has been very limited. It has been merely one component in ASEAN's identity-building.

The Thai group did not suggest a strategy for negotiating the differing authority levels of ASEAN member parliaments. But the differences between member countries in this regard would be an issue if the AIPO were to become an independent organ integrated more closely into the

ASEAN decision-making system along the lines of the federalist model. The AIPO proposal did not have any federalist ambitions. At the same time, since legal developments in the ASEAN countries have taken place – formally or actually – in national parliaments, the study group noted the crucial need for co-operation among legislative bodies in the areas of trade liberalization and economic co-operation. Following the neo-functionalist model, the group suggested that the AIPO be linked to the ASEAN decision-making system by traditional means, that is, without trespassing on traditional consensus-building. The normative emphasis of the group further referred to neo-functionalism. The authors stated, "Once they [the ASEAN members] independently reach a satisfactory level of trade liberalization and investment, economic convergence would require them to work on related monetary and fiscal policies. In overall terms, regional integration is based on the concept of a point of no return."[3] Economic integration, which is a response to globalization, requires, in the present stage of ASEAN's economic co-operation, deeper "regional integration at the policy level".[4] An existing organization, such as the AIPO, offers a point of departure for this kind of integration. The AIPO should now take on the role of coordinating national legislative institutions critical to regional integration. The first step should be to integrate the AIPO into the existing ASEAN institutional structure, establishing important linkages between the AEM and the ASEAN secretariat. Next, the AIPO should focus on issues critical to ASEAN's integration process, primarily, the practical realization of trade and service liberalization as well as financial co-operation.[5]

The AIPO proposal made some of the most concrete suggestions for developing ASEAN's political integration. The nature of those suggestions reveals the underlying functionalism in ASEAN, already emphasized in Estrela Solidum's early writings. Now regional economic developments have made these functionalist ideas a reality.

At the Fourth ASEAN Informal Summit in November 2000, ASEAN issued an *Initiative for ASEAN Integration* (IAI). The initiative avoided addressing political integration, although the concept of regional integration had already been established as the norm. Seeing ASEAN as a single economy requiring integration in every sector, the *IAI* argued for the exploitation of new information technology (IT) among ASEAN, including common training, scholarships and exchange programs, and noted that particular concern should be paid to less developed ASEAN economies which require economic and technological support. While the *IAI* avoided the political aspects of integration, thus adhering to the traditional ASEAN way of developing regionalism, its emphasis on integration clearly indicated ASEAN's post-crisis trend of "functionalism in institutionalism".[6]

ASEAN AND EAST ASIAN INTEGRATION

Perhaps even more important than its proposals for ASEAN's internal evolution, was the reference the *Initiative for ASEAN Integration* made to East Asia. China, Japan and South Korea supported and contributed to the IAI in order to integrate information technology between ASEAN and East Asia, giving evidence for the growing importance of *ASEAN + 3* co-operation and offering another application of the old EAEC idea. Japan contributed 15 billion US dollars for a "Comprehensive Co-operation Package" of IT in Asia, and China gave 5 million USD to the ASEAN-China Co-operation Fund in order to create the "Asian IT Belt".[7] This kind of co-operation, touted openly in unofficial ASEAN circles, could have far reaching consequences. Clearly the EAEC idea has not lost its potency. The ex-President of the Philippines, Fidel Ramos, suggested that a convenient way for the EAEC to become a reality would be for the East Asian countries – China, Japan and South Korea – to accede to the AFTA treaty.[8] Officially, there has been no discussion of East Asia's joining AFTA. The negative stand of the US toward the EAEC has prevented Japan, in particular, from engaging in such discussions. However, the Asian economic crisis clearly proved the need for real co-operation between East Asian economic powers and ASEAN.

To accomplish this co-operation in a more practical, lower-profile way than through EAEC, ASEAN initiated the *ASEAN + 3*, which appeared for the first time in the middle of the crisis – December 1997 – during the second ASEAN Informal Summit in Kuala Lumpur. Originally the summit was planned as a festive occasion proclaiming the *ASEAN Vision 2020*. The economic crisis eclipsed those plans. Preceded by ASEAN's own initiatives to solve the Southeast Asian financial situation, the summit focused on the financial crisis. The IMF and the Western powers had rejected the ASEAN proposal – the Asian Fund – to which the East Asian countries would have contributed notable shares. The invitation of China, Japan and South Korea to this summit, then, can be understood in light of this rejection.

In Kuala Lumpur the East Asian countries were represented at the highest political level. The point of departure of *ASEAN + 3* co-operation was then financial and economic. The heads of states and the governments of *ASEAN + 3* met again in Hanoi in December 1998 and again in November 1999 at the third ASEAN Informal Summit in Manila, where, while carefully ignoring the ideological emphasis on the Asian model, they agreed to broaden practical economic and political co-operation. Not all of the ideas underlying the EAEC had disappeared, however. In fact, the *ASEAN + 3* political co-operation confirmed in the Joint Statement on East Asia Co-operation paralleled those areas already articulated in the EAEC, especially the co-ordination of policies in international forums such as the WTO and APEC.[9]

The Joint Statement pressed the need for Southeast Asian countries to rely, when confronted with global economic and political pressures, on powerful Asian countries. Among the member governments of ASEAN, different perceptions of East Asian co-operation have prevailed. For example, for Mahathir, East Asian co-operation would play an important role in preventing the United States from dividing East Asia; it would also help to form a defensive wall against economic, as well as ideological and cultural, attacks from the US.[10] In contrast to this, the Filipino ex-president Fidel Ramos, believes the EAEC or East Asian co-operation in general would provide for ASEAN a "continuing effort to keep in balance the three legs of the stool of global interdependence – Europe, East Asia and North America".[11]

At the Chiang Mai Meeting in Thailand *ASEAN + 3* was further institutionalized. The economic ministers' and the senior officials' meetings were regularized, and the decision-making mechanism were defined. *ASEAN +3* adopted practices similar to those established in ASEAN. *ASEAN +3* works by the *13-x* principle – if an issue has majority support, the countries that do not agree can retire from action. Absolute consensus is not needed.[12]

Although the East Asian countries signed neither a formal agreement of trade – such as AFTA – nor an important agreement on financial issues, ASEAN's attempts to strengthen ties with East Asia demonstrate an obvious trend in the post-economic-crisis era. The economic crisis demonstrated both Southeast Asia's dependency on US economic power as projected by the international economic regime and the political vulnerability of the ASEAN countries when hit by economic recession. Given the various permutations of political interest and the variety of co-operative possibilities, however, it remains to be seen when the intention to co-operate will turn into real political action.

ASEAN AND THE ENVIRONMENT: FROM TRADE ISSUES TO SUSTAINABLE DEVELOPMENT

Several factors suggest that a regional framework is most favorable for environmental policies. Most environmental problems are too large for single states to handle, while international agreements have proved too general and abstract to achieve concrete solutions. The EU's environmental policies provide a promising example of this regional approach. But, despite the fact that environmental issues have long been on ASEAN's agenda of functional co-operation, ASEAN's actual record in environmental protection is very modest. With the assistance of the United Nations Environmental Program (UNEP), ASEAN co-operation on the environment started with the ASEAN Subregional Environment Program (ASEP) in 1977. ASEP II and ASEP III followed, along with the ASEAN Strategic Plan of Action on the Environment in 1994 and again in 1998. These programs were supplemented with several ASEAN declarations, joint communiqués and agreements.[13] But because of ASEAN's basic axiom of non-interference in member countries' domestic affairs, the organization's good intentions of forming regional environmental governance have run into problems of monitoring and control.

ASEAN inefficiency in environmental matters can be compared with the inefficiency of international conventions and can be understood in light of the nature of the organization. The differences between ASEAN and the EU are huge: The EU has its own extensive environmental legislation that must be implemented by each member country's own legislation. Environmental governance in the EU, however, has not been an end in itself. Rather, through environmental legislation, the EU has tried to accommodate the conditions for competition among different parts of the community, taking the principle of free trade as a priority. If one member country's environmental legislation restrains free trade, it needs to be abolished; if the EU has passed an environmental law, each country has to execute it in the name of free competition.[14] Unlike the EU, ASEAN has not formed a common free trade area inside its common borders but has instead promoted open regionalism and open global competition. The ASEAN members' participation in APEC has further enforced this situation. Despite its several environmental initiatives, the nature of APEC as well as the aim of its de facto leader, the US, has been to open Asian and Pacific markets. Effective environmental protection would in effect set non-tariff barriers and run counter to that aim.

In this way, ASEAN's attempts to take advantage of globalization have always overridden its environmental considerations. Its activities in the GATT and in the WTO clearly continue this pattern. The eagerness of some ASEAN members – particularly Malaysia – to blame the concerns of Western environmentalists on colonialism should be understood in this light.[15] ASEAN's basic strategy to access world markets combined with its loose organizational structure and strong emphasis on national sovereignty, has made inevitable its poor environmental record and justified its image as an organization which talks much but does little.

The huge differences among ASEAN member countries in environmental legislation and management as well as in environmental circumstances also accounts for ASEAN's very modest environmental record. The addition to ASEAN of the four new and poor members has further complicated the situation. Singapore, a small but well-organized city-state, has advanced the furthest on this front, developing an umbrella environmental agency and investing considerable resources in environmental management. On the other side, environmental protection and management has fared poorly in the Philippines and Indonesia. Both countries consist of very fragmented territories, and in both weak administrations have had difficulties in management. Political changes have altered environmental priorities in some countries, particularly in the Philippines after the fall of Marcos.[16] And Indonesia's disordered political and economic situation leaves little possibility for coherent environmental management.

ASEAN has had more success in managing trade-related environmental issues than it has in protecting its members' environments. These trade-related environmental issues have revolved largely around the question of the deforestation taking place in Indonesia, Malaysia, the Philippines and Thailand caused largely by uncontrolled logging of the rain forests. Despite several ASEAN statements and agreements, ASEAN had assumed a defensive posture on the issue instead of acknowledging the problem. But in the late 1990s two factors came together to force a change in the ASEAN posture. Environmentalist and consumer movements started affecting the trade regime, and haze from illegal burning of the rain forests on several occasions severely degraded Southeast Asian air quality. ASEAN responded to these challenges in two ways. Both the ASEAN countries and the ASEAN organization started to activate environmental standardization and eco-labeling. The ASEAN Strategic Plan of Action had laid down common environmental quality standards in 1994, and now ASEAN started to develop an eco-labeling system based on ISO 14000 standardization. Single ASEAN countries also developed their own eco-labeling and forest standardization systems based on different certification schemes, as discussed earlier.

The effect of attempts at environmental standardization is questionable, however. For example, much of the demand which burdens the environments of the ASEAN countries comes from Japan. Japanese consumers have not required certified products to the extent that Western consumers have. In the short run, as Southeast Asia increases its exports to Japanese and Chinese markets, the insistence on eco-labeling in the Western countries may shift timber trade away from the West and toward Asian countries.[17]

The haze problem, however, which coincided with the financial crisis in 1997, cannot be so easily sidestepped. Trying to solve it has forced ASEAN to link trade policies with environmental considerations. The forest fires, largely caused by illegal logging by farmers and big timber companies, reached dimensions impossible to ignore. The fires burned mostly on the Indonesian side of Borneo and Sumatra, but also in some parts of the Malaysian Peninsula. The problem was so severe that truly effective environmental measures became necessary. In East Kalimantan about 4 million hectares of forests and other lands burned, the equivalent of twice the area of Taiwan.[18] The haze pollution caused by the fires endangered the quality of air in large areas of the region, in Sumatra, Kalimantan, Sarawak, but also in mainland Malaysia and Singapore. Health problems and setbacks in the economy resulted.

The Strategic Plan of Action for the Environment, 1999–2004, and particularly the Regional Haze Action Plan (RHAP), endorsed by the ASEAN Environment Ministers in December 1997, acknowledged that this transboundary haze problem caused by forest fires in one member country called for a regional monitoring system. In April 1999, ASEAN adopted a zero-burning policy and obligated all member countries to enforce the laws and regulations of this policy.[19] The ASEAN Environmental Ministers in April 2000 agreed to take measures to deal with offenders and enforce the zero-burning policy. According to ASEAN secretary sources, these measures resulted in the investigation and prosecution of a number of plantation companies accused of illegal open burning.[20]

Interestingly enough, the common ASEAN policy to solve the haze problem led to supranational development in the region. It became absolutely clear that regional policies had to be realized at the local level or the problem would reoccur. More environmentally friendly forest management standards and mechanisms for their effective implementation had to be devised. In the *Special Report on Forest Fires and Haze Situation in Indonesia and Action Taken* ASEAN urged its member countries to adopt the zero-burning policy into their national legislation.[21] Even though the problem of the haze in 1997 and 1998 had centered on Indonesia, the ASEAN measures covered the whole region. The efficiency of implementation of ASEAN policy at the local level is still an open question and will surely depend on the responses of the individual countries. Even though the concern for environmental protection did not particularly determine ASEAN policy in this issue, the tendency signaled by that policy was clear and important – the institutionalist mechanism of ASEAN was directing the organization into a functionalist development of integration.

ASEAN AND THE NGOS: REGIONALISM FROM BELOW[22]

In discussions either of *new* or *old* regionalism, regionalist theories have been concerned with regional integration mostly as governments' efforts toward regional co-operation. I have examined Southeast Asian regionalism from this point of view, too. Functionalist theories do provide paradigms in which regional integration follows economic and social integration and governmental roles become less significant. During the 1990s communication technology, particularly information technology, advanced to such an extent that non-governmental interaction in cultural, social and political fields increased significantly. The general trends of this regionalism *from below* need to be noted. These trends hold true not only for interaction on the Southeast Asian regional level but also on the global level.

In fact, ASEAN has a long record of taking advantage of the NGOs. ASEAN's diplomacy has been partly based on the second-track discussions of so-called ASEAN NGOs, a network of semi-official NGOs. The ASEAN web-site acknowledges 54 such affiliated organizations. They include a variety of associations, from the ASEAN Chambers of Commerce to the ASEAN Chess Association. Other groups, such as ASEAN-ISIS, have played significant roles in ASEAN's decision-making system. I am not discussing here such ASEAN affiliated NGOs, but rather those groups which deal with the more politically delicate social, environmental, and ethnic issues.

Two particular characteristics mark these NGOs. First, the boundaries familiar to regional co-operation do not bind them. The environmental and human rights NGOs have embraced a more global context, while the NGOs concerned with social, labor and trade issues have situated themselves in a more regional context, although they have not limited their activities only to the ASEAN area. Their activities often have global linkages or even global co-ordination, although some organizations operate solely on the local level. Secondly they may be part of global governance in the field of their activities, in environmental, social or human rights sectors. The governance can be direct or indirect through their donors – often development agencies, international organizations such as the UN, the World Bank and the ADB or globally acting mother organizations as is particularly the case with many environmental organizations. Many NGOs have close connections to academic institutions and important opinion-makers. Increasingly, the growing funding for developmental and consultative projects funneled through these NGOs has created hundreds or thousands of careers for educated English-speaking academics in these countries.

These groups increasingly use internet networks and co-operate globally with other groups in their fields. Often large politico-economic themes unite them globally. NGOs came together to oppose the Multilateral Agreement on Investments (MAI) negotiated by the OECD and intended for adoption by the WTO. More locally, for example, NGOs worked together to support the campaign of Anwar Ibrahim during his trial.

Because of their economic and philosophical ties, these organizations, although operating regionally, do not necessarily ascribe to the ASEAN concept of regionalism. For some, the reason for this rejection is that they apply for funding from international donors. They often adopt attitudes critical toward the economic and cultural aspects of globalism and economic liberalism. These attitudes flow from a variety of sources – from nationalist tendencies to more sophisticated economic and social analyses. Many of these organizations view some ASEAN innovations, such as AFTA, quite negatively, largely because of ASEAN's officially uncritical stance toward global trade liberalization. Some make a more complex analysis. The Bangkok-based *Focus on the Global South*, a particularly expertise-based NGO, for example, examines critically the premises of economic liberalism but does not reject ASEAN, since it sees the regional organization as exerting a force counterbalancing US economic power. Some NGOs ignore ASEAN because of the sectors they operate in. For example, NGOs working with environmental issues and having global mother organizations often do not work regionally.

Southeast Asian NGOs have attracted a good deal of media coverage, and their activities have sometimes been surprisingly successful. It is still open to question, though, whether they can offer, in regard to regional co-operation, alternatives to governmental co-operation. Perhaps it is unproductive to see NGOs and governmental regional organizations as oppositional. As international relations change all over the world, the channels NGOs use may open up new pathways for regional co-operation. Characteristically, these new networks have so far – as in the case of forest certification – eliminated altogether the need for governmental intervention, although the situation varies among Southeast Asian countries. Furthermore, the new networks are promoting through their channels alternative information and expressing interests unheard of from official sources or the mainstream media.

9 Conclusion: Southeast Asian Regionalism: Old or New?

Estimating the success of ASEAN as a regional organization is difficult. ASEAN has had obvious success in maintaining a peaceful international environment. The ASEAN governments readily refer to this absence of war among the members during the last 30 years as well as to the organization's growth – especially its incorporation of the old socialist countries. On the other hand, ASEAN has not been able to influence real economic cooperation or make significant impact on important sectors such as environmental protection. These failings make it difficult to value ASEAN as an example of regionalism.[1] From the point of view of *open regionalism*, however, these failings do not lessen ASEAN's value. Within the paradigm of *open regionalism*, ASEAN's success in economic terms can be measured, not by the levels of integration achieved in the region, but by how effectively ASEAN cooperation has attracted foreign direct investments into the region.

These two standards of success for regional cooperation – valuing, on the one hand, intra-regional trade, and valuing, on the other hand, supra-national institutions, conveniently fits the dichotomy of the *new* and the *old* regionalism. This dichotomy justifies Norman Palmer's thesis at the same time as it confirms the basic axioms of Hettne's *new regionalism* program. The *new regionalism* refers to regional developments undertaken after the Cold War within a multilateral international system, whereas "the old regionalism was marked by bipolarity" and describes Cold War regional developments, especially in Europe.[2] Within this general historical framework, however, Hettne found the identification of new patterns of regionalization to be more fruitful than the identification of a new period of regionalization.[3] If the distinction between the old and new regionalism rests only on historical periods, moreover, the operational value of the distinction for future discussions disappears. This analytical struggle obscures the whole *new regionalism* program.

This study has not tried to evaluate Southeast Asian regionalism by referring to stages of regional cooperation – the estimations made here on intra-ASEAN trade, for example, refer only to the context of the regionalist debate. This study has, rather, traced the development of regional thinking in the ASEAN region in the post-Cold War period of 1990–2000, dealing with the construction of regionalism in Southeast Asia and in the ASEAN organization as well as with political responses to certain global and regional challenges. This study takes the same point of departure as the *new regionalism* debate in the sense that it discusses globalization as power, economic influence, and interdependence and understands regionalism as government-led processes developed in response to that globalization.

This study argues that regionalist discourse, when regional governments and regional organizations are included, follows some general trends and that institutionalism, functionalism and realism not only describe European regionalist discourse, but also articulate general approaches that take shape within particular regional and political contexts.

This study traces an interesting example of regionalism as a response to globalization in the Southeast Asian context and, to that end, examines both intra-ASEAN and extra-ASEAN relations. In that examination intra-ASEAN cooperation with regard to political, economic and security issues sheds light on regionalist ideas and regionalist construction in ASEAN co-operation. ASEAN's relations toward the external world show ASEAN's concrete attempts to deal with globalization. The Southeast Asian economic crisis, examined in the last part of the book, in particular provides an opportunity to analyze regional responses toward the challenges of globalism.

This study suggests that the main form of ASEAN political cooperation is institutionalism. This institutionalism alone, which emphasizes the role of common norms and rules in intergovernmental cooperation and underestimates the importance of supra-national governance, guided ASEAN's political cooperation in the beginning of the 1990s. Before the creation of AFTA, it prescribed the terms of economic cooperation as well. In fact, ASEAN institutionalism, as a mode of political cooperation, inspired the concept of the *new regionalism* and for good reason. ASEAN regionalism grew out of the need for political co-operation, for the most part free from the kind of economic motivation that drove European integration. The initiative for cooperation came from the regional governments, not from the economic sector. Since the purpose of those governments was to maintain regional peace, the levels of practical and functional intergovernmental cooperation remained low. Nonetheless, the distinction between European and ASEAN regionalism is not as clear as many proponents of the *new regionalism* suggest. In the European functionalist approach regional peace originally provided a very important motive for cooperation. And even though the emphasis on the institutionalist approach was much stronger in Southeast Asian regionalism than in Europe, as discussed earlier, the ideas of regional economic relations, co-operation and interdependence were not totally missing from Southeast Asian regionalist discourse.

The institutionalist approach further guided the ASEAN enlargement process when the economically backward Indochinese countries and the politically difficult Burma joined the organization. During the enlargement process, the emphasis on national sovereignty, non-intervention and the principle of *constructive engagement* gained strength and were confirmed as the norms and rules of ASEAN interstate relations and the bases of regional cooperation.

The ASEAN trac- two expertise groups took part in the constructive efforts to establish ASEAN cooperation on an institutionalist foundation. The same method was used in ASEAN's extended security approach, the ASEAN Regional Forum. Since by the mid-1990s it seemed obvious that possible threats to Southeast Asian security came from external sources – such as China in the South China Sea issues and in its relations with Taiwan and the unresolved situation in the Korean Peninsula – the goal of the ARF was to extend the ASEAN code of behavior to a greater Asia-Pacific environment. In this way the second-track expertise community criticized the narrowness of ASEAN's approach at the same time as it tried to construct a broader base for ASEAN's norms.

In fact, the ASEAN expertise group turned against the ASEAN institutionalist approach even earlier in the field of economic cooperation. Before AFTA, ASEAN tried to apply to economic relations the same concept that had worked in political co-operation – decision-making based on consensus. The ASEAN Preferential Trade Agreement subscribed to the idea that ASEAN decisions should not harm the vital interests of any member country. But since the structure of production was very similar in the member countries, achieving effective trade liberalization in important sectors became difficult. The constraint of consensus made the ASEAN PTA a dead letter.

The ASEAN economists, then, first challenged the institutionalist approach in ASEAN regionalism. Unlike the advocates of the *new regionalism,* the economists saw integration as an important part of regional cooperation. The world *integration* appeared for first time in ASEAN regional discourse as economists argued against the PTA and for a more comprehensive regional trade agreement. The PTA failed because of the lack of co-ordination among the governments. A more comprehensive trade agreement – a free trade agreement or even a customs union – would necessitate supra-national developments to allow for monitoring and governing the participating members.

Economic arguments for regional cooperation appeared elsewhere, too. In Vietnam, in the early 1990s, membership in ASEAN was seen as an economically important step allowing Vietnam to take advantage of Southeast Asian regionalism and even broader globalization trends. Similarly, the old ASEAN members saw economic possibilities in new Indochinese markets. It came as a surprise, then, that the new ASEAN Free Trade Agreement, AFTA, did not remarkably boost intra-ASEAN trade. The idea as such was good, and the trade liberalization program was comprehensive. The schedule of reducing intra-ASEAN trade was even hastened several times. At the same time as the creation of AFTA, the position of the ASEAN Secretary was strengthened and some authority to monitor the agreement was given to a supranational body. Still, the agreement shied away form overstepping national sovereignty and permitted governments the possibility of later reservations. When similar regional trade agreements promoting regionalization and globalization appeared elsewhere, it became obvious that AFTA's schedule for tariff reductions and the absence of the measures against non-tariff barriers rendered the process ineffective.

The AFTA process proved the need for economic integration in ASEAN, the organization said to represent the *new regionalism* in the Asia-Pacific area. I am inclined to argue not only that integration and functionalist arguments are part of regionalist debate all over the world, but also that the tendency toward integration is apparent in all regional organizations having political and economic motives.

Realism in ASEAN regionalism appeared particularly in relation to questions of economic power and ASEAN's external relations. In the 1980s it worked to unite ASEAN members in the diplomatic stand they took in international organizations against Vietnam's occupation of Cambodia – the Kampuchean issue. During the 1990s the realism approach surfaced again when the GATT negotiations and the WTO offered to ASEAN a possibility to unite its ranks, first against protective trade measures – particularly in Europe – and then against environmental, social and political conditioning in world trade issues.

Two different realism-type approaches have guided ASEAN responses to external trade issues. The neorealist approach, represented particularly by the Singaporean leadership, sees the global system as composed of actors pursuing economic interests and political power. In this context, ASEAN countries should work together and find allies so that ASEAN may gain advantage whenever possible. In the other realist approach, represented by Malaysian Premier Mahathir, political power in the present world system is particularly projected by economic means. The powerful Western countries try to dominate developing countries in order to preserve their economic and political position. In this scheme, governments do not act alone. Western trade unions together with environmental and human rights organizations join forces with the US in an attempt to preserve its hegemony. In order to resist this Western economic and cultural dominance, the ASEAN countries should ally with the powerful Eastern economic and political powers – Japan and China.

These two realist-based approaches inform ASEAN's policies toward Asian and Pacific co-operation as well as ASEAN relations with the EU. ASEAN's policies in Asia and the Pacific are dominated both by economic relations and by security concerns. As a regional organization, ASEAN has articulated a plainer policy in politico-economic matters, expressed particularly in the ARF, than in security issues. The latent tension between the ASEAN approach and the US policy on trade liberalization has dominated politico-economic matters. The conflict of interest between ASEAN and the US has come into sharp focus on the question of the EAEC, although that situation is apparently less straightforward than those who interpret the US as nullifying East Asian economic and political cooperation suggest.[4] ASEAN member states express a variety of distinct interests in East Asian cooperation, too. For Malaysia, the EAEC is a test of economic and political struggle between East Asia and the US, while for many ASEAN governments it is a bargaining tool important to maintaining the tripolar world order between the US, East Asia and the EU.

The ASEAN-EU relationship, developed in the Europe-Asia meeting, reflects this tripolar world order. Despite the two regional organizations' obviously different interests in the liberalization of world trade and in the linkage between world trade regulations and certain social, political and environmental issues, ASEAN has tried to reinforce this tripolarity with the EU. This move boldly reveals the realism at work in ASEAN's regionalism. From the perspective of economic and political power relations, a world order based on multilateralism would benefit ASEAN.

The weaknesses of Southeast Asian regionalism came into sharp relief during the Asian economic crisis. The crisis revealed the importance of the multilateral approach, the limits of institutionalism as an organizing principle in regional cooperation, and the inability of a regionalism bereft of functioning common institutions to manage the economies of its members.

First of all, the economic crisis exploded the image of the economic superiority of ASEAN economies; that image had been an important part of constructing Asian values. Although Asian values had played an ambiguous role in ASEAN cooperation, the success of the ASEAN economies argued against any criticism of ASEAN cooperative practices. When economic growth and success was linked to the Asian values debate, this growth shielded institutionalism and seem to prove its efficacy. But when the growth turned negative, Southeast Asian regionalism seemed powerless to support economic welfare.

The political crises that followed the depressions in Malaysia and particularly in Indonesia also eroded the image of regionalism and the ASEAN organization. The political turmoil called into question the basic ASEAN principles of sovereignty and non-intervention at the same time as it rendered possible the intervention from outside the region. Although, as the discussion of *constructive intervention* proved, some ASEAN countries wanted to have a stronger hold on ASEAN's affairs, it remains doubtful that effective intervention could have been mounted from the ASEAN side into the domestic affairs of its members, most of whom continued the strong tendency to defend old principles of sovereignty and non-intervention. These governments obviously preferred foreign intervention to ASEAN intervention, fearing that intervention from inside the organization would cause unbearable tensions and, in the worst case, armed conflict between member countries.

Besides highlighting ASEAN's own internal weakness, the economic crisis showed ASEAN's vulnerability to economic pressure from the international financial regime. Long-standing economic growth had veiled ASEAN members' economic vulnerability to international capital flows and ASEAN's own structural inability to undertake common measures to stabilize member economies. During the crisis, the world financial regime and international financial authorities totally ignored the ASEAN organization, dealing bilaterally with the ASEAN countries. The members had to confront huge economic power without any regional support.

Prior to the crisis, the economic success of the individual countries and the organization's ability to find allies had earned ASEAN some bargaining power in international organizations, particularly in the world trade regime. In the critical moment of the economic crisis, however, this bargaining power collapsed. That collapse produced two kinds of suggestions from within ASEAN. The first kind proposed that ASEAN protect itself from external economic pressure by developing its own internal coherence through more profound economic and political cooperation. Although ASEAN's concrete moves toward economic cooperation had come largely from IMF and World Bank demands to liberate its member countries' trade and economies, the plans and suggestions offered by different ASEAN governments revealed a real tendency toward supranational integration in ASEAN. Despite rather utopian suggestions for currency cooperation, unworkable because the economic crisis had made the governments extremely weak, these proposals indicated that ASEAN governments had given up their old claim of absolute sovereignty. Although ASEAN is not yet ready to develop supra-national institutions, owing to heterogeneous member economies and post-crisis political instabilities, clearly current trends in Southeast Asian regionalism point in the direction of new integration in the neofunctionalist mode. The haze problem, which occurred simultaneously with the crisis, also called for effective common measures that presuppose integration in environmental policies and legislation.

The second kind of crisis-inspired suggestion coming from within ASEAN proposed that ASEAN enforce the policy of multilateralism in external relations. This means that ASEAN should abandon none of its relations with the US, East Asia or Japan. In the post-economic crisis period ASEAN's *ASEAN + 3* policy toward East Asia most obviously illustrates this approach. This policy not only seeks to achieve a more balanced interdependence but acknowledges the fact that East Asia, rather than more remote markets in the US and Europe, forms the most natural environment for ASEAN's trade and investments. Important security concerns, however, continue to give to the US an important position in the area. This multilateralist approach indicates a change in ASEAN's external policy – it will operate no longer only as a pressure group but will work to forge common policies between world political and economic centers. Especially with regard to political and social issues connected with trade, for example, ASEAN's adoption of more accommodating attitudes reflects this change.

Regionalist ideas in Southeast Asia in general and ASEAN cooperation in particular have made use of the principles of institutionalism, functionalism and realism. Similarly, these ideas have also structured the concrete measures taken in the region to deal with the questions of regionalism and globalism. Owing to the phase of nation-building common in Southeast Asian countries, intergovernmental cooperation has predominated in these efforts. ASEAN has not given up consensus-based decision-making or non-intervention, although new ideas seriously challenge these old ideas.

Far from being a Southeast Asian peculiarity, intergovernmentalism is a very important tendency in the EU, too. Various institutions – governmental or private – push either in this direction or in the supra-nationalist direction. I argue here that these tendencies are common to regional organizations in general. I am inclined to avoid dichotomizing different types of regionalism. Instead, I see the varying balances between the forces of intergovernmentalism and supra-nationalism in regional organizations as indicative of the stage of development of member countries, the structure of production and trade within member countries, and the nature of the interdependencies those countries have formed with the external world. Regionalism is thus composed of these elements, although in ASEAN responses to globalization have been largely framed by individual member countries.

The Asian economic crisis proves the weakness of regionalism and regional organization based only on the constructivist idea of institutionalism. Similarly, the crisis challenges the current constructivist tendency of the social sciences to shy away from assigning differential value to various constructions of reality. The Asian economic crisis has shown us the high stakes of such hesitancy. In that crisis a largely imaginary form of economic activity – international currency trade – shook governments, threw large strata of the regional population into economic turmoil and caused famine and ethnic violence. The institutionalist kind of regionalism developed by ASEAN was powerless to help its member countries or their people. This sobering realization should urge social scientists to understand as limited the workable patterns of regional cooperation.

Notes and References

1 INTRODUCTION: ANALYZING SOUTHEAST ASIAN REGIONALIST EFFORTS

[1] Volumes 1–4 were available in December 2000.
[2] Hettne 1999a, xix.
[3] Hettne 1994, 1–2 and 1999b, 7.
[4] Palmer 1991.
[5] Eliassen and Monsen 1998, 2, 19–26.
[6] For example, Dewi Anwar Fortuna (1994, 2–3) warns of those cleavages which Western observers have made when they analyze ASEAN from the point of view of Western European model.
[7] Clark 1997, Hettne 1997, Sideri 1997 and Payne and Gamble 1996.
[8] Acharya 1999, 6 and Acharya 1997.
[9] Solidum 1974, 172.
[10] Ibid. 10.
[11] Ibid. 8, 170, see also Kurus 1995, 405–6.
[12] Haas 1989, Antolik 1990 and Palmer 1991.
[13] Solidum 1974, 171, 174–7.
[14] See Ariff 1996.
[15] Kartadjoemena 1996, 12.
[16] Akrasanee and Stifel 1994, 11.
[17] Paderanga 1995, 15.
[18] Ibid.
[19] See, Suthiphand Chirathivat et al. 1999 and Ortuoste 1999.
[20] Whether this is a "hard fact" is an open question, as the whole concept of Southeast Asia is rather a new construction and, for example, Laos and Cambodia may have much more common with Sri Lanka than with the Philippines. Anderson 1998, 3–8.
[21] Bunn Nagara 1996, 44–48.
[22] Solidum 1981, 130.
[23] Ibid., 135.
[24] See, Jusuf Wanandi 1996, 10–11.
[25] Noordin Sopiee 1992, 20.
[26] A good example in which institutionalist expert advice turns to neo-functionalist ideas is Maria Consuelo C. Ortuoste's contemplation on the future of ASEAN in a post-economic crisis situation. Ortueste's suggestions to develop the ASEAN organization include the development of another decision-making mechanism on the side of mushawarah and mufakat and to abandon the concept of absolute sovereignty among the ASEAN states. Ortuoste 1999.
[27] Sideri 1997.

28 MacIntyre 1995, 162.
29 See Malay 1997, 81–84 and Din Merican 1996, 9.
30 Nesadurai 1996.
31 Talib 1998.
32 Sopiee 1992, 18.
33 *Diliman Review* 1997, 1.
34 Rethinking the Thirld World, 50.
35 Parreñas 1995, 22.
36 Ibid., 26.
37 Paribatra 1994, 256.
38 Abdad 1996, 241–2.
39 Hernandez 1997.
40 Tay and Talib 1997.
41 See Caballero-Anthony 1998.
42 Lam Lai Sing 1994.
43 Lim 1998, 121–2.
44 See, for example, Evans and Rowley 1984, 204–216.
45 Acharya 1998, xvii.
46 See, for example, a long-serving Malaysian cabinet member, Tan Sri Muhammad Ghazali bin Shafie, October 22, 1974, in Shafie 1982, 226 and Minister of Foreign Affairs of Thailand, Chatichai Choonhavan, August 5, 1975, FAB, Vol. XV, No. 3, 59–60.
47 Malaysian Minister of Foreign Affairs, YBM Tengku Ahmad Rithauddeen, November 24 1977, FAM December 1977, 40. See also A. Rahim Ishak, Singaporean Senior Minister of State for Foreign Affairs, March 29, Speeches Vol. 1, No. 10, April 1978, 56–57.
48 S. Rajaratnam, Singaporean Minister of Foreign Affairs, June 14, 1978 and January 19, 1979, Speeches Vol. 2, No. 1, July 1978, 23 and Speeches Vol. 2, No. 8. February 1979, 25. See also S. Dhanabalan, Singaporean Senior Minister of State for Foreign Affairs, March 11, 1980, Speeches Vol. 3, No. 10, April 1980, 107.
49 Hänggi 1991, 15–16.
50 Ibid., 12–20.
51 Malaysian Minister of Foreign Affairs, Tengku Datuk Ahmad Rithauddeen, March 20, 1976, FAM March 1976, 69, see also Tan Sri Muhammad Ghazali bin Shafie, October 22, 1974, in Shafie 1982, 223–26, 230.
52 See, for example, S. Dhanabalan, Singaporean Senior Minister of State for Foreign Affairs, March 11, 1980, Speeches Vol. 3, No. 10, April 1980, 106.
53 Ismail Kassim "Why Singapore Begs to Differ", New Nation, November 4, 1977.
54 Tan Sri Muhammad Ghazali bin Shafie, October 22, 1974, in Shafie 1982, 230.
55 Mahathir 1995, 119–121.

56 Interestingly enough, Thailand's Deputy Prime Minister Thanat Khoman's analysis followed rather closely the Singaporean view on the role of external powers in Southeast Asia. See "National Threat Perceptions in East Asia and the Pacific", FAN 4, 1982, 7–8.

57 Even Thanat Khoman, who signed the Bangkok Declaration for Thailand, emphasized ASEAN's role as an instrument for breaking up colonial ties in Southeast Asia. Thanat Khoman 1992, xvii–xviii.

58 The Speech Delivered by Dr Ahmed Soekarno, President of the Republic of Indonesia, September 1, 1961. In The Conference of Heads of State or Government of Non-Aligned Countries, Belgrade, September 1–6, 1961. Beograd: Publicisticko-Izdavacki Zavod "Jugoslavija" 1961, 31.

59 Sukarno's hostile attitude toward the establishment of the Malaysian Federation is explained as his attempt to resist British neo-colonialism. See, Anwar 1994, 24–25.

60 See Lee Kuan Yew's speech at the Socialist International Conference Council on September 3, 1964, in One Hundred Years of Socialism, a Ministry of Culture Publication, Malaya Engraving & Litho Printing Co., 19–24, also Kwok Kian-Woon 1999, 55–57 and Hong Lysa 1999, 98–99.

61 Vatikiotis 1996, 76–77.

62 Accordingly, the role of older colonialists was now taken by the trade unions in Western Europe, which want to reject the economic development of the former colonies. See, for example, Singaporean Minister for Foreign Affairs, S Rajaratnam, October 4, 1977, Speeches Vol. 1, No. 5, November 1977, 37–38 and parliamentary discussion in Singapore, Singapore Parliament, Parliamentary Debates, Official Report, January 12, 1979, 182–3.

63 Anwar 1994, 51–52.

64 See Palmujoki 1997, 104.

65 The decision had certain internal bases as the dominating Chinese businesses have had traditionally close ties with the British. (See particularly Mahathir's famous book "the Malay Dilemma", 1970). Therefore this was a part of creating opportunities for bumiputra (Malay) business.

66 Rajaratnam, June 14, 1978, Speeches, Vol. 2, No. 1, July 1978, 23.

67 Senior Minister of State for Foreign Affairs, March 29, 1978, Speeches Vol. 1, No. 10, April 1978, 52.

68 See, Harris & Bridges 1983.

69 Sudo 1992, 77–109.

70 See, Ajanant 1997, 15 and Anwar 1994, 69–70, Tan 1992.

71 The weakness of the secretariat has been, according to Thanat Khoman (1992, p. xx) due to the suspicion of the member countries toward each other.

72 The Straits Times, September 18, 1989.

[73] Anwar 1994, 2–3.
[74] Rajaratnam, November 18, 1977, Speeches Vol . 1, No. 5, November 1977, 26.
[75] See, for example, Beng-Huat Chua 1995 and Hill & Lian Kwen Fee 1995.
[76] Asian Development Bank 1997, 16–18.
[77] Ibid., 34.
[78] Tu Wei-ming 1990.
[79] Bangkok Declaration 1993.
[80] See early NGOs' critic "Human Rights in the Region", Statement of the Third General Assembly. Regional Council on Human Rights in Asia, Penang, Malaysia December 7–10, 1985. See also "The Asia Pacific Non-Governmental Organizations' Bangkok Statement and Response to the Bangkok Declaration" (1993).
[81] See particularly the papers of the conference arranged by Just World Trust, International Conference on Rethinking Human Rights, 6–7 December 1994, Kuala Lumpur where the question of human rights was changed to the question of the Western attempt to dominate the developing countries.
[82] Chan Heng Chee 1993, 17.
[83] Ibid., 21–25.

2 WIDENING OR DEEPENING REGIONAL COOPERATION?

[1] See, for example, Mayall 1990, 111–125.
[2] TAC, Article 2, *ADS*, 35.
[3] Declaration of ASEAN Concord, Bali 24 February 1976, *ADS*, 32.
[4] Joint Communique of the Twenty-Third ASEAN Ministerial Meeting, Jakarta, 24–25 July 1990.
[5] Ibid.
[6] Palmujoki 1990, 140.
[7] See, for example, Mahathir 1992, 3.
[8] Surin Maisrikrod 1992, 299.
[9] Palmujoki 1997, 173–196.
[10] Ibid., 195.
[11] See particularly Wurfel 1999.
[12] Mahathir, January 4 and March 4 1991, <www.smpke.jpm.my>.
[13] *Interaction for Progress* 1991.
[14] Tran Quang Co 1996, *Nghien Cuu Quoc Te*, No.1, 5.
[15] *Shared Destiny* 1993, 20.
[16] Ibid., 26.
[17] Hoang An Tuan 1994, 261–264.

[18] *VIII National Congress Documents*.
[19] Thayer 1999, 12.
[20] *Shared Destiny* 1993, 20–27.
[21] Ibid., 25.
[22] Ibid., 26–27.
[23] For these critical expectations, see Sukhumbhand Paribatra 1994, 253.
[24] Bangkok Summit Declaration of 1995, <www.aseansec.org/summit/5th/summit5.html>.
[25] Kusuma Snitwongse 1995, 3–7.
[26] Mahathir, September 26, 1991, <www.smpke.jpm.my/pm/speeches.html>.
[27] Keynote address by the Minister of Foreign Affairs on "ASEAN – Shared Identities, Interests and Values" at the forum in Kuala Lumpur on 4 March 1996, *FAM*, 29 (1) March 1996, 31.
[28] Ariff 1997, 66.
[29] Mahathir, October 14, 1992 and January 6, 1993, <www.smpke.jpm.my/pm/speeches.html>.
[30] Mahathir, December 14, 1995, <www.smpke.jpm.my/pm/speeches.html>.
[31] Press Statement, The First Informal ASEAN Heads of Government Meeting, Jakarta, November 1996, <www.aseansec.org./summit/prias96.htm>.
[32] See for example, Professor S. Jayakumar, Singaporean Foreign Minister at Georgetown University April 22, 1996, <app.internet.gov.sg/scripts/mfa/>.
[33] Sukhumphand Paribatra 1997, 6.
[34] Kavi Chongkittavorn 1997, 24.
[35] Kusuma Snitwongse 1995, 7 and Sukhumbhand Paribatra 1997, 9–12.
[36] Thaung Tun 1997, 14.
[37] Thu My 1997, 204.
[38] Sukhumbhand Paribatra, *ASEAN-ISIS Monitor*, no.13, March 1996, 7.
[39] K.S. Balakrishnan, 1995, 19.
[40] Thitinan Pongsudhirak, 1995.
[41] ASEAN Standing Committee, Annual Report 1996–1997, <www.asean.or.id>
[42] *FEER*, December 12, 1996, 18.
[43] Press Statement The First Informal ASEAN Heads of Government Meeting Jakarta, 30 November 1996, <www.asean.or.id>.
[44] See for example, *Bangkok Post*, April 27, 1997 "Thailand rejects US appeal".
[45] Singaporean Prime Minister Goh Chok Tong's interview, *FEER*, December 24, 1998, <www.feer.com/Restricted/98dec_24/cover2.html>.

46 See, for example, Thai Prime Minister Chuan Leekpai at the Opening Ceremony of the Sixth ASEAN Summit, 15 December 1998, Hanoi, <www.asean.or.id/summit/6th/prg_opth.htm>.

47 Ibid.

48 See Thanat Khoman 1992, xx and Akrasanee and Stifel 1992, 30–31.

49 Sree Kumar 1992, 73.

50 Ibid., 73–75.

51 Bowles 1997, 225.

52 Naya and Imada 1987, 22–24, Alburo 1992, 205.

53 See, for example, Singaporean Prime Minister Lee Kuan Yew's opening address at the 15th ASEAN Ministerial Meeting. *15th ASEAN Ministerial Meeting and Post-Ministerial Meeting with the Dialogue Countries, Singapore 14–18 June 1982.*

54 Alburo 1992, 203.

55 Alburo 1992, 205.

56 Naya 1987, 39–45.

57 Imada, Montes & Naya 1991, 34.

58 See for example, *the Informal Meeting of the ASEAN Economic Ministers*, Singapore, 29–30 October 1987, Press Release.

59 Mahathir, October 7, 1991, <www.smpke.jpm.my/pm/speeches.html>.

60 Gochoco-Bautista and Faustino 1994, 39–40.

61 Mahathir, January 27, 1992, <www.smpke.jpm.my/pm/speeches.html>.

62 Singapore Declaration, 28 January 1992, <www.asean.or.id/>.

63 Those product groups are: 1) Ceramic and Glass products, 2) Cement, Chemicals, 4) Copper cathodes, 5) Electronics, 6) Fertilizers, 7) Gems and Jewelry, 8) Leather products, 9) Plastics, 10) Pharmaceutics, 11) Pulp, 12) Rubber products, 13) Textiles, 14) Vegetable oils, 15) Wooden/Rattan furniture.

64 Press Statement. The 3rd AFTA Council Meeting, Indonesia, 11 December 1992, <www.asean.or.id/>.

65 For example, on the comparison of 6-digit and 8/9 digit levels of classification: wires of iron or non-alloy steel, 7217.23, duty free, copper plated wire, 7217.2310, 20 percent duty. See, Azarcan and Tecsan 1995, 19, also Agreement on the Common Effective Preferential Tariff Scheme for the ASEAN Free Trade Area, January 28, 1992, <www.asean.or.id/>.

66 The so called AFTA-Plus means the measures taken by the ASEAN Framework Agreement on Intellectual Property Cooperation and ASEAN Framework Agreement on Services, Bangkok, 15 December 1995, highlighting ASEAN's attempt to penetrate "non-border areas" of regional trade.

67 Singapore Declaration, 28 January 1992, <www.asean.or.id/>.

68 Opening Statement by Prime Minister Goh Chok Tong at the Fifth ASEAN Summit, Bangkok, 14 December 1995, <www.gov.sg/mfa/pmopen.html>.

69 Ibid.

70 Ibid.

71 Chng Meng-Kng 1995, 2–3, see also Suthiphand Chirathivat 1997, 29.

72 Chia Siow Yue 1997, 43.

73 Ibid., 62.

74 Protocol on Dispute Settlement Mechanism, November 20, 1996, <www.asean.or.id>.

75 Ministerial Understanding on ASEAN Cooperation in Finance, March 1, 1997, <www.asean.or.id>.

76 Suthiphand Chirathivat 1997, 36–38.

77 Mahathir, January 6, 1993, <www.smpke.jpm.my/pm/speeches.html>.

3 REGIONALISM AND SECURITY IN SOUTHEAST ASIA

1 A good presentation of different security policies of the ASEAN countries can be found in Alagappa 1998.

2 See, for example, Mahathir's speech at the 39th United Nations' General Assembly, October 10, 1984, <www.smpke.jpm.my>.

3 See, Hay 1997, 10, Wanandi 1998, 193–196, da Cunha 1999, 14–19.

4 Panitan Wattanyagorn 1995.

5 Ahmad 1992. See also da Cunha 1999, 16–18.

6 See, for example, Leifer 1996.

7 Mahathir writes in his book with Shintaro Ishihara (1995, p. 119): "Malaysia has always maintained a very different stance from that of some of our ASEAN neighbors in asserting that there is no necessity for a U.S. military presence in our region. The United States assumes that we are afraid of Japan, of China. But we feel there is no threat, for the simple reason that all the countries of East Asia realize that you don't have to conquer others to become prosperous."

8 Ahmad 1992.

9 da Cunha 1999, 19.

10 *The Straits Times*, 13 January 1998.

11 See, Singapore Declaration, 28 January 1992.

12 ASEAN Declaration on the South China Sea, Manila, Philippines, 22 July 1992, <www.asean.or.id>.

13 Treaty on Southeast Asia Nuclear Weapon-Free Zone, December 15, 1995, <www.asean.or.id>.

14 Hay 1997, 9.
15 Jusuf Wanandi, *CSCAP Newsletter*, October 1994, No. 2, 3.
16 See, Habib 1996.
17 Jim Rolfe, *CSCAP Newsletter*, August 1995, No. 3, 2.
18 Ibid.
19 Ibid.
20 Wanadi 1996b, 157.
21 Rolfe 1995, 3 and Rolfe, *CSCAP Newsletter*, February 1996, No. 4, 3.
22 Jim Rolfe, *CSCAP Newsletter*, August 1995, No. 3, 3.
23 See, *CSCAP Memorandum*, No. 2, 3 and 7.
24 Jim Rolfe, *CSCAP Newsletter*, August 1995, No. 3, 3.
25 See, Chairman's statement, the First ASEAN Regional Forum, Bangkok, 25 July 1994, Chairman's Statement, the Second ASEAN Regional Forum, Brunei Darulsalam, 1 August 1995, <www.asean.or.id>.
26 The ASEAN Regional Forum: A Concept Paper, <www.asean.or.id>.
27 Ibid.
28 The ASEAN Regional Forum: A Concept Paper, Annex A, <www.asean.or.id>.
29 Bloed 1992, 6.
30 The ASEAN Regional Forum: A Concept Paper, Annex A and Annex B, <www.asean.or.id>.
31 Acharya 1996, 24.
32 See, Camilleri 1997, "Promoting Human Rights in Asia Pacific" <aus-cscap.anu.edu.au> and Galharague 1999, "Challenges to the principle of non-intervention" <www.cscapeurope.org/report>.
33 See, Wanadi 1996, 159–160.
34 *Asian Defense Journal*, September 1996, 12–14.
35 Chairman's Statement, The Third ASEAN Regional Forum, Jakarta, 23 July 1996, <www.asean.or.id/>
36 See, for example, Mahathir Mohamad 14 December 1995, <www.smpke.jpm.my/pm/speeches.html>.
37 Chairman's Statement, the Seventh Meeting of Regional Forum, Bangkok, 27 July 2000, <www.asean.or.id/>
38 See, for example, *the Straits Times*, September 10 and 14, 1999 and *Bangkok Post*, September 10, 1999.
39 See, for example Chairman's Statement, the Sixth Meeting of the ASEAN Regional Forum, Singapore, 26 July 1999, <www.asean.or.id/>.
40 Habib 1996, 5–6.
41 See, for example, SIPRI Yearbook 1995, 259–386, SIPRI Yearbook 2000, 244–248.
42 Hay 1997, 16–22.

4 ASEAN IN THE ASIA-PACIFIC CONTEXT

1 Stubbs 1994, 372–373.
2 Mahathir at the Dinner in honour of Singaporean Prime Minister Goh Chok Tong, January 11, 1991 <www.smpke.jpm.my>.
3 *FEER* December 20 1990, 57.
4 ASEAN Economic Ministers' Declaration on the Uruguay Round, Luxembourg, June 1, 1991 <www.asean.or.id>.
5 *FEER* December 20 1990, 58.
6 Mahathir's speech at the International Conference on "the ASEAN countries and the World Economy: Challenge of Change", Bali, Indonesia, March 4, 1991 <www.smpke.jpm.my>.
7 Ibid.
8 Mahathir Mohamad to the foreign correspondents, October 14, 1992 <www.smpke.jpm.my>.
9 *FEER*, January 24, 1991, 22.
10 *FEER*, March 21, 1991, 18–19.
11 Mahathir's speech at the International Conference on "the ASEAN countries and the World Economy: Challenge of Change", Bali, Indonesia 3, April 1991 <www.smpke.jpm.my>.
12 The Singapore Declaration 1992 <www.asean.or.id>.
13 US-Australia Joint Communique, October 1, 1992, US Department of State Dispatch, October 5,1992, Vol. 3, No. 40 , 756.
14 Richard Solomon in *FEER*, January 31, 1991, 33.
15 Richard Solomon's address before the Pacific Rim Forum, San Diego, California May 15, 1992, US Department of State Dispatch Vol.3. No 21, May 25, 1992, 414.
16 U.S. Department of State Daily Press Briefing, July 20, 1994.
17 *FEER*, January 17, 1991, 11–12.
18 See for example, Former Japanese Prime Minister Yasuhiro Nakasone keynote speech at the World Bank's "International Conference on Democracy, Market Economy and Development, February 26–27, 1999.
19 *FEER*, November 24, 1994, 18.
20 See Korhonen 1998, 180.
21 See Malaysian Deputy Prime Minister Anwar Ibrahim "Japan and Southeast Asia in the Twenty-First Century" September 9, 1994, Hotel Ohkura, Tokyo <www.smpke.jpm.my/tpm/TPMMain.html>.
22 In fact Lee Kuan Yew saw the dangers in the EAEC of the division of the Pacific and preferred APEC, see Antolik 1992, 146. On the other hand, an eminent Singaporean author, Tommy Koh (1998, 214) saw "ASEAN, EAEC and APEC as three intersecting circles and not as contradictory institutions".
23 Lam Lai Sing 1994, 458.

24 Kishore Mahbubani, Speech at Europe Asia Forum in Singapore, 21 February 1998, in Mahbubani 1998, 153.
25 Joint Press Statement, the First Meeting of the ASEAN Economic Ministers and the Ministers of People's Republic of China, Japan and Republic of Korea, 2 May 2000, <www.asean or.id/economic>.
26 Asian Development Bank 1997, Root 1996, A.H. & Geete Somjee 1995, Castells 1992. For the critique of these explanations, see Jomo 1997 and 1998.
27 Krugman (1994) compares the economic growth of East and Southeast Asia to what happened in the Soviet Union in the 1950s, referring particularly to the studies of Lawrence Lau, Jong-Il Kim and Alwyn Young.
28 Huntington 1993, 22.
29 Ibid., 28.
30 Ibid., 48–49.
31 For example, Sato 1997, 9.
32 Huntington 1993, 40–41.
33 See for example Kishore Mahbubani's article from 1992 "West and the Rest" in Mahbubani 1998, 37–56.
34 Mahathir & Ishihara 1995 and Zakaria's (1994) interview with Lee Kuan Yew.
35 See Mahbubani 1995.
36 See Bodde 1994, 66.
37 See *FEER* March 16 and May 11, 1989.
38 *FEER*, April 20, July 20 and August 10, 1989
39 Joint Communique of the 23rd ASEAN Ministerial Meeting, Jakarta, 24–25 July 1990 <www.asean.or.id>.
40 The Commission for a New Asia (1994) was a group composed of prominent Asian ex-state leaders and academics.
41 Manning and Stern 1994, 83.
42 Bodde 1994, 55.
43 Funabashi 1993, 83.
44 Lee Kuan Yew's interview in *FEER*, November 18, 1993, 18.
45 Nesadurai 1996, also Bodde 1994, 36–38.
46 Joint Statement, Third Ministerial Meeting, Seoul, Korea, Nov 12–14, 1991, <www.apecsec.org.sg/virtualib/>.
47 See Mahathir, November 15 and December 5, 1993, <www.smpke.jpm.my>.
48 *FEER,* December 2, 1993, 12.
49 Thai ambassador Kasit Pyromya according to FEER, November 10, 1994, 29.
50 See, *FEER*, November 10, 1994, 30
51 *FEER,* November 24, 1994, 14.
52 Halloran 1996.

[53] Bodde 1994, 45.
[54] *FEER*, December 5, 1996, 18.
[55] *FEER*, November 27, 1997, 79–80.

5 ASEAN AND THE EU: POLITICO-IDEOLOGICAL CONFLICT AND ECONOMIC NECESSITIES

[1] See Harris and Bridges 1983.
[2] Holland 1995.
[3] *COM(94) 314 final*, 7.
[4] Ibid., 3.
[5] A former Unilever executive, Sir Michael Perry (1994) asked whether falling European competitiveness is due to its inefficiency and Asian efficiency. See also the critique of Committee on External Economic Relations (CEER) on conditionalizing and the social clause in the Commission's proposal for the new Asia strategy, *PE 211.248/fin.*, 26–27, 29.
[6] In the beginning of 1997 among the EU's anti-dumping countermeasures, 22 percent concerned Southeast Asia. The percentage is remarkable if the whole of Southeast Asian imports to the EU, which is only 10 percent, is taken into account. If China is included the number of sanctions increases to 42 percent, while the total amount of imports is 25 percent. EU External Trade Statistics in *Kauppapolitiikka* 3/1997, 21.
[7] CEPHCP, *PE 211.248/fin.*, 31.
[8] CDC, *PE 211.248/fin.*, 33–35.
[9] FAC, *PE 211.248/fin.*, 11–12 and CEER, *PE 211.248/fin.*, 25.
[10] Kurus 1995, 406.
[11] Statement by Malaysian Foreign Minister Ahmad Baldawi at the ASEAN-EC Dialogue Session, Kuala Lumpur, 22–24 July 1991, *24th AMM*, 90.
[12] Opening Statement by the Honourable Dato' Seri Dr. Mahathir bin Mohamad, *Fifth ASEAN Summit*, 14.
[13] Mahbubani 1992, 16–17.
[14] Mahbubani 1995, 105.
[15] Ibid., 106.
[16] Mahbubani 1992, 14–17, also Wanandi 1992.
[17] Opening Statement by H.E. Mr. Soeharto, at the 5th Meeting of ASEAN Heads of Government, Bangkok, 14 December 1995, *Fifth ASEAN Summit*, p. 11, Opening Statement by The Honourable Dato' Seri Mahathir bin Mohamad, at the 5th Meeting of ASEAN Heads of Government, Bangkok, 14 December 1995, *Fifth ASEAN Summit*, pp. 13–16, Opening Statement by H.E. Mr. Vo Van Kiet, at the 5th Meeting

of ASEAN Heads of Government, Bangkok, 14 December 1995, *Fifth ASEAN Summit*, p. 32, 33.

18 Overview of the state-of-play of WTO disputes, 27 October 2000, <www.wto.org>.

19 Commission proposes WTO role in labour standards debate, IP/96/692, Brussels, July 24, 1996, <europa.eu.int/en/comm/dg01/prlabour.htm>.

20 *Business Times*, May 13, 1998.

21 *COM(96) 314 final*, 28.

22 According to *Le Monde* (March 3, 1996) the absence of the Prime Ministers of two Nordic countries, Denmark and Sweden, was due to a TV programme dealing with Chinese orphans.

23 Chairman's statement of the Asia-Europe Meeting, Bangkok, 2 March 1996. <www.asean.or.id/world/asempr1.htm>.

24 *Manila Bulletin* March 2, 1996 and Jusuf Wanandi in *the Jakarta Post*, March 8, 1996.

25 *Declaration by the European Union*, 2 June 1997. Leon Brittan stated in Berlin, 15 September that "a constructive and frank dialogue will benefit us more than allegations and recriminations." Sir Leon Brittan, Vice President of the European Commission, Speech/97/180, 1997–09–15, p. 4.

26 See, *the Straits Times*, September 2 and 3, 1997.

27 *The Nation*, February 26 and March 1, 1996.

28 *The Straits Times*, October 21, 2000.

29 ASEM Asian Financial Chrises Response Fund: A preliminary assessment, The World Bank, July 25, 2000.

30 See Lim 1999, 6–7.

31 Chris Patten, "The EU and Asia in the New Millenium", Hong Kong 18 October 2000, <www.europa.eu.int/comm/external_relations/news/patten>.

32 See, Asia-Europe Cooperation Framework 2000, October 21, 2000, <www.asem3.go.kr> and Perspectives and Priorities for the ASEM Process into the New Decade, Com 2000 (241), 18 April 2000, <www.europaeu.int/commm/external_relations/asem>.

33 *The Straits Times*, February 16, 1996.

34 See, *Manila Bulletin*, March 3, 1996 and *the Jakarta Post*, February 29, 1996.

6 THE ASIAN ECONOMIC CRISIS, THE SOUTHEAST ASIAN COUNTRIES AND ASEAN

1 Woronoff 1986, 5.

2 The World Bank 1993, 1–26.

[3] See Jomo 1997, 2, See also Hunter 1993.

[4] See ASEAN GDP Growth Rates (%) (1994–96, <www.asean.or.id>.

[5] Anagariya 1993.

[6] The World Bank, 1993, 7.

[7] Root 1996, 16.

[8] ADB 1997, 130.

[9] *FEER* April 24, 1997, 36.

[10] See the Economy Report of the member countries, <www.apecsec.org.sg/member/memberecreport>.

[11] See *FEER*, February 19, 1998, 14–20 and *Business Times*, May 4, 1998 <biztimes.asia1.com>.

[12] *The Star* (Kuala Lumpur) 24 September, 1997 <thestar.com.my>.

[13] *The Star* 9 June, 1998 <thestar.com.my>.

[14] *The Star* 25 May, 1998 <thestar.com.my>.

[15] *The Star* 22 May and 9 June 1998 <thestar.com.my> and *the Straits Times* 9 and 10 June, 1998 <straitstimes.asia1.com>.

[16] *The Star,* 21 June, 1998 <thestar.com.my>.

[17] See, Sukma 1998, 106–116.

[18] Mallet 1999.

[19] Rosenberger 1997.

[20] Mallet 1999, 38–43.

[21] In fact the European socialists' inability to separate anti-colonialism from Third World Communism estranged the PAP from the European social democrats. See Lee Kuan Yew's Speeches at the Socialist International Conference September 3 and 5, 1964 in *One Hundred Years of Socialism*, and a Speech at the Congress of Socialist International in Stockholm on May 7, 1966, in *Socialism and Reconstruction in Asia*, the Government Printing Office, Singapore 1966.

[22] See for example Lee Kuan Yew's lecture at Harvard University, 17 October 2000, <www.gov.sg/sprinter/archieves>.

[23] Mahathir 1986, 44–47.

[24] See, for example, Just World Trust 1994a, 1994b and 1995.

[25] See Mahbubani 1998, 12.

[26] Mahathir 1986, 48–55.

[27] Lee Kuan Yew's, speech at the Europe–Asia Forum 20, February 1998, <www.gov.sg/sprinter>.

[28] Lee Kuan Yew's speech at Rice University, Houston, 23 October 1998, <www.gov.sg/sprinter/archives>.

[29] Lee Kuan Yew's address at the Commemoration Conference of Confucius' 2550th Birthday, Beijing, 7 October 1999, <www.gov.sg/sprinter/archives>.

[30] Lee Kuan Yew's address at the Institute of Strategic and International Studies (ISIS) Malaysia Forum, Kuala Lumpur, 16 August 2000, <www.gov.sg/sprinter/archives>.

31 Mahathir's speech at the Annual Seminar of the World Bank, Hong Kong, 20 September 1997, <www.smpke.jpm.my>.

32 Ibid.

33 Mahathir's speech at the 12th General Meeting of Pacific Economic Co-operation Council (PECC), Santiago, Chile, 30 September 1997, <www.smpke.jpm.my>.

34 See Thai Foreign Minister's comments after the ASEAN Ministerial Meeting in July, 1995, *Bangkok Post,* July 25, 1997.

35 Joint Press Statement, the 29th ASEAN Economic Ministers Meeting 16, October 1997, Subang Jaya, <www.asean.or.id>.

36 Joint Press Communiqué The First ASEAN Finance Ministers Meeting Phuket, 1 March 1997, <www.asean.or.id>.

37 *Bangkok Post*, November 10, 1997.

38 Ibid.

39 *Bangkok Post*, December 1, 1997.

40 Ibid.

41 *The Star,* March 1, 1998, <www.jaring.my/star>.

42 *Bangkok Post*, April 5, 1998.

43 Terms of Understanding on the Establishment of the ASEAN Surveillance

44 See for example, ASEAN's homepages on finance, <www.asean.or.id/economic/ov_fin.htm>.

45 See *New Straits Times,* February 7, 1998, *the Star*, March 1 and March 2, 1998, <www.jaring.my/star>, and Joint Press Statement, the Second ASEAN Finance Ministers Meeting, Jakarta, 28 February 1998, <www.asean.or.id>.

46 *The Star*, March 18 and December 18, 1998, <www.thestar.com.my>.

47 This was particularly expressed by the Singaporean Premier Goh Chok Tong, see *the Straits Times*, December 16, 1998.

7 GLOBAL GOVERNANCE AND REGIONALIST SOLUTIONS

1 Lee Kuan Yew, *the Straits Times*, September 18, 1989.

2 *The Straits Times*, November 16, 1998.

3 Nicolaides 1994, 230–232.

4 Skogstad 1994, 251, 256.

5 ASEAN statement on the Uruguay Round at the Asia Pacific Economic Cooperation Ministerial Meeting Seoul, 12–14 November 1991, <www.asean.or.id>.

6 Jomo 1998b, 19.

7 Joint Press Statement the 23rd ASEAN Economic Ministers Meeting, Malaysia, 7–8 October 1991 and Joint Press Statement the 24th

ASEAN Economic Ministers Meeting, Philippines, 22–23 October 1992, <www.asean.or.id>.

8 Sampson 2000, 144–151.

9 Joint Press Statement the 24th ASEAN Economic Ministers Meeting, Philippines, 22–23 October 1992, <www.asean.or.id>.

10 DeSombre 1999, 56.

11 Informal Consultations between AEM and the Ministers from the CER countries, 9 September 1995, Brunei Darussalam, <www.asean.or.id>.

12 Mahathir, 27 April 1992 The Official Opening of the 2nd Ministerial Conference of Developing Countries on Environment and Development and Mahathir 8 November 1994, The Asian Parliamentarian Conference on Environment and Sustainable Development, <www.smpke.jpm.my/pm/speeches.html>.

13 Bullard, Bello and Malholtra 1998, 86–87, 92–93.

14 Pauly 1994, 204.

15 IMF Executive Directors and Voting Power, December 22, 2000, <www.imf.org>.

16 Pauly 1994.

17 Bullard, Bello and Malholtra 1998, 120–121.

18 See *FEER*, November 6, 1997, 14–16.

19 See, *the Straits Times* editorial, January 15, 1998 and *the Straits Times*, February 20 and June 5 1998.

20 The IMF's Response to the Asian Crisis, April 1998, <www.imf.org/External/np/exr/facts/asia.HTM>.

21 This view is condensed in Jomo's (1998a) study.

22 Bullard, Bello and Malholtra 1998, 94 and Lauridsen 1998, 149–150.

23 *The Straits Times*, March 3 1998, <straitstimes.asia1.com.sg> and FEER, March 19, 1998, 18–19.

24 *The Star*, Monday, May 25, 1998, <thestar.com.my>.

25 Mahathir, "Case Study for a Country under Economic Stress" Aug. 2, 1999, <www.smpkje.jpm.my>.

26 Anwar, *the Star* Friday May 4, 1998, <thestar.com.my>.

27 *Business Times* (Singapore), 23 September 1998, <business-times.asia1.com.sg/focus25html>.

28 *FEER*, February 26, 1998, 14–15 and March 19, 1998, 18–19.

29 See *the Straits Times*, September 16, 1998, <straitstimes.asia1.com.sg>, Business Times, September 17 and 22, 1998, <business-times.asia1.com.sg>.

30 *The Straits Times*, September 22, 1998, <straitstimes.asia1.com.sg>.

31 *The Straits Times,* September 17, 1998, <straitstimes.asia1.com.sg>, *the Star,* September 17, 29 and October 6, 1998, <thestar.com.my>.

32 Mosley, Harrigan and Toye 1991a, 29–39.

33 Ibid. 51.

34 Mosley, Harrigan and Toye 1991b, 44–53.

[35] Ibid, 72–122.

[36] See, for example, the World Bank chief James Wolfensohn's comments, *New Straits Times* (Malaysia) February 5, 1998.

[37] *EDI Annual Report 98*, 9 and the World Bank 1999, 21.

[38] Conference Report, presentation by Vinod Thomas, Director, Economic Development Institute, February 27, 1999 at the World Bank's *International Conference on Democracy, Market Economy and Development*, see also the World Bank's chief economists Joseph Stiglitz's (1999a) luncheon keynote "Participation and Development: Perspectives from the 'Comprehensive Development Paradigm'" and his presentation (1999b) "Labour Participation and the East Asian Crisis", both at the same conference. Also "New frontiers in diagnosing and combating corruption", *the World Bank Notes*, Public Sector, October 1998. The former Japanese Prime Minister Yasuhiro Nakasone at the World Bank's Korea conference forcefully defended the opposite view that democracy should follow economic development, i.e., the Asian model. See Nakasone's keynote speech at the World Bank Conference (Nakasone 1999).

[39] See, *the World Bank Media Advisory*, February 26, 1999.

[40] The World Bank Group, *Corporate Governance Reform in East Asia – Responding to the Global Financial Crisis.* Private Sector Development Department.

[41] Zakaria 1994, 109–126.

[42] Kim Dae Jung 1994, 189–194.

[43] At the World Bank's Korea conference Kim Dae Jung stalwartly attacked the authoritarian Asian model. See, Opening Address by President Kim Dae Jung of the Republic of Korea at the *International Conference on Democracy, Market Economy and Development*, Seoul, Korea February 26–27, 1999.

[44] *Newsweek*, July 21, 1997, 29.

[45] Ibid.

[46] ASEAN Troika Statement, Bangkok, 19 April 1998, <www.asean.or.id/news/troika2.htm>.

[47] The Filipino Government's news release on the 3rd ASEAN Informal Summit, <www.summit99.ops.gov.ph/nov28.htm>.

[48] The ASEAN Troika, <www.asean.or.id>.

[49] See, Opening Statement by His Excellency Dr. Surin Pitsuwan, Minister of Foreign Affairs of Thailand at the 31st ASEAN Ministerial Meeting Manila, Philippines, 24 July 1998 <www.asean.or.id>.

[50] See the Closing Statements of Singaporean and Filipino Foreign Ministers, Professor S. Jayakumar and Domingo L. Siazon, 31st AMM, 24–25 July 1998, Manila, Philippines, <www.asean.or.id>. See also Opening Statement of H.E. Dato' Seri Abdullah Ahmad Badawi Minister of Foreign Affairs of Malaysia at 31st ASEAN Ministerial Meeting Manila, 24 July 1998, <www.asean.or.id> and

FEER, July 23, 1998, 20. Also Smith 1999, 250.

51 See, *FEER* December 17, 1998.

52 See, *FEER* February 26, 1998, 16–17, also Funston 1999, 206 and Smith 2000, 511–512.

53 Palmujoki 1997, 124. Kishore Mahbubani said later that although Singapore was against Indonesia's occupation, "over the last quarter century Indonesia has de facto been governing East Timor and this has been generally accepted by the World at large". See, Statement to the UNSC by Ambassador Kishore Mahbubani on the question of East Timor, 11 September 1999, <app.internet.gov.sg/scripts/mfa/pr/>.

54 See *Bangkok Post*, November 13, 1997 and March 4, 1998 and *the Straits Times*, October 13, 1998.

55 See *FEER*, January 28, 1999, 26–27.

56 Kivimäki 2000, 538–39.

57 See, Statement to the UNSC by Ambassador Kishore Mahbubani on the question of East Timor, 11 September 1999, <app.internet.gov.sg/scripts/mfa/pr/>, see also the other ASEAN members statements, the UN Press Release SC/6724, 11 September 1999.

58 See *the Straits Times*, September 10,1999 <straitstimes.asia1.com.sg>, *the Star*, October 5, 1999, <thestar.com.my> and *the Nation* (Bangkok), November 1, 1999.

59 AFP "East Timor prefers South Pacific Forum ahead of ASEAN: Ramos Horta", reported on the web page of East Timor Action Network (ETAN) <etan.org/et99/july/25–31/26etprefer.htm>.

60 Joint Communique of Thirty Third ASEAN Ministerial Meeting, Bangkok, Thailand, 24–25 July, 2000, <asean.or.id>.

61 *The Straits Times,* October 7, 1998, <straitstimes.asia1.com.sg>.

62 *The Strait Times*, October 13, 17 and 20, 1998 <straitstimes.asia1.com.sg>.

63 Remarks as Prepared for Delivery by Vice President Gore, AEC Business Summit, Kuala Lumpur, November 16, 1998, <www.whitehouse.gov>.

64 See *the Straits Times*, October 7, 1998, <straitstimes.asia1.com>.

65 See, *the Business Times*, September 22, 1998, <biztimes.asia1.com>.

66 See, *the Star*, September 17, 1998 <thestar.com.my> and *the Straits Times*, September 18, 1998 <straitstimes.asia1.com>.

8 SOUTHEAST ASIAN REGIONALIST TRENDS IN THE BEGINNING OF THE NEW MILLENNIUM

1 See Suthiphand Chirathivat 1999, 21.

2 See, for example, the Philippines' former president, Fidel Ramos' address in Washington D.C., 17 May 2000, <www.asean.or.id./secgen/articles>.

[3] Suthiphand Chirathivat et. al. 1999, 30.
[4] Ibid., 31.
[5] Ibid., 46–47.
[6] Press Statement by Chairman, 4th ASEAN Informal Summit, Singapore, 25 November 2000 <www.asean.or.id>.
[7] Ibid.
[8] Fidel Ramos' address in Washington D.C., 17 May 2000, <www.asean.or.id./secgen/articles>.
[9] Joint Statement on East Asia Cooperation, 28 November 1999, <www.asean.or.id>.
[10] Mahathir's article of 5 July 1999 "Looking for an Asia that can pull together" for international circulation, <www.smpke.jpm.my>.
[11] Fidel Ramos' address in Washington D.C., 17 May 2000, <www.asean.or.id./secgen/articles>.
[12] The Second Meeting of the ASEAN Economic Ministers and the Ministers of the People's Republic of China, Japan and Republic of Korea, 7 October 2000, Chiang Mai, Thailand <www.asean.or.id>.
[13] See, *ASEAN Strategic Plan of Action on the Environment.*
[14] Geradin 1997, 79–88 and Haigh 1992, 235–238.
[15] Alley 1998, 96–98.
[16] Dauvergne, 1998, 2, 4–5.
[17] Cameron 1996.
[18] Cotton 1999, 332.
[19] Joint Press Statement, Sixth ASEAN Ministerial Meeting on Haze, 16 April 1999, Brunei Darussalam, <www.asean.or.id.>.
[20] Environment: Overview, <www.asean.or.id/function/ov_env.htm>.
[21] Special Report on Forest Fires and and Haze Situation in Indonesia and Action Taken (2000), <www.asean.or.id>.
[22] See Francis Loh Kok Wah's (1996) and Suthy Prasartset's (1996) articles.

9 CONCLUSION: SOUTHEAST ASIAN REGIONALISM: OLD OR NEW?

[1] Öjendal 2000, 11.
[2] Hettne 1999a, xx and 1999b, 7.
[3] Hettne 1999b, 8.
[4] Leong 2000.

Bibliography

DOCUMENTS AND DOCUMENT SERIES

ADS. *ASEAN Document Series 1967–1986*. Compiled by the ASEAN Secretariat. Second (revised) Edition, Jakarta 1986.

ASEAN Strategic Plan of Action on the Environment. Jakarta: ASEAN Secretariat, July 1994.

"The Asia Pacific Non-Governmental Organizations' Bangkok Statement and Response to the Bangkok Declaration" (1993). In James T.H. Tang, *Human Rights and International Relations in the Asia-Pacific Region*. London: Pinter 1995.

"Bangkok Declaration 1993". In James T.H. Tang *Human Rights and International Relations in the Asia-Pacific Region*. London: Pinter 1995.

COM(94) 314 final (Commission of the European Communities, Communication from the Commission to the Council, "Towards a New Asia Strategy) – the EU document.

The Commission for a New Asia (1994) *Towards A New Asia. A Report of the Commission for a New Asia.*

The Conference. *The Conference of Heads of State or Government of Non-Aligned Countries, Belgrade, September 1–6, 1961*. Beograd: Publicisticko-Izdavacki Zavod "Jugoslavija".

"Conference Report". A presentation by Vinod Thomas, Director, Economic Development Institute, February 27, 1999 at the World Bank's *International Conference on Democracy, Market Economy and Development*, Seoul, Korea, February 26–27, 1999.

CSCAP Memorandum.

CSCAP Newsletter.

Declaration by the European Union on the accession of Cambodia, Laos and Burma/Myanmar to ASEAN, Luxembourg, 2 June 1997, 8637/97 (Presse 1989) E/59/97 – the EU document.

FAB. *Foreign Affairs Bulletin*. Bangkok: Information Department, Ministry of Foreign Affairs.

FAM. *Foreign Affairs Malaysia*. Kuala Lumpur: Ministry of Foreign Affairs.

FAN. *Foreign Affairs Newsletter*. Bangkok: Information Department, Ministry of Foreign Affairs.

15th ASEAN Ministerial Meeting and Post-Ministerial Meeting with the Dialogue Countries, Singapore 14–18 June 1982. Jakarta: The ASEAN Secretariat.

VIIIth National Congress Documents. Communist Party of Vietnam. Hanoi 1996: The Gioi Publishers.
Fifth ASEAN Summit, Bangkok 14–15 December 1995. Jakarta: The ASEAN Secretariat, 1996.
"Human Rights in the Region", *Statement of the Third General Assembly*. Regional Council on Human Rights in Asia, Penang, Malaysia December 7–10, 1985.
The Informal Meeting of the ASEAN Economic Ministers, Singapore, 29–30 October 1987, Press Release.
Interaction for Progress (1991) Report of an International Symposium on *Interaction for Progress – Vietnam's New Course and ASEAN Experience*. Westlake Guest House, Hanoi, 20–23 August 1991.
Joint Communique of the Twenty-third ASEAN Ministerial Meeting, Jakarta, 24–25 July 1990. Jakarta: The ASEAN Secretariat.
One Hundred Years of Socialism. A Ministry of Culture Publication, Singapore: Malaya Engraving & Litho Printing Co.
"Opening Address" by President Kim Dae Jung of the Republic of Korea at the *International Conference on Democracy, Market Economy and Development*, Seoul, Korea February 26–27, 1999.
PE 211.248/fin. (Report on the Communication from the Commission to the Council "Towards a New Asia Strategy", Committee on Foreign Affairs, Security and Defence Policy) – the EU document.
Shared Destiny – Southeast Asia in the 21st Century. Report of the ASEAN-Vietnam Study Group, February 1993.
Singapore Parliament, *Parliamentary Debates*, Official Report, Singapore.
Sir Leon Brittan, Vice President of the European Commission, Speech/97/180, 1997–09–15 – the EU document.
Socialism and Reconstruction in Asia. Speeches of Lee Kuan Yew. Singapore: The Government Printing Office 1966.
Speeches. A Selection of Ministerial Speeches. Singapore: The Information Division, Ministry of Culture.
24th AMM – The Twenty-Fourth ASEAN Ministerial Meeting and Post Ministerial Conferences with Dialogue Partners, Kuala Lumpur, 19–24, July 1991. Jakarta: The ASEAN Secretariat.
US Department of State Daily Press Briefing.
US Department of State Dispatch.
The World Bank Group, *Corporate Governance Reform in East Asia – Responding to the Global Financial Crisis*. Private Sector Development Department.
The World Bank Media Advisory, February 26, 1999.
The World Bank Notes, Public Sector, October 1998.

NEWSPAPERS AND WEEKLIES

Bangkok Post (Bangkok).
Business Times (Singapore).
FEER, Far Eastern Economic Review (Hong Kong).
The Jakarta Post *(Jakarta).*
Le Monde (Paris).
Manila Bulletin (Manila).
The Nation (Bangkok).
New Nation (Singapore).
New Straits Times (Kuala Lumpur).
Newsweek (Washington).
The Straits Times (Singapore).

WEBSITES

http://www.apecsec.org.sg – Asia-Pacific Economic Cooperation (APEC) Website.

http://app.internet.gov.sg – MFA Ministry of Foreign Affairs, Singapore, Speeches and Statements.

http://www.asean.or.id (http://www.aseansec.org) – Website maintained by the ASEAN Secretariat, 70A Jl. Sisingamangaraja, Jakarta 12110 Indonesia.

http://www.asem3.go.kr – The Third Asia-Europe Meeting. Korean Website.

http://aus-cscap.anu.edu.au – Australian Member Committee of the Council for Security Cooperation in the Asia Pacific, AUS-CSCAP Home Page.

http://biztimes.asia1.com (http://business-times.asia1.com.sg) – *Business Times* (Singapore) Online.

http://www.cscapeurope.org - European Committee, CSCAP Europe. Council for Security Cooperation in the Asia-Pacific.

http://etan.org – East Timor Action Network.

http://europa.eu.int – The European Union's server.

http://www.feer.com – *Far Eastern Economic Review* Online. Review Publishing Company Limited, Hong Kong.

http://www.focusweb.org – Website maintained by Focus on the Global South, c/o CUSRI, Wisit Prachuabmoh Building, Chulalongkorn University, Phayathai Road, Bangkok 10330, Thailand.

http://www.gov.sg/mfa/ (http://www.mfa.gov.sg) – MFA Ministry of Foreign Affairs, Singapore.

http://www.gov.sg/sprinter/ – Singapore Press Releases on the Internet. The Singapore Government.

http://www.imf.org – International Monetary Fund (IMF) Website.
http//: www.summit99.ops.gov.ph/nov28.htm – News Release, ASEAN Informal Summit, November 29, 1999.
http://www.smpke.jpm.my – The Government of Malaysia, Prime Minister's Office, Official Website.
http://straitstimes.asia1.com – *The Straits Times* (Singapore) Online.
http://thestar.com.my (http:// www.jaring.my/star) – *The Star* (Kuala Lumpur) Online.
http://www.whitehouse.gov – The White House Website.
http://www.wto.org – The WTO Website. World Trade Organization, rue de Lausanne 154, CH-1211 Geneva 21, Switzerland.

OTHER LITERATURE

Abdad, M.C. Jr. (1996) "Re-engineering ASEAN". *Contemporary Southeast Asia,* 18 (3): 237–53.
Acharya, Amitav (1996) "Regional Security in the Asia Pacific: Trends and Prospects". In Jusuf Wanandi, *Regional Security Arrangements – Indonesian and Canadian Views.* Jakarta: Centre for Strategic and International Studies.
Acharya, Amitav (1997) "Ideas, Identity, and Institution Building: from the 'ASEAN way' to the 'Asia-Pacific way'"? *The Pacific Review,* 10 (3): 319–346.
Acharya, Amitav (1998) "The Essence of a Pragmatic Idealist: Reconciling National Interest with Common Good". An Introduction to the Book, Tommy Koh: *The Quest for World Order. Perspectives of a Pragmatic Idealist.* Singapore: Times Academic Press.
Acharya, Amitav (1999) "Realism, Institutionalism, and the Asian Economic Crises". *Contemporary Southeast Asia,* 21 (1): 1–29.
Ahmad, Zakaria Haji (1992) "The United States Military: Southeast Asian Views". *Strategi,* 1 (1): 67–87.
Ajanant, Juanjai (1997) "AFTA: An Introduction". In Kao Kim Hourn & Kanter S., *Asean Free Trade Agreement. Implications & Future Directions.* London: ASEAN Academic Press.
Akrasanee, Narongchai and Stifel, David (1992) "The Political Economy of the ASEAN Free Trade Area". In Pearl Imada and Seiji Naya, *AFTA. The Way Ahead.* Singapore: Institute of Southeast Asian Studies.
Akrasanee, Narongchai and Stifel, David (1994) "A Vision of Southeast Asia in the Year 2000: Towards a Common Economic Regime". *Contemporary Southeast Asia,* 16 (1): 1–13.
Alagappa, Mutiah (ed.)(1998) *Asian Security Practice – Material and Ideational Influences.* Stanford, California: Stanford University Press.

Alburo, Florian A. (1992) "The ASEAN Summit and ASEAN Economic Co-operation". In K.S. Sandhu, Sharon Siddique, Chandran Jeshurun, Ananda Rajah, Joseph L.H. Tan, Pushpa Thambipillai, *The ASEAN Reader*. Singapore: Institute of Southeast Asian Studies.

Alley, Roderic (1998) *The United Nations in Southeast Asia and the South Pacific*. Houndmills and London: Macmillan and New York: St. Martin's Press.

Anderson, Benedict (1998) *The Spectre of Comparisons. Nationalism, Southeast Asia and the World.* London and New York: Verso.

Antolik, Michael (1990) *ASEAN and the Diplomacy of Accommodation.* New York and London: M.E.Sharpe, Inc.

Antolik, Michael (1992) "ASEAN's Singapore Rendezvous: Just Another Summit"? *Contemporary Southeast Asia,* 14 (2): 142–153.

Anwar, Dewi Fortuna (1994) *Indonesia in ASEAN. Foreign Policy and Regionalism.* New York: St. Martin's Press and Singapore: Institute of Southeast Asian Studies.

Ariff, Mohamed (1997) "From ASEAN-Six to ASEAN-Ten: Issues and Prospects". In *AFTA in the Changing International Economy.* Singapore: Institute of Southeast Asian Studies.

ASEAN-ISIS Monitor, (13), March 1996.

Asian Defense Journal, September 1996.

Asian Development Bank (1997) *Emerging Asia. Changes and Challenges.* Manila: Asian Development Bank.

Axeline, Andrew W. (1977) "Underdevelopment, dependence, and integration: the politics of regionalism in the Third World". *International Organisation,* 31 (1): 83–105.

Azarcan, Chulia and Tecson, Gwendolyn (1995) *Threats and Opportunities in AFTA*. The Philippines: The AFTA Advisory Commission Secretariat and the Center for Research and Communication.

Balakrishnan, K.S. (1995) "Slorc and Myanmar: The Struggle for Identity". *ASEAN-ISIS Monitor,* (10), 17–19.

Beng-Huat Chua (1995) *Communitarian Ideology and Democracy in Singapore.* London and New York: Routledge.

Bloed, Arie (1992) "The CSCE Process from Helsinki to Vienna: An Introduction". In Arie Bloed, *From Helsinki to Vienna: Basic Documents of the Helsinki Process.* Dordrecht: Martinus Nijhoff Publishers.

Bodde, William Jr (1994) *View from the 19th Floor. Reflections of the First APEC Executive Director.* Singapore: Institute of Southeast Asian Studies.

Bowles, Paul (1997) "ASEAN, AFTA and the 'New Regionalism'". *Pacific Affairs*, 70 (2): 219–233.

Bullard, Nicola, Bello, Walden and Malhotra, Kamal (1998) "Taming the Tigers: The IMF and the Asian Crisis". In Jomo K.S. *Tigers in*

Trouble. Financial Governance, Liberalization and Crises in East Asia. London: Zed Books.

Bunn Nagara (1996) "Political Cooperation – Amid Challenges and Opportunities". In ASEAN in the 21st Century: Opportunities and Challenges [the supplement of *International Studies Review* (Hanoi) No. 11, March], 43–58.

Caballero-Anthony, Melly (1998) "Mechanisms of Dispute Settlement: The ASEAN Experience". *Contemporary Southeast Asia,* 20 (1): 38–66.

Cameron, Owen (1996) "Japan and South-East Asia's Environment". In Michael J.G. Parnwell and Raymond L. Bryant, *Environmental Change in South-East Asia. People, Politics, and Sustainable Development.* London: Routledge.

Castells, Manuel (1992) "Four Asian Tigers With a Dragon Head: A Comparative Analysis of the State, Economy and Society in Asia Pacific Rim". In Richard P. Appelbaum and Jefrey Henderson, *States and Development in the Asia Pacific Rim.* Newsbury Park, California: Sage Publications.

Chan Heng Chee (1993) "Democracy: Evolution and Implementation. An Asian Perspective". In Robert L. Bartley, Chan Heng Chee, Samuel P Huntington and Shijuro Ogata, *Democracy & Capitalism. Asian and American Perspectives.* Singapore: Institute of Southeast Asian Studies.

Chia Siow Yue (1997) "Foreign Direct Investment in Southeast Asia". In Chia Siow Yue and Marcello Pacin, *ASEAN in the New Asia – Issues & Trends.* Singapore: Institute of Southeast Asian Studies.

Chng Meng-Kng (1995) "Regional Business Development in ASEAN: The ASEAN Free Trade Area (AFTA)". In *AFTA Reader, Volume II.* Jakarta: ASEAN Secretariat.

Clark, Ian (1997) *Globalization and Fragmentation. International Relations in the Twentieth Century.* Oxford: Oxford University Press.

Cotton, James (1999) "The 'haze' over Southeast Asia: Challenging the ASEAN Mode of Regional Engagement". *Pacific Affairs,* 72 (3): 331–351.

da Cunha, Derek (1999) *Southeast Asia's Security Dynamics: A Multiplicity of Approaches Amidst Changing Geopolitical Circumstances.* International Politics and Security Issues No. 4(99). Singapore: Institute of Southeast Asian Studies.

Dauvergne, Peter (1998) *Environmental Insecurity, Forest Management, and State Responses in Southeast Asia.* Working Paper 1998/2. Canberra: Department of International Relations, Australian National University.

DeSombre, Elizabeth R. (1999) "Environmental Harm as Economic Subsidy: New Perspectives on the Feasibility of Trade Sanctions for

Environmental Protection". *International Journal of Peace Studies*, 4 (1): 47–62.

Diliman Review 1997, 45 (1).

Din Merican (1996) "Democracy: A matter of choice". *Cambodia Times*, August 19.

EDI Annual Report 98 – The World Bank Economic Development Institute Annual Report 1998. Washington, D.C.: The World Bank.

Eliassen, Kjell A. and Monsen, Catherine (1998) *Institutions and Networks: A Comparison of European and Southeast Asian Integration.* Sandvika: Centre for European and Asian Studies at the Norwegian School of Management.

Evans, Grant and Rowley, Kevin (1984) *Red Brotherhood at War. Indochina since the Fall of Saigon.* London: Verso.

Foot, Rosemary (1996) "Thinking Globally from Regional Perspective: Chinese, Indonesian and Malaysian Reflections on the Post-Cold War Era." *Contemporary Southeast Asia,* 18 (1): 17–35.

Funabashi, Yoichi (1993) "The Asianization of Asia." *Foreign Affairs,* 72 (5): 75–85.

Geradin, Damien (1996) "Lessons from the European Community". In Simon S.C. Tay and Daniel C. Esty, *Asian Dragons and Green Trade.* Singapore: Times Academic Press.

Gochoco-Bautista, Maria Socorro and Faustino, Jaime (1994) *AFTA and the Philippines: National Economic Policy-Making and Regional Economic Cooperation.* Quezon City: The Institute for Strategic and Development Studies.

Funston, John (1999) "Challenges Facing ASEAN in a More Complex Age". *Contemporary Southeast Asia,* 21 (2): 205–219.

Haas, Michael (1989) *The Asian Way to Peace. A Story of Regional Cooperation.* New York: Praeger.

Haas, Peter M. (1992) "Introduction: epistemic communities and international policy coordination". *International Organization,* 46 (1): 1–37.

Habib, Hasnan (1996) "Regional Security: Trends and Prospects". In Jusuf Wanandi, *Regional Security Arrangements. Indonesian and Canadian Views.* Jakarta: Centre for Strategic and International Studies.

Haig, Nigel (1992) "The European Community and International Environmental Policy". In Andrew Hurrel and Benedict Kingsbury, *The International Politics of the Environment.* Oxford: Clarendon Press.

Halloran, Richard (1996) "The Rising East". *Foreign Policy,* 102: 3–21.

Hängi, Heiner (1991) *ASEAN and the ZOPFAN concept. Singapore*: Institute of Southeast Asian Studies.

Haris, S. and Bridges, B. (1983) *European Interests in ASEAN.* London: Routledge & Kegan Paul.

Hay, Simon J. (1997) *ASEAN's Regional Security Dialogue Process: From Expectation to Reality?* International Politics and Security Issues No. 1(97). Singapore: Institute of Southeast Asian Studies.

Hernandez, Carolina G. (1997) "Governments and NGOs in the Search for Peace: The ASEAN-ISIS and CSCAP Experience". A paper prepared for *the Alternative Security System Conference, Focus on the Global South*, Bangkok, Thailand 27–30 March (WWW-document: http://focusweb.org/focus/announce/hernandez.html).

Hettne, Björn (1994) "The New Regionalism: Implications for Development and Peace". In Björn Hettne and András Inotai, *The New Regionalism – Implications for Global Development and International Security.* Helsinki: UNU World Institute for Development Economics Research.

Hettne, Björn (1997) "Development, Security and World Order". *The European Journal of Development Research,* 16 (1): 83–106.

Hettne, Björn (1999a) "The New Regionalism: A Prologue". In Björn Hettne, András Inotai and Osvaldo Sunkel, *Globalism and the New Regionalism.* Houndmills and London: Macmillan and New York: St Martin's Press.

Hettne, Björn (1999b) "Globalization and the New Regionalism". In Björn Hettne, András Inotai and Osvaldo Sunkel, *Globalism and the New Regionalism.* Houndmills and London: Macmillan and New York: St Martin's Press.

Hill, Michael and Lian Kwen Fee (1995) *The Politics of Nation Building and Citizenship in Singapore.* London: Routledge.

Hoang Anh Tuan (1994) "Vietnam's Membership in ASEAN: Economic, Political and Security Implications". *Contemporary Southeast Asia,* 16 (3): 259–273.

Holland, Martin (1995) *European Union Common Foreign Policy: From EPC to CFSP Joint Action and South Africa.* Houndmills and London: Macmillan.

Hong Lysa (1999) "Making the history of Singapore: S Rajaratnam & CV Devan Nair". In Lam Peng Er and Kevin YL Tan, *Lee's Lieutenants – Singapore Old Guard.* St Leonards: Allen & Unwin.

Hunter, Janet E. (1993) *The Japanese Experience of Economic Development.* EDI Working Papers. Washington, DC: Economic Development Institute of the World Bank.

Huntington, Samuel P. (1993) "The Clash of Civilization?" *Foreign Affairs,* 72 (3): 22–49.

Imada, Pearl, Montes, Manuel and Naya, Seiji (1991) *A Free Trade Area – Implications for ASEAN.* Singapore: Institute of Southeast Asian Studies.

Jomo, K.S. (1997) *Southeast Asia's Misunderstood Miracle.* Boulder, Colorado: Westview.

Jomo, K.S. (ed.) (1998a) *Tigers in Trouble. Financial Governance, Liberalization and Crises in East Asia.* London: Zed Books.

Jomo, K.S. (1998b) "Introduction: Financial Governance, Liberalisation and Crises in East Asia". In Jomo K.S. *Tigers in Trouble. Financial Governance, Liberalization and Crises in East Asia.* London: Zed Books.

Just World Trust (1994a) *Just Viewpoints – A critical reflection on events in the international political arena.* Penang: Juta Print.

Just World Trust (1994b) *International Conference on Rethinking Human Rights*, 6–7 December 1994, Kuala Lumpur.

Just World Trust (1995) *Dominance of the West over the Rest.* Penang: Just World Trust.

Kartadjoemena, H.S. (1996) "Global interdependence, WTO, ASEAN and APEC: Challenge for the legal profession in ASEAN". *ASEAN Update,* (2): 10–12.

Kauppapolitiikka, 3 1997.

Kawi Chongkittavorn (1997) "The Evolution of 'Constructive Engagement'". In Ralph Bachoe and Debbie Stothard, *From Consensus to Controversy. ASEAN's Relationship with Burma's Slorc.* Bangkok: ALTSEAN-Burma.

Kim Dae Jung (1994) "Is Culture Destiny? The Myth of Asia's Anti-Democratic Values". *Foreign Affairs,* 73 (6): 189–194.

Kivimäki, Timo (2000) "U.S.–Indonesian Relations During the Economic Crisis: Where Has Indonesia's Bargaining Power Gone"? *Contemporary Southeast Asia*, 22 (3): 527– 549.

Koh, Tommy (1998) *The Quest for World Order – Perspectives of A Pragmatic Idealist.* Edited with an introduction by Amitav Acharya. Singapore: The Institute of Policy Studies and Times Academic Press.

Korhonen, Pekka (1998) *Japan and Asia Pacific Integration. Pacific Romances 1968–1996.* London and New York: Routledge.

Krugman, Paul (1994) "The Myth of Asia's Miracle." *Foreign Affairs,* 73 (6): 64–78.

Kurus, Bilson (1995) "The ASEAN Triad: National Interest, Consensus Seeking, and Economic Co-operation." *Contemporary Southeast Asia,* 16 (4): 404–20.

Kusuma Snitwongse (1995) "An Expanding Asean: The Political Dimension". *ASEAN-ISIS Monitor,* (10), 3–7.

Kwok Kian-Woon (1999) "The social architect". In Lam Peng Er and Kevin YL Tan, *Lee's Lieutenants – Singapore Old Guard.* St Leonards: Allen & Unwin.

Lam Lai Sing (1994) "A Short Note on ASEAN-Great Power Interaction". *Contemporary Southeast Asia* 15 (4): 451–63.

Lauridsen, Laurids S. (1998) "Thailand: Causes, Conduct, Consequences". In Jomo K.S. *Tigers in Trouble. Financial Governance, Liberalization and Crises in East Asia.* London: Zed Books.

Leifer, Michael (1996) "The ASEAN Regional Forum". *Adelphi Paper* 302.

Leong, Stephen (2000) "The East Asian Economic Caucus (EAEC): 'Formalized' Regionalism Being Denied". In Björn Hettne, András Inotai and Osvaldo Sunkel, *National Perspectives on the New Regionalism in the South.* Houndmills and London: Macmillan and New York: St. Martin's Press.

Lim, Robyn (1998) "The ASEAN Regional Forum: Building on Sand". *Contemporary Southeast Asia,* 20 (2): 115–36.

Loh Kok Wah, Francis (1996) "ASEAN NGOs in the Post Cold War World". In Jayant Lele and Wisdom Tettey, *Asia – Who Pays for Growth? Women, Environment and Popular Movements.* Aldershot: Dartmouth.

MacIntyre, Andrew (1995) "Ideas and experts: Indonesian approaches to economic and security cooperation in the Asia-Pacific region". *The Pacific Review,* 8 (1): 159–72.

Mahathir, Mohamad (1970) *The Malay Dilemma.* Singapore: Times Books International 1996, originally published 1970.

Mahathir, Mohamad (1986) *The Challenge.* Selangor Darul Ehsan: Pelanduk Publications.

Mahathir, Mohamad (1992) "ASEAN: The Next Generation". *ASEAN-ISIS Monitor,* (5): 1–4.

Mahathir, Mohamad and Shintaro Ishihara (1995) *The Voice of Asia: Two Leaders Discuss the Coming Century.* Tokyo: Kodansha International Ltd.

Mahbubani, Kishore (1992) "New Areas of Asean Reaction: Environment, Human Rights and Democracy". *ASEAN-ISIS Monitor,* (5): 13–17.

Mahbubani, Kishore (1995) "The Pacific Way". *Foreign Affairs,* (74) 1: 100–111.

Mahbubani, Kishore (1998) *Can Asians Think?* Singapore and Kuala Lumpur: *Times Books International.*

Malay Jr., Armado S. (1997) "An Asia That Can Say No". *Kasarinlan* 12 (3): 81–84.

Mallet, Victor (1999) *The Trouble with Tigers – The Rise and Fall of Southeast Asia.* London: HarperCollins Publishers.

Manning, Robert and Stern, Paula (1994) "The Myth of the Pacific Community". *Foreign Affairs,* 73 (6): 79–93.

Mayall, James (1990) *Nationalism and International Society.* Cambridge: Cambridge University Press.

Mosley, Paul, Harrigan Jane and Toye, John (1991a) *Aid and Power – The World Bank and Policy-based Lending. Volume I: Analysis and Policy Proposals.* London and New York: Routledge.

Mosley, Paul, Harrigan Jane and Toye, John (1991b) *Aid and Power – The World Bank and Policy-based Lending. Volume II: Case Studies.* London and New York: Routledge.

Nakasone, Yasuhiro (1999) "Journey into Democracy and Market Economy", a Keynote Speech, Political Leader's Symposium, the *International Conference on Democracy, Market Economy and Development*, Seoul, Korea February 26–27.1999.

Naya, Seiji (1987) *Toward an ASEAN Trade Area.* Kuala Lumpur: The Institute of Strategic and International Studies Malaysia.

Naya, Seiji & Imada, Pearl (1992) "The Long and Winding Road Ahead for AFTA". In Pearl Imada and Seiji Naya, *AFTA. The Way Ahead.* Singapore: Institute of Southeast Asian Studies.

Nesadurai, Helen E.S. (1996) "APEC: A tool for US regional domination"? *The Pacific Review,* 9 (1): 31–57.

Nghien Cuu Quoc Te, (1) 1996.

Nicolaides, Phedon (1994) "The Changing GATT System and the Uruguay Round Negotiations". In Richard Stubbs and Geofrey R.D. Underhill, *Political Economy and The Changing Global Order.* Houndmills and London: Macmillan.

Öjendal, Joakim (2000) "To Be or Not to Be? Regionalization in East and South East Asia". In Björn Hettne, András Inotai and Osvaldo Sunkel, *National Perspectives on the New Regionalism in the South.* Houndmills and London: Macmillan and New York: St. Martin's Press.

Ortuoste, Maria Consuelo C. (1999) *The Prospect of a Concert of ASEAN Nations and Leadership in the Asia Pacific.* ISIS Paper 1. Institute of Security and International Studies (ISIS) Thailand.

Paderanga, Cayetano, Jr. (1995) "Asia-Pacific Economic Conference: The Goods Market". *Foreign Relations Journal,* 10 (4): 13–19.

Palmer, Norman D. (1990) *The New Regionalism in Asia and the Pacific.* Lexington, Massachusetts: Lexington Books.

Palmujoki, Eero (1990) "Diplomacy over the Kampuchean Question". In Ng Chee Yuen and Chandran Jeshurun, *Southeast Asian Affairs 1990.* Singapore: Institute of Southeast Asian Studies.

Palmujoki, Eero (1997) *Vietnam and the World. Marxist-Leninist Doctrine and the Changes in International Relations, 1975–93.* Houndmills and London: Macmillan and New York: St. Martin's Press.

Panagariya, Arvind (1993) *Should East Asia Go Regional? No, No, and Maybe.* The World Bank Policy Research Working Papers, Trade Policy.

Panitan Wattanayagorn (1995) "ASEAN's arms modernization and arms transfers dependence." *The Pacific Review*, 8 (3): 494–507.

Parreñas, Julius Caesar (1995) "Prospects for Free Trade and Co-operation: APEC's Osaka Summit". *Foreign Relations Journal*, 10 (4): 20–42.

Pauly, Louis W. (1994) "Promoting a Global Economy: The Normative Role of the International Monetary Fund". In Richard Stubbs and Geofrey R.D. Underhill, *Political Economy and The Changing Global Order.* Houndmills and London: Macmillan.

Payne, Andrew and Gamble, Anthony (1996) "Introduction: The Political Economy of Regionalism and World Order". In Andrew Payne and Anthony Gamble, *Regionalism and World Order*. Basingstoke and London: Macmillan.

"Rethinking the Third World: A Roundtable Discussion". *Kasarinlan* 12 (3), 1997: 39–77.

Root, Hilton L. (1996) *Small Countries, Big Lessons. Governance and the Rise of East Asia.* New York: Oxford University Press.

Rosenberger, Leif Roderick (1997) "Southeast Asia's Currency Crisis: A Diagnosis and Prescription". *Contemporary Southeast Asia,* 19 (3): 223–251.

Sato, Seizaburo (1997) "The Clash of Civilizations: A View of Japan". *Asia-Pacific Review,* 4 (2): 7–24.

Shafie, M. Ghazali (1982) *Malaysia: International Relations. Selected Speeches.* Kuala Lumpur: Creative Enterprise Sendirian Berhad.

Sideri, Sandro (1997) "Globalisation and Regional Integration". *The European Journal of Development Research,* 16 (1): 38–82.

SIPRI Yearbook 1995. Armaments, Disarmament and International Security. Oxford: Oxford University Press.

SIPRI Yearbook 2000. Armaments, Disarmament and International Security. Oxford: Oxford University Press.

Skogstad, Grace (1994) "Agricultural Trade and the International Political Economy". In Richard Stubbs and Geofrey R.D. Underhill, *Political Economy and The Changing Global Order.* Houndmills and London: Macmillan.

Smith, Anthony L. (2000) "Indonesia's Foreign Policy under Abdurrahman Wahid: Radical or Status Quo State"? *Contemporary Southeast Asia,* 22 (3): 498–526.

Soesastro, Hadi (1996) "Challenges to AFTA in the 21st Century". *The Indonesian Quarterly* 24 (2): 112–120.

Solidum, Estrella D. (1970) *The Nature of Cooperation among the ASEAN States as Perceived through Elite Attitudes – A Factor for Regionalism.* Ph.D. dissertation, University of Kentucty.

Solidum, Estrella D. (1974) *Towards a Southeast Asian Community.* Quezon City: University of the Philippines Press.

Solidum, Estrella D. (1981) "The Role of Certain Sectors in Shaping and Articulating the Asean Way". In R.P. Anand and P.V. Quisumbing, *ASEAN Identity, Development & Culture*. Quezon City: University of the Philippines Law Center & East-West Center Culture Learning Institute.

Somjee, A.H. and Somjee, Geete (1995) *Development Success in Asia Pacific – An Exercise in Normative-Pragmatic Balance.* Houndmills and London: Macmillan.

Sopiee, Noordin (1992) "Asean into the Second Generation: Potentials and Proposals in the Political and Security Dimension". *ASEAN-ISIS Monitor*, (5): 18–23.

Sree Kumar (1992) "Policy issues and the formation of the ASEAN free trade area". In Pearl Imada & Seiji Naya (eds.), *AFTA. The Way Ahead*. Singapore: Institute of Southeast Asian Studies.

Stiglitz, Joseph (1999a) "Participation and Development: Perspectives from the 'Comprehensive Development Paradigm'". A luncheon keynote at the *International Conference on Democracy, Market Economy and Development*, Seoul, Korea, February 26–27.1999.

Stiglitz, Joseph (1999b) "Labour Participation and the East Asian Crisis". A presentation at the *International Conference on Democracy, Market Economy and Development*, Seoul, Korea, February 26–27.1999.

Stubbs, Richard (1994) "The Political Economy of the Asia-Pacific Region". In Richard Stubbs and Geofrey R.D. Underhill, *Political Economy and The Changing Global Order*. Houndmills and London: Macmillan.

Sudo, Sueo (1992) *The Fukuda Doctrine and ASEAN. New Dimensions in Japanese Foreign Policy*. Singapore: Institute of Southeast Asian Studies.

Sukhumbhand Paribatra (1994) "From ASEAN Six to ASEAN Ten: Issues and Prospects". *Contemporary Southeast Asia*, 16 (3): 243–258.

Sukhumbhand Paribatra (1997) "ASEAN and the SLORC Conundrum: Is Burma Ready for Membership?" In Ralph Bachoe and Debbie Stothard, *From Consensus to Controversy. ASEAN's Relationship with Burma's Slorc*. Bangkok: ALTSEAN-Burma.

Sukma, Rizal (1998) "Indonesia. A Year of Politics and Sadness". In Derek da Cunha and John Funston, *Southeast Asian Affairs 1998*. Singapore: Institute of Southeast Asian Affairs.

Surin Maisrikrod (1992) "Thailand's Policy Dilemmas Towards Indochina". *Contemporary Southeast Asia*, 14 (3): 287–300.

Suthiphand Chirathivat (1997) "ASEAN Economic Integration with the World through AFTA". In *AFTA in the Changing International Economy*. Singapore: Institute of Southeast Asian Studies.

Suthiphand Chirathivat (1999) "Crisis and Impact on ASEAN Economic Integration". In Suthiphand Chirathivat, Carlo Filippini and Corrado Molteni, *ASEAN–EU Relations: The Long-term Potential beyond the Recent Turmoil*. Milano: E.G.E.A.

Suthiphand Chirathivat, Chumporn Pachusanond and Patcharawalai Wongboonsin (1999) "ASEAN Prospects for Regional Integration and the Implications for the ASEAN Legislative and Institutional Framework". *ASEAN Economic Bulletin* 6 (1): 28–50.

Suthy Prasartset (1996) "The Rise of NGOs as Critical Social Movements in Thailand". In Jayant Lele and Wisdom Tettey, *Asia – Who Pays for Growth? Women, Environment and Popular Movements*. Aldershot: Dartmouth.

Talib, Shaharil (1998) "Southeast Asia: For Your Eyes Only". A keynote address, International Conference on Economy and Polity: Historical and Contemporary Studies of Some Southeast Asian States, 10–12th January 1998, Yangon Myanmar, presented also at *the International Conference on Southeast Asia in the 20th Century*, University of the Philippines, 28–30 January.

Tan, Gerald (1992) "ASEAN Preferential Trading Arrangements. An Overview". In K.S. Sandhu, Sharon Siddique, Chandran Jeshurun, Ananda Rajah, Joseph L.H. Tan, Pushpa Thambipillai, *The ASEAN Reader*. Singapore: Institute of Southeast Asian Studies.

Tay, Simon and Talib, Obood (1997) "The ASEAN Regional Forum: Preparing for Preventive Diplomacy". *Contemporary Southeast Asia*, 19 (3): 252–268.

Thanat Khoman (1992) "ASEAN. Conception and Evolution". In K.S. Sandhu, Sharon Siddique, Chandran Jeshurun, Ananda Rajah, Joseph L.H. Tan, Pushpa Thambipillai, *The ASEAN Reader*. Singapore: Institute of Southeast Asian Studies.

Thaung Tun (1997) "Constructive Engagement on Trial". In Ralph Bachoe and Debbie Stothard, *From Consensus to Controversy. ASEAN's Relationship with Burma's Slorc*. Bangkok: ALTSEAN-Burma.

Thayer, Carlyle A. (1999) "Vietnamese Foreign Policy: Multilateralism and the Threat of Peaceful Evolution". In Carlyle A. Thayer and Ramses Amer, *Vietnamese Foreign Policy in Transition*. Singapore: Institute of Southeast Asian Studies.

Thitinan Pongsudhirak (1995) "Myanmar and ASEAN: Obstacles to a Regional Order". A paper presented at the *Conference Myanmar Towards the 21st Century: Dynamics of Continuity and Change*, Rimkok Hotel, Chiang Rai, June 1–3.

Thu My (1997) "From ASEAN 7 to ASEAN 10: Opportunities and Challenges". In International Symposium *ASEAN Today and Tomorrow*, Organized by National Center for Social Sciences and Humanities of Vietnam, Hanoi, September 18–17, 1997.

Tu Wei-ming (1990) "The Confucian Dimension in the East Asian Development Model". *Kasarinlan*, 5, (4): 59–70.

Wanandi, Jusuf (1992) "Human Rights and Democracy in the ASEAN Nations: The Next 25 Years". *ASEAN-ISIS Monitor*, (5): 7–12.

Wanandi, Jusuf (1996a) "ASEAN Summit yields major results". *ASEAN Update*, 1 (1): 10–11.

Wanandi, Jusuf (1996b) "The Regional Role of 'Track Two' Diplomacy: ASEAN, ARF and CSCAP". In Hadi Soestro and Anthony Bergin, *The Role of Security and Economic Cooperation Structures in the Asia Pacific Region – Indonesian and Australian Views.* Jakarta: Centre for Strategic and International Studies.

Wanandi, Jusuf (1998) "ASEAN, the Wider Region and the World: The Political-Security Agenda". In Stephen Leon, *ASEAN towards 2020. Strategic Goals and Future Directions.* London: ASEAN Academic Press.

The World Bank (1993) *The East Asian Miracle. Economic Growth and Public Policy.* New York: Oxford University Press.

The World Bank (1999) *The World Development Report. Knowledge for Development.* New York: Oxford University Press.

Woronoff, Jon (1986) *Asia's "Miracle" Economies.* Armonk, New York: M.E. Sarpe, Inc.

Wurfel, David (1999) "Between China and ASEAN: The Dialectics of Recent Vietnamese Foreign Policy". In Carlyle A. Thayer and Ramses Amer, *Vietnamese Foreign Policy in Transition.* Singapore: Institute of Southeast Asian Studies.

Vatikiotis, Michael R.J. (1996) *Political Change in Southeast Asia. Trimming the Banyan Three.* London and New York: Routledge.

Zakaria, Fareed (1994) "Culture is Destiny. A Conversation with Lee Kuan Yew". *Foreign Affairs*, 73 (2): 109–126.

Index